PRINCE
Freya

4

STORY AND ART BY
KEIKO ISHIHARA

4

CONTENTS

Characters & Story

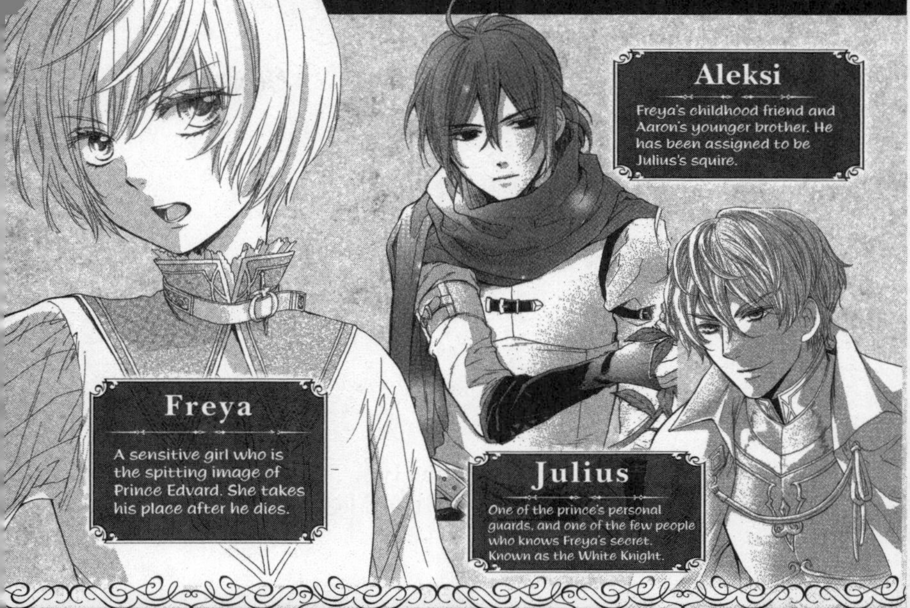

Aleksi

Freya's childhood friend and Aaron's younger brother. He has been assigned to be Julius's squire.

Freya

A sensitive girl who is the spitting image of Prince Edvard. She takes his place after he dies.

Julius

One of the prince's personal guards, and one of the few people who knows Freya's secret. Known as the White Knight.

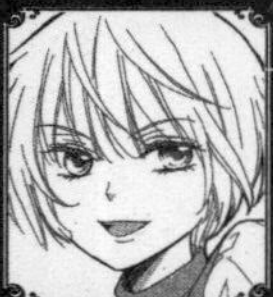

Prince Edvard

Crown prince of Tyr. Once known as the Prince of Hope, he was recently assassinated via poison.

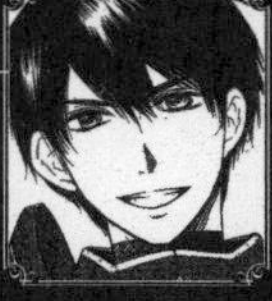

Aaron

Freya's childhood friend and one of the prince's personal guards. Known as the Black Knight. Slain by a villain's sword.

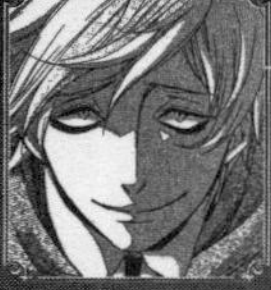

Sable Nerasof

A Sigurdian officer and Aaron's killer.

The Prince's Personal Guard

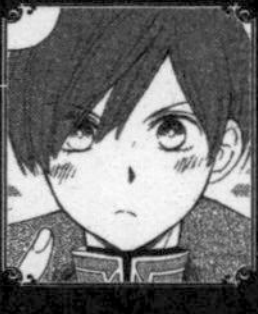

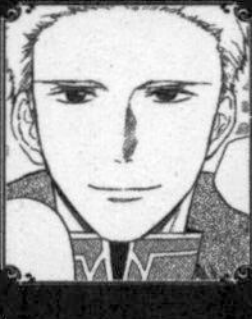

Mikal

Yngvi

Pro-Sigurd Faction and Adversaries

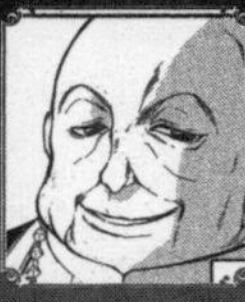

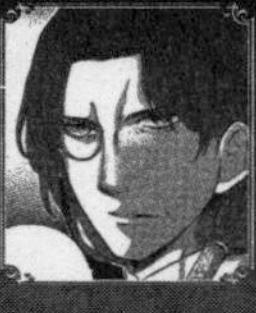

Minister Lars Eikthrynir

Chancellor Mahrukh Khan

Prince Edvard is dead, and Freya has no choice but to impersonate him in order to save the kingdom of Tyr. When Aaron is killed by the enemy, Freya is plunged into despair and Alek becomes Julius's' squire so he can stay by her side and protect her.

Upon receiving word of a Sigurdian attack on Fort Leren, Freya and her guards ride out to provide reinforcements. Along the way, Alek is struck by arrows and falls into a gorge. Freya takes command of the fort, fights the traitor Hugo and struggles to prevent the Sigurdians getting in. The enemy's relentless attack eventually breaches the gates, but on the brink of defeat a mysterious armed force suddenly arrives!

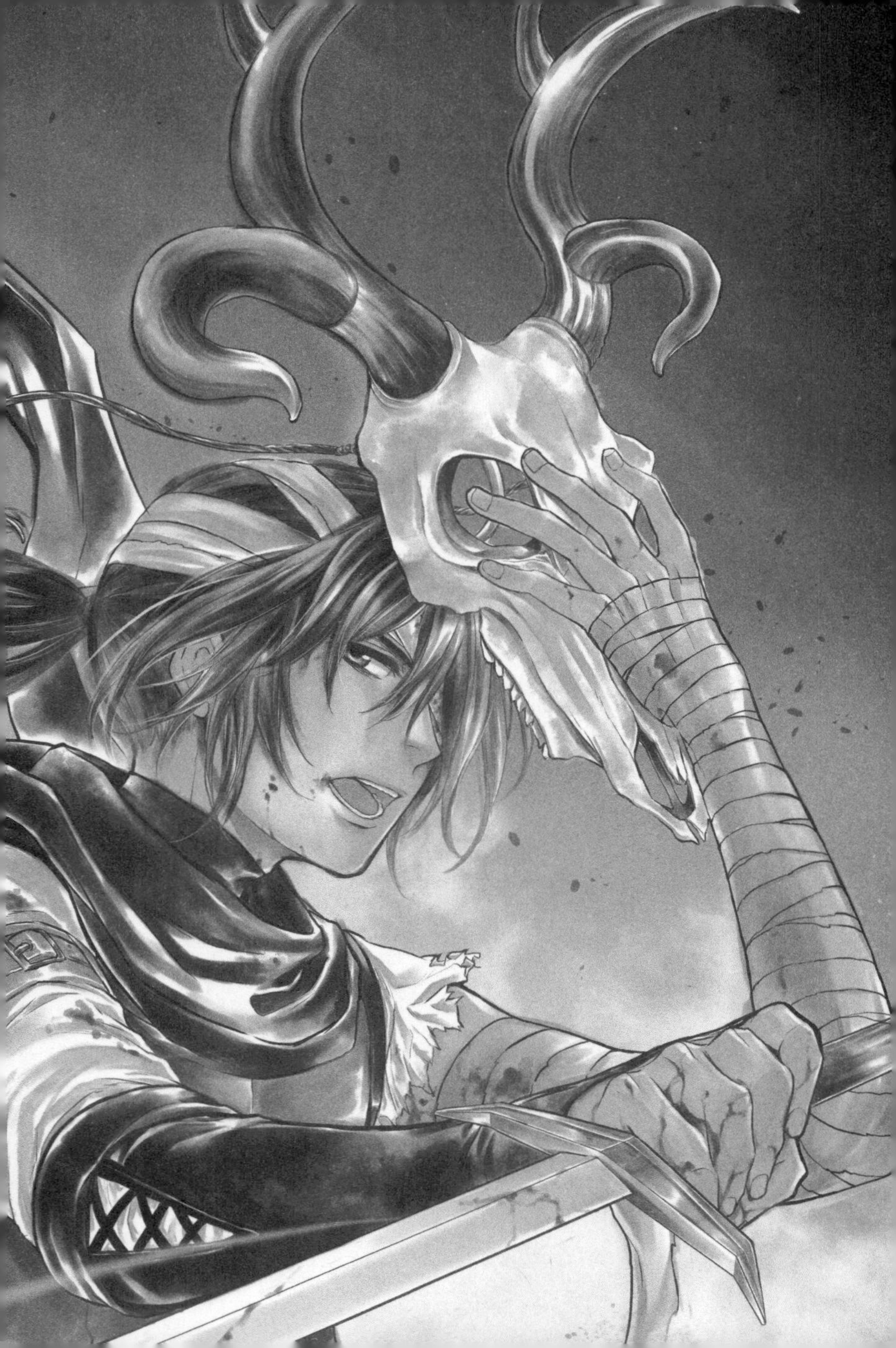

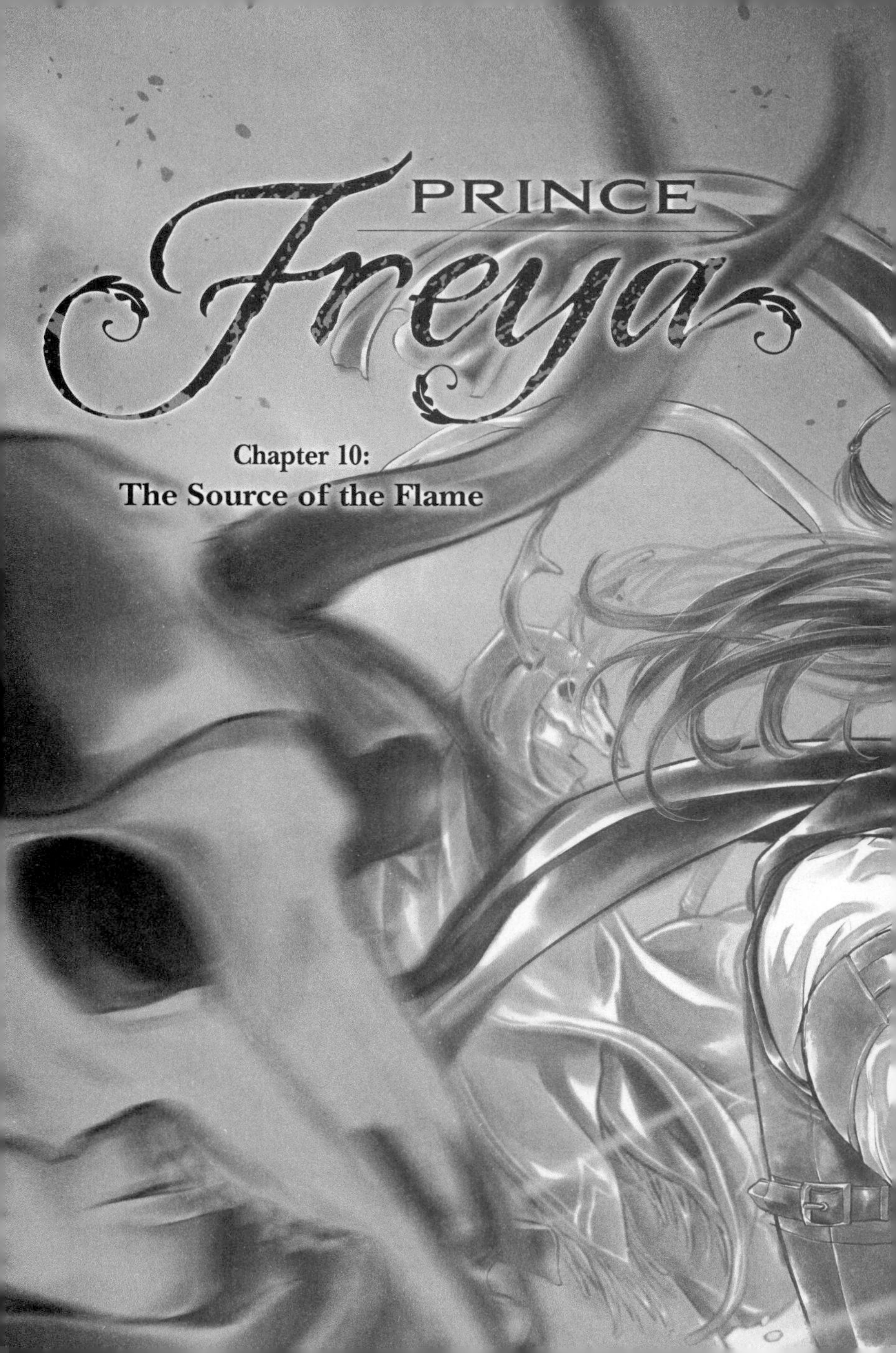
PRINCE
Freya
Chapter 10:
The Source of the Flame

PRINCE
Freya

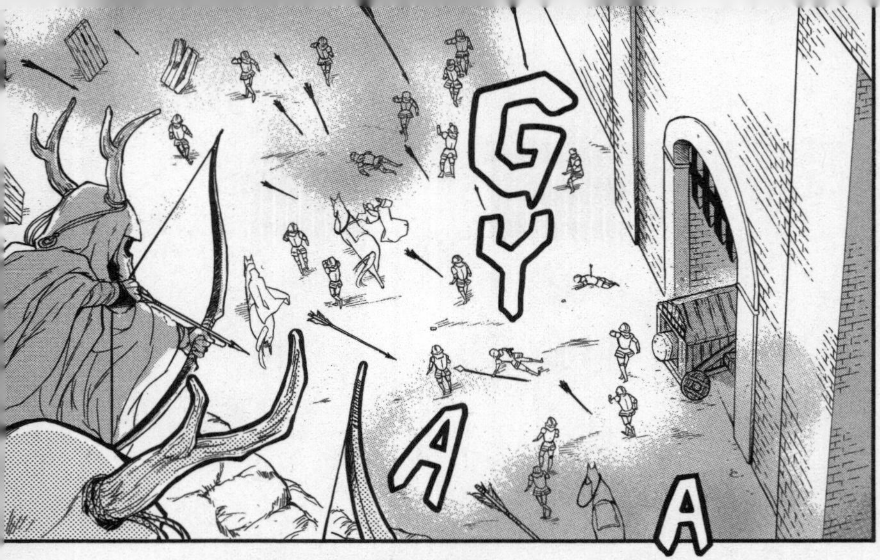
G
Y
A
A

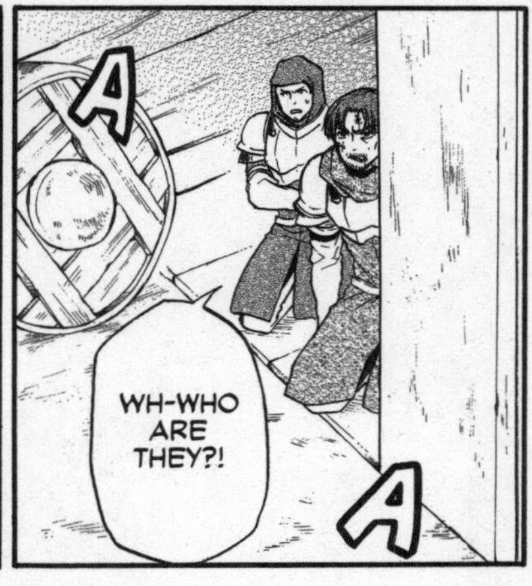
A
WH-WHO ARE THEY?!
A

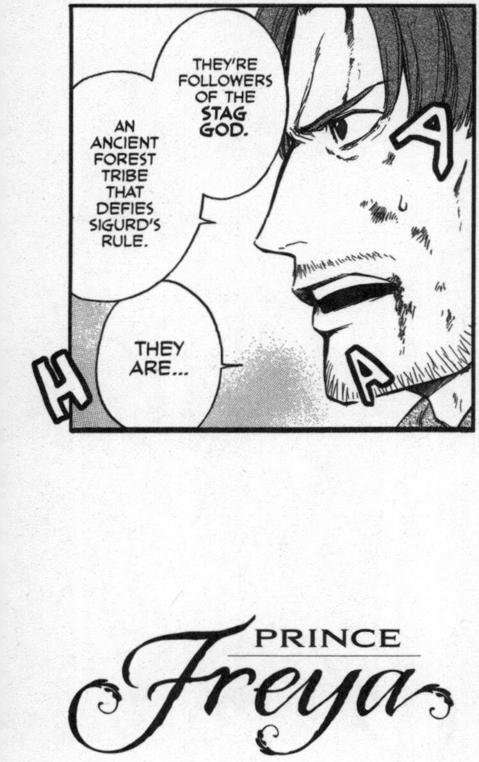
THEY'RE FOLLOWERS OF THE STAG GOD.
AN ANCIENT FOREST TRIBE THAT DEFIES SIGURD'S RULE.
A
THEY ARE...
A
H

PRINCE
Freya

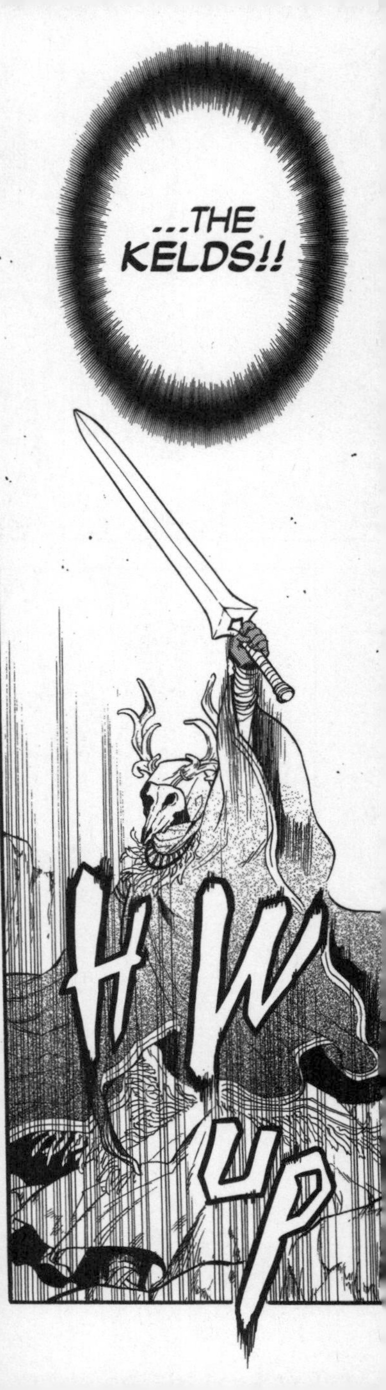
...THE KELDS!!
HWUP
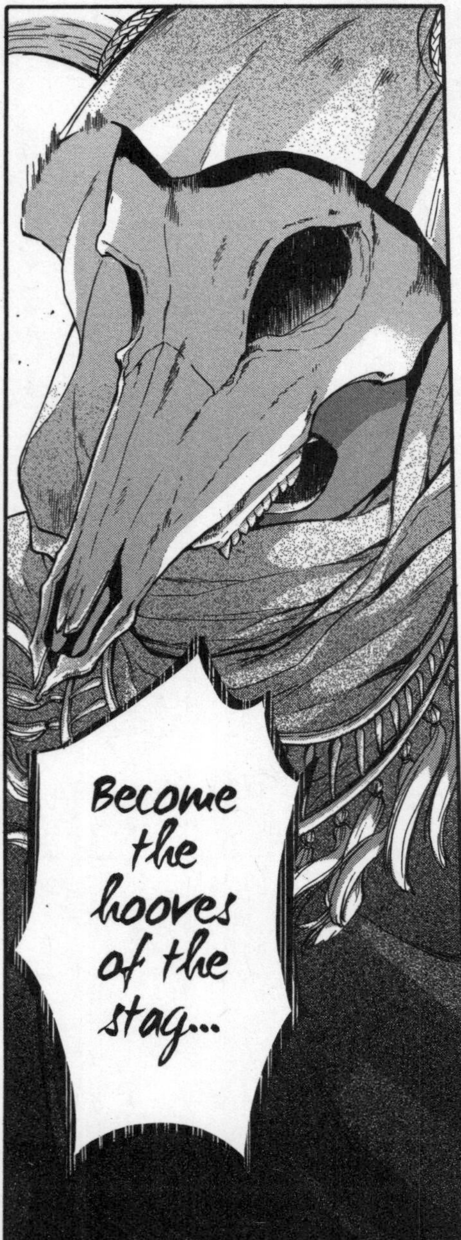
Become the hooves of the stag...

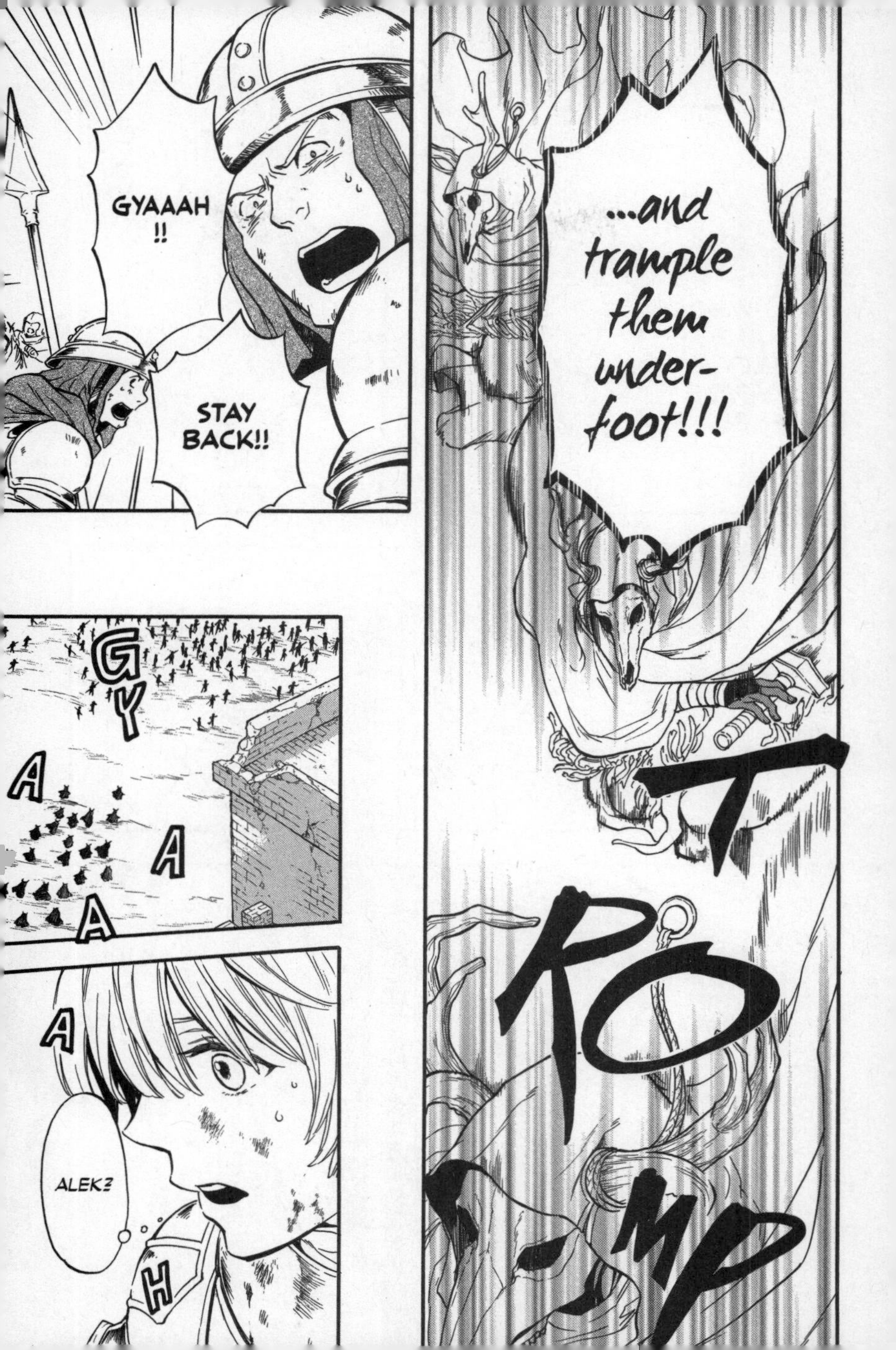

...and trample them under-foot!!!
TROMP
GYAAAH!!
STAY BACK!!
GYAAAAAH
ALEK?

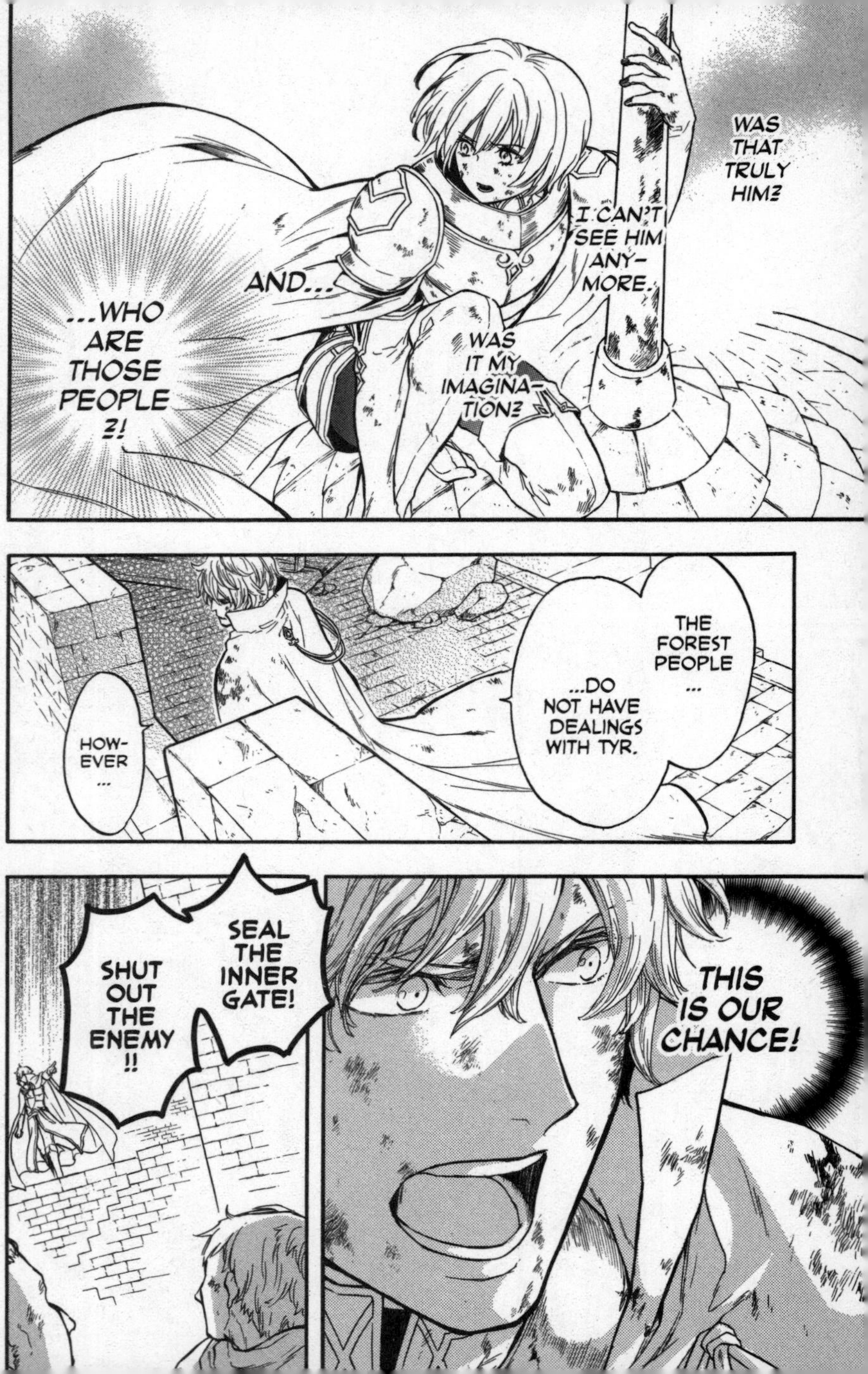
WAS THAT TRULY HIM?
I CAN'T SEE HIM ANYMORE.
WAS IT MY IMAGINATION?
AND...
...WHO ARE THOSE PEOPLE?!
THE FOREST PEOPLE...
...DO NOT HAVE DEALINGS WITH TYR.
HOWEVER...
THIS IS OUR CHANCE!
SEAL THE INNER GATE!
SHUT OUT THE ENEMY!!

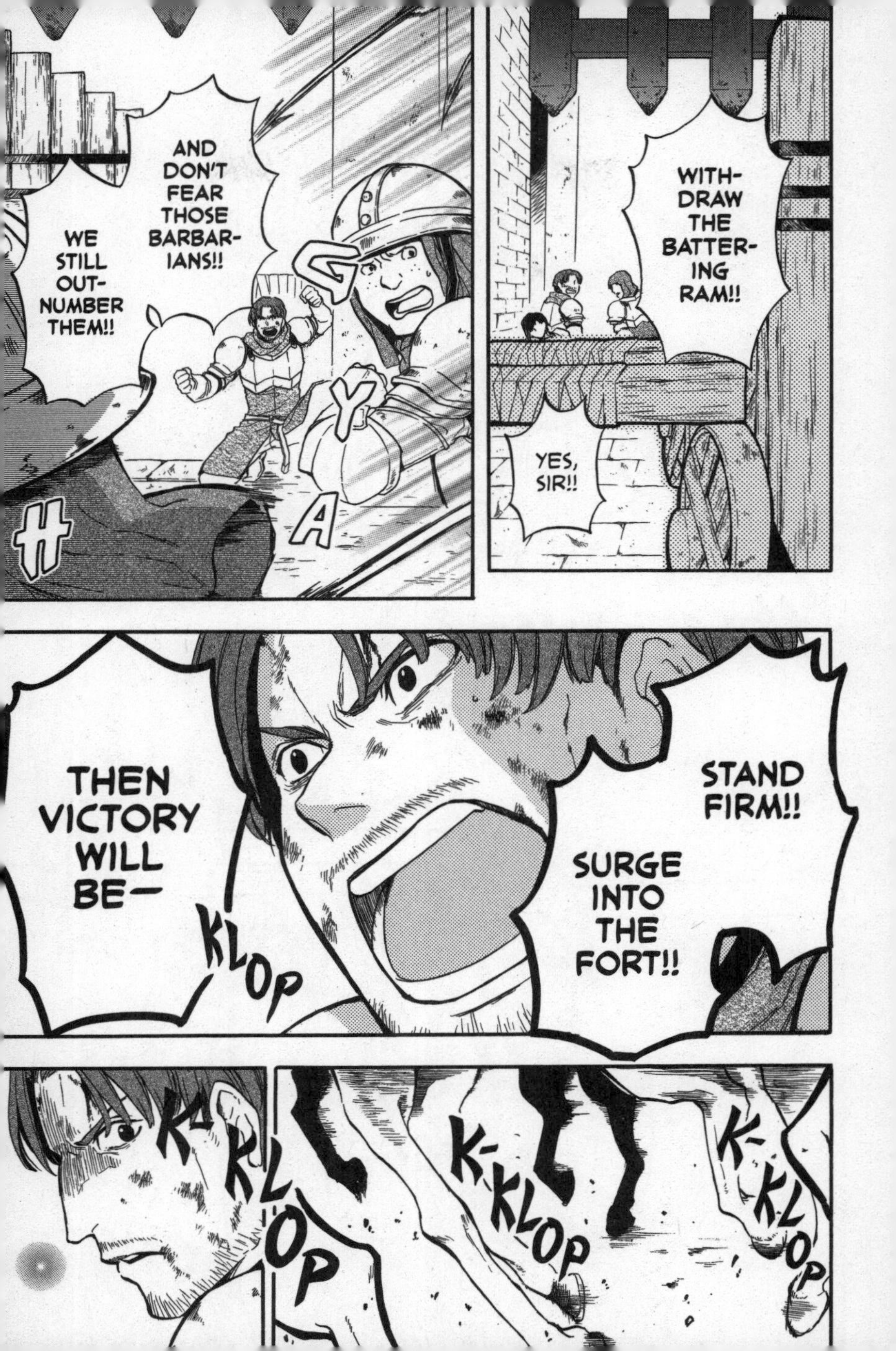
WITH-DRAW THE BATTER-ING RAM!!
YES, SIR!!
AND DON'T FEAR THOSE BARBAR-IANS!!
WE STILL OUT-NUMBER THEM!!
GYAH
STAND FIRM!!
SURGE INTO THE FORT!!
THEN VICTORY WILL BE—
KLOP
K-KLOP
K-KLOP
K-KLOP

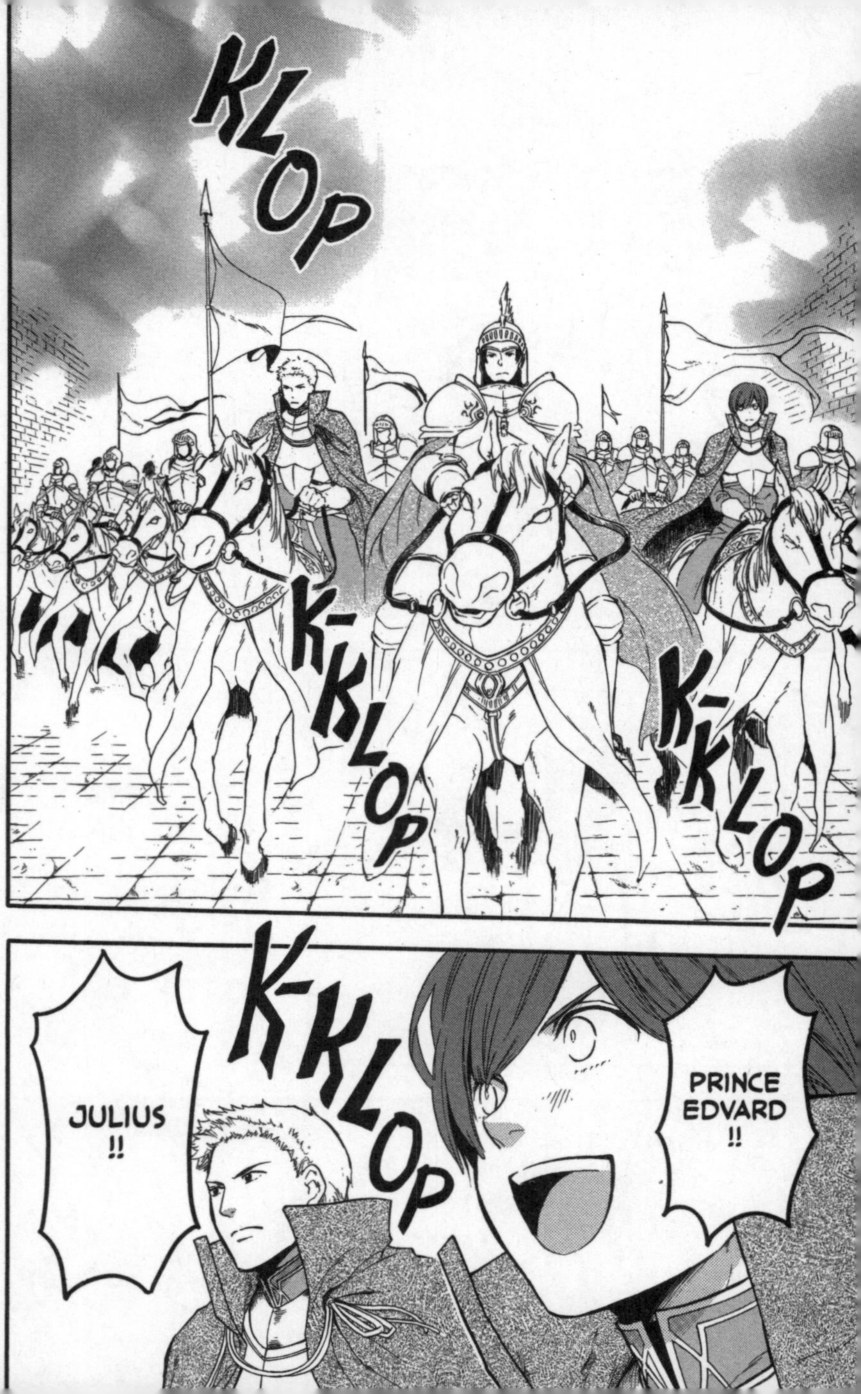
KLOP
K-KLOP
K-KLOP
PRINCE EDVARD !!
K-KLOP
JULIUS !!

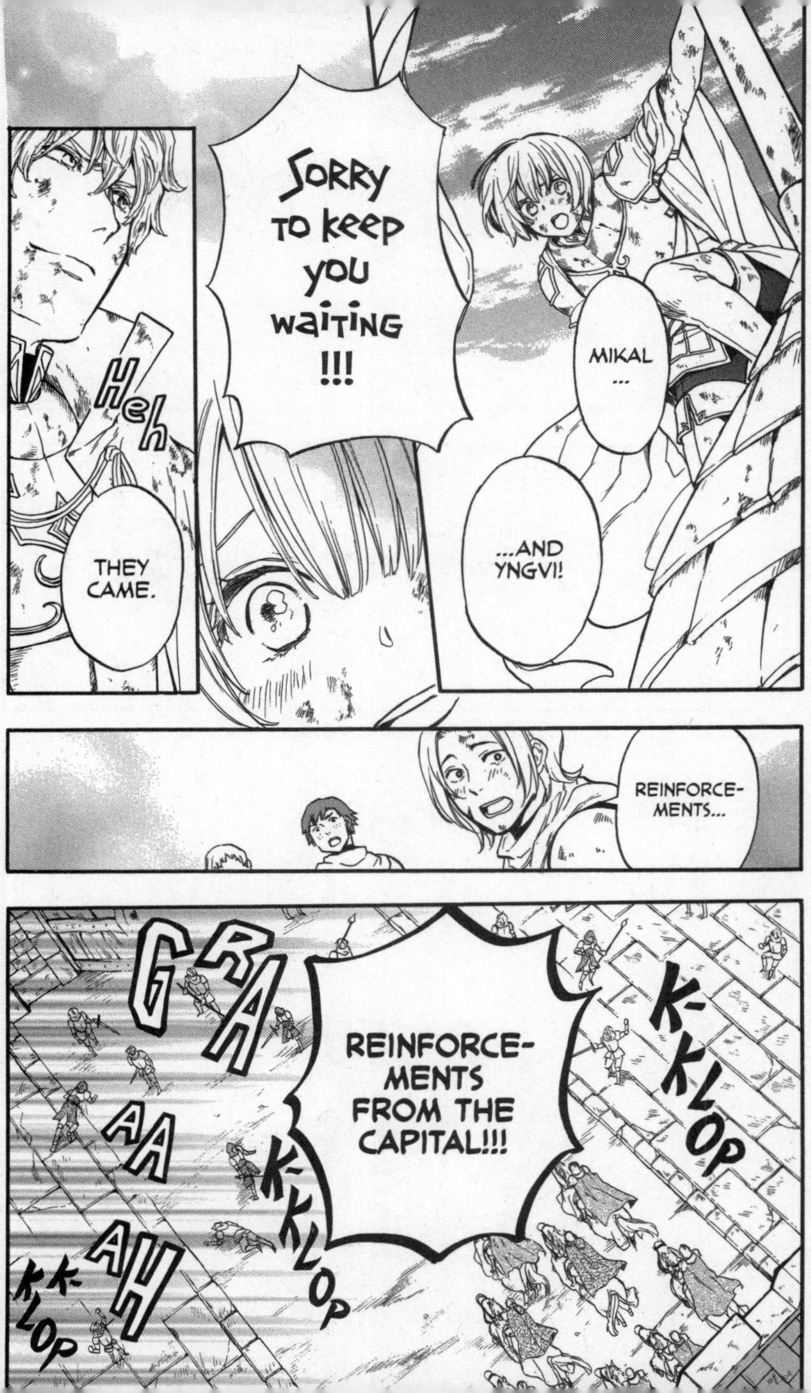
SORRY TO KEEP YOU WAITING!!!
MIKAL...
...AND YNGVI!
Heh
THEY CAME.
REINFORCEMENTS...
K-KLOP
REINFORCEMENTS FROM THE CAPITAL!!!
GRAAAAH
K-KLOP
K-KLOP

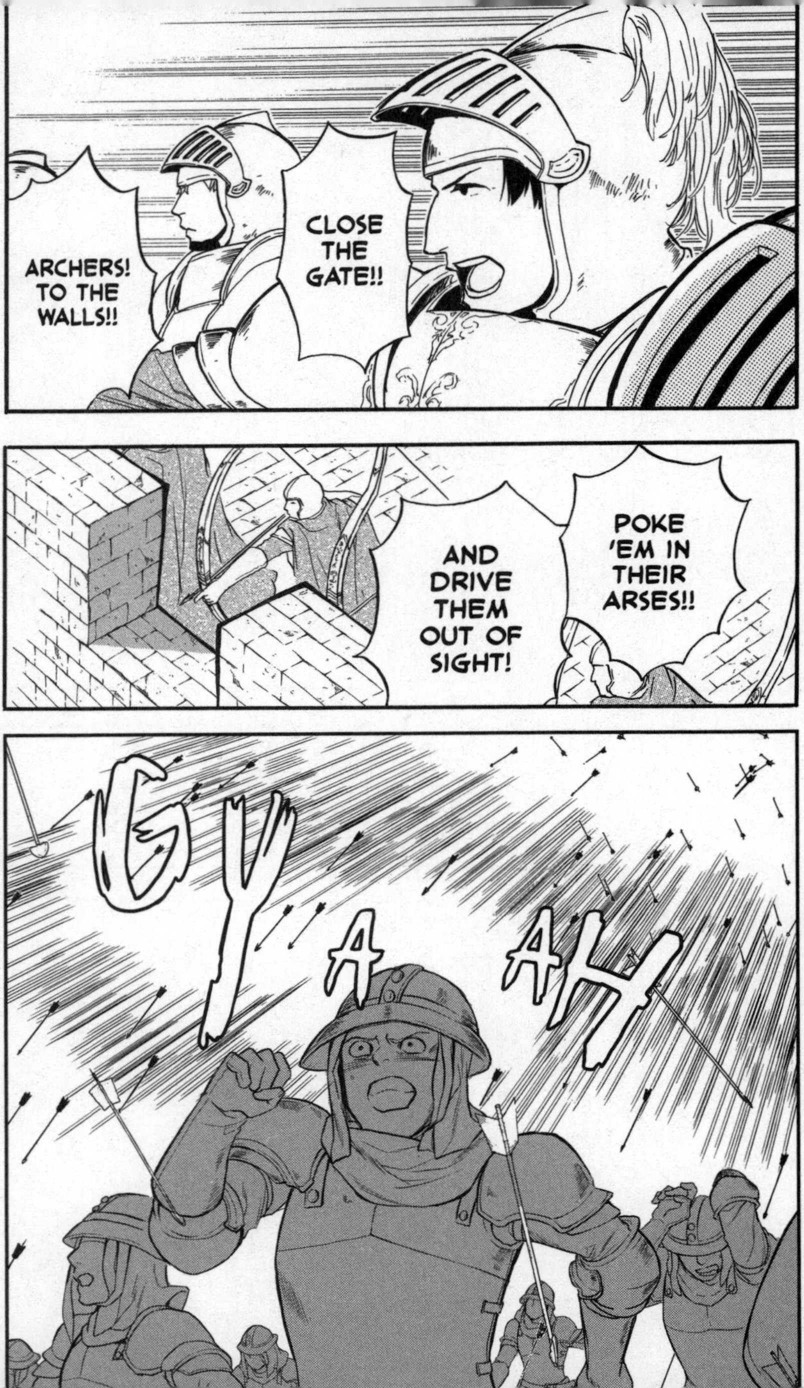
CLOSE THE GATE!!
ARCHERS! TO THE WALLS!!
POKE 'EM IN THEIR ARSES!!
AND DRIVE THEM OUT OF SIGHT!
GYAAH

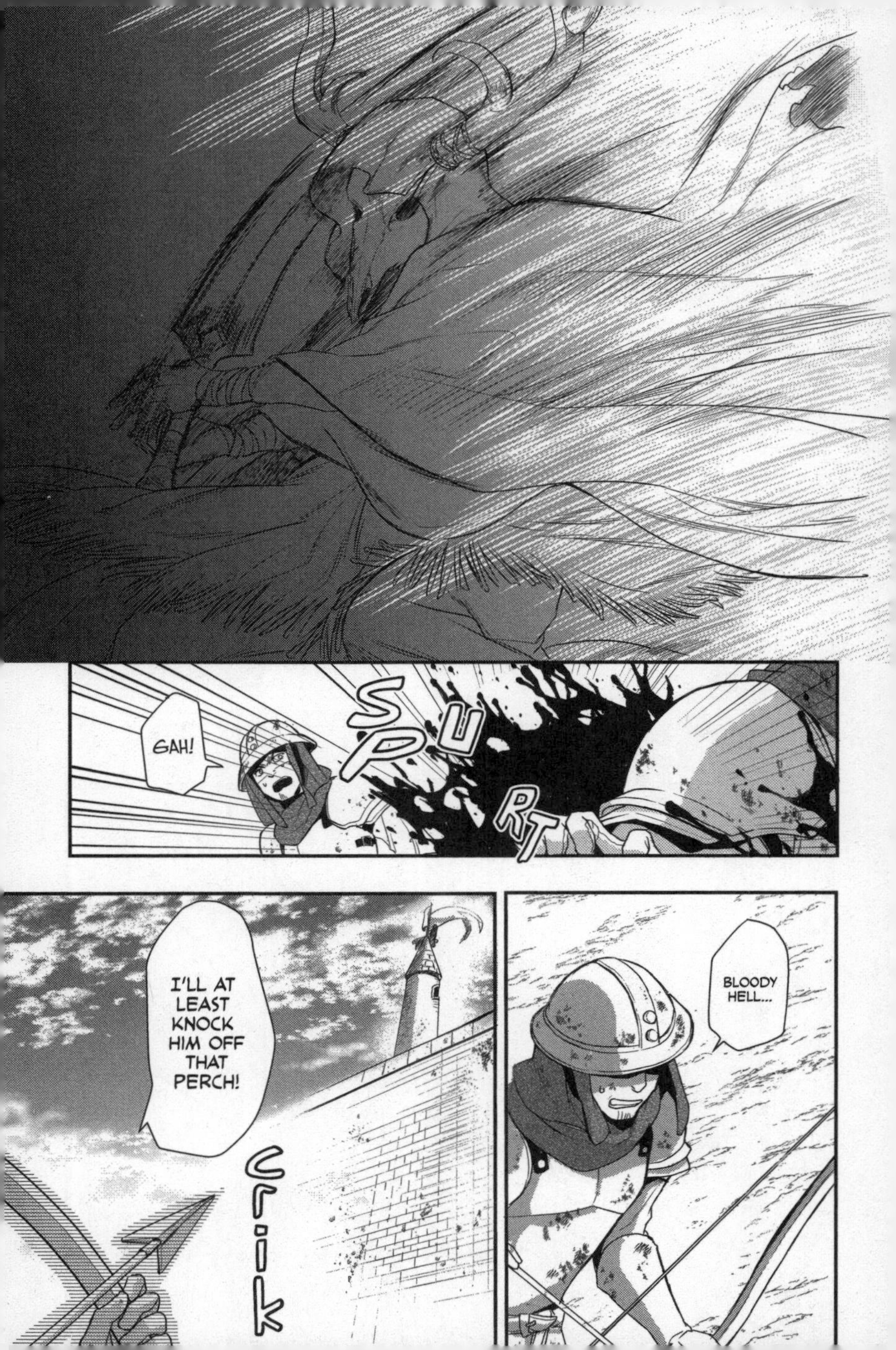
SPURT
GAH!
BLOODY HELL...
I'LL AT LEAST KNOCK HIM OFF THAT PERCH!
CREAK

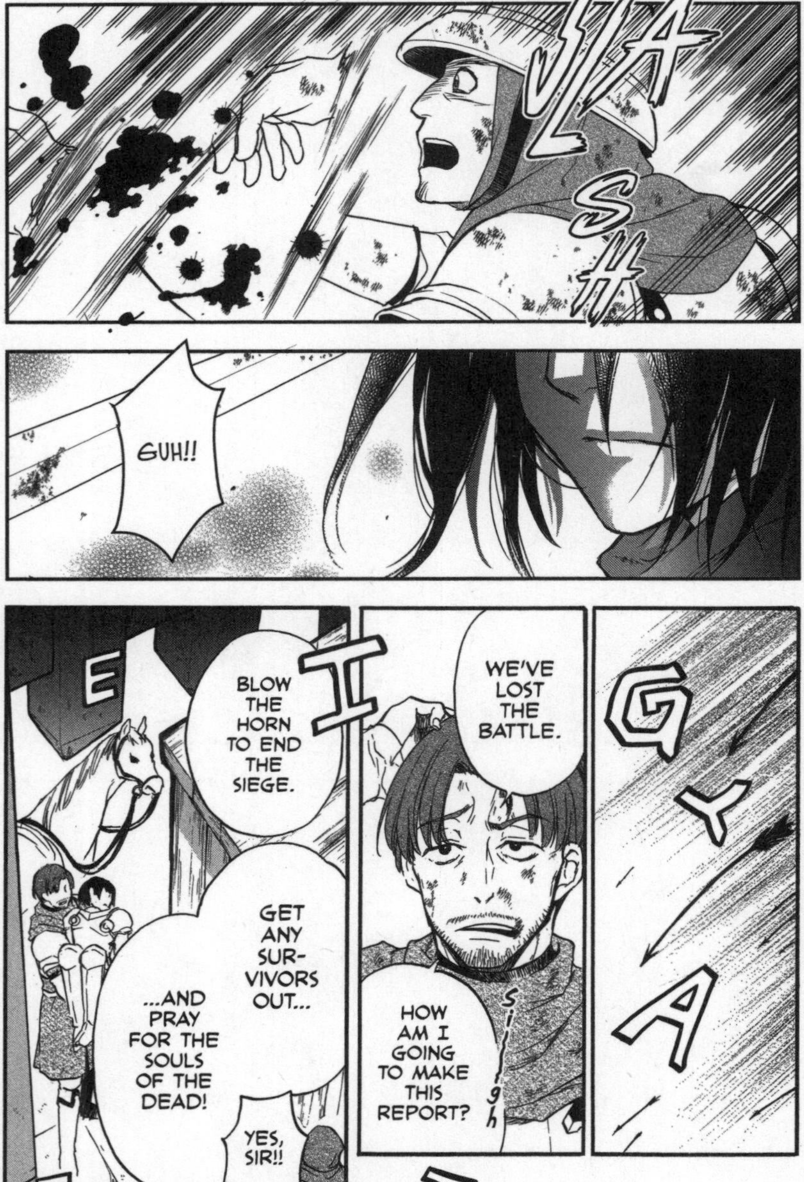
SLASH
GUH!!
GYA
WE'VE LOST THE BATTLE.
HOW AM I GOING TO MAKE THIS REPORT?
sigh
EI EI
BLOW THE HORN TO END THE SIEGE.
GET ANY SUR-VIVORS OUT...
...AND PRAY FOR THE SOULS OF THE DEAD!
YES, SIR!!

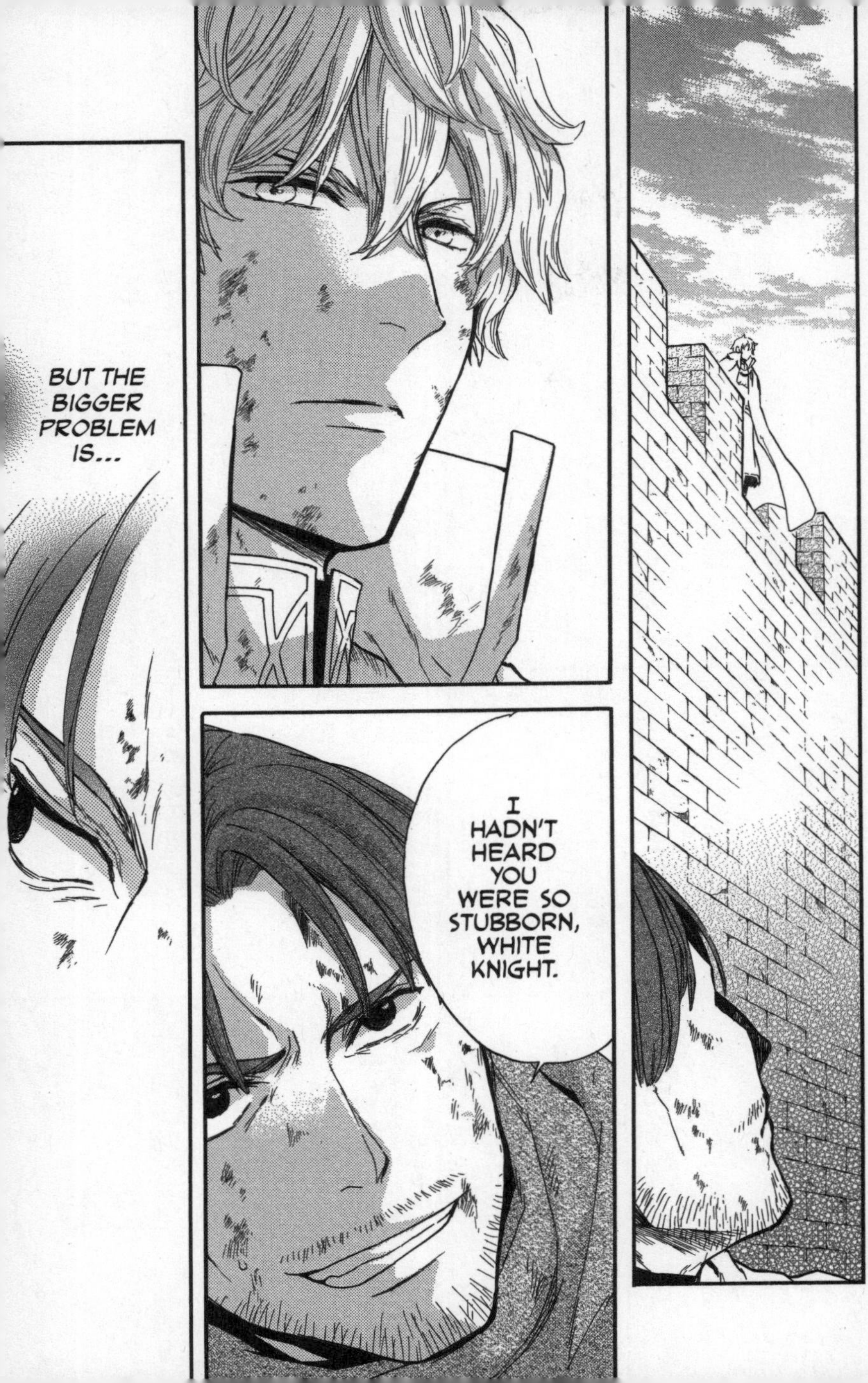
I HADN'T HEARD YOU WERE SO STUBBORN, WHITE KNIGHT.
BUT THE BIGGER PROBLEM IS...

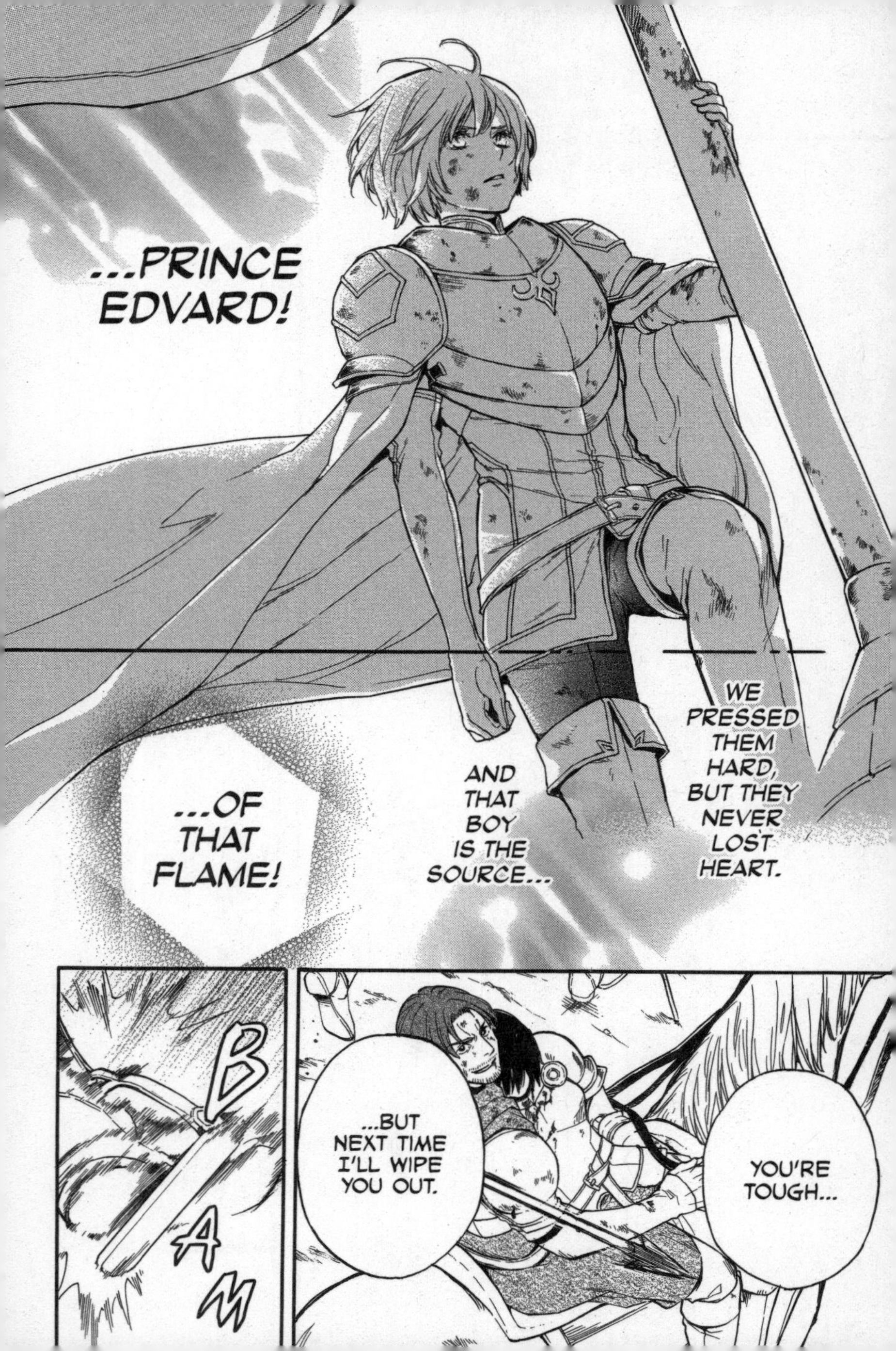
...PRINCE EDVARD!
WE PRESSED THEM HARD, BUT THEY NEVER LOST HEART.
AND THAT BOY IS THE SOURCE...
...OF THAT FLAME!
YOU'RE TOUGH...
...BUT NEXT TIME I'LL WIPE YOU OUT.
BAM

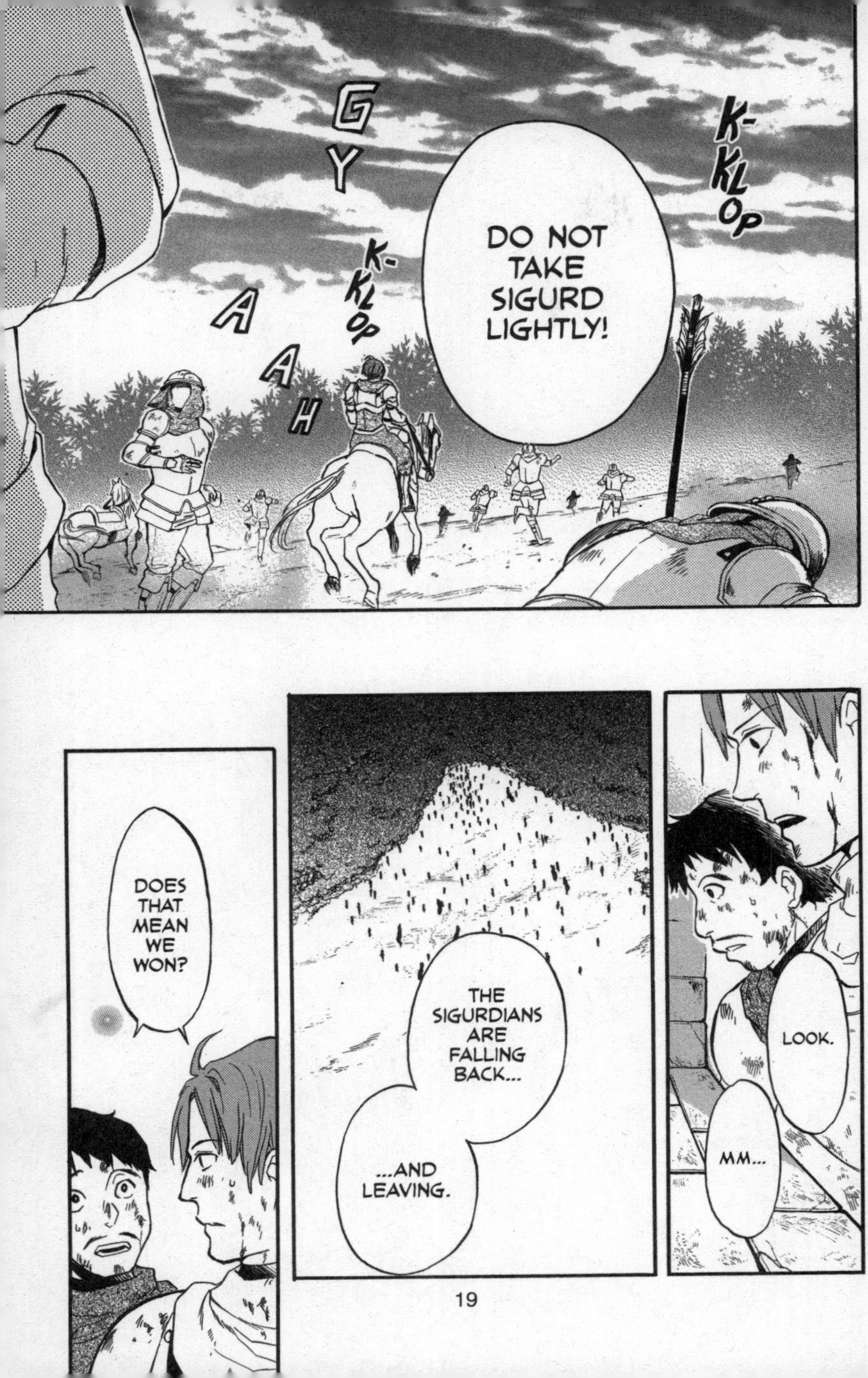
K-KLOP
DO NOT TAKE SIGURD LIGHTLY!
K-KLOP
GYAAAH
LOOK.
MM...
THE SIGURDIANS ARE FALLING BACK...
...AND LEAVING.
DOES THAT MEAN WE WON?

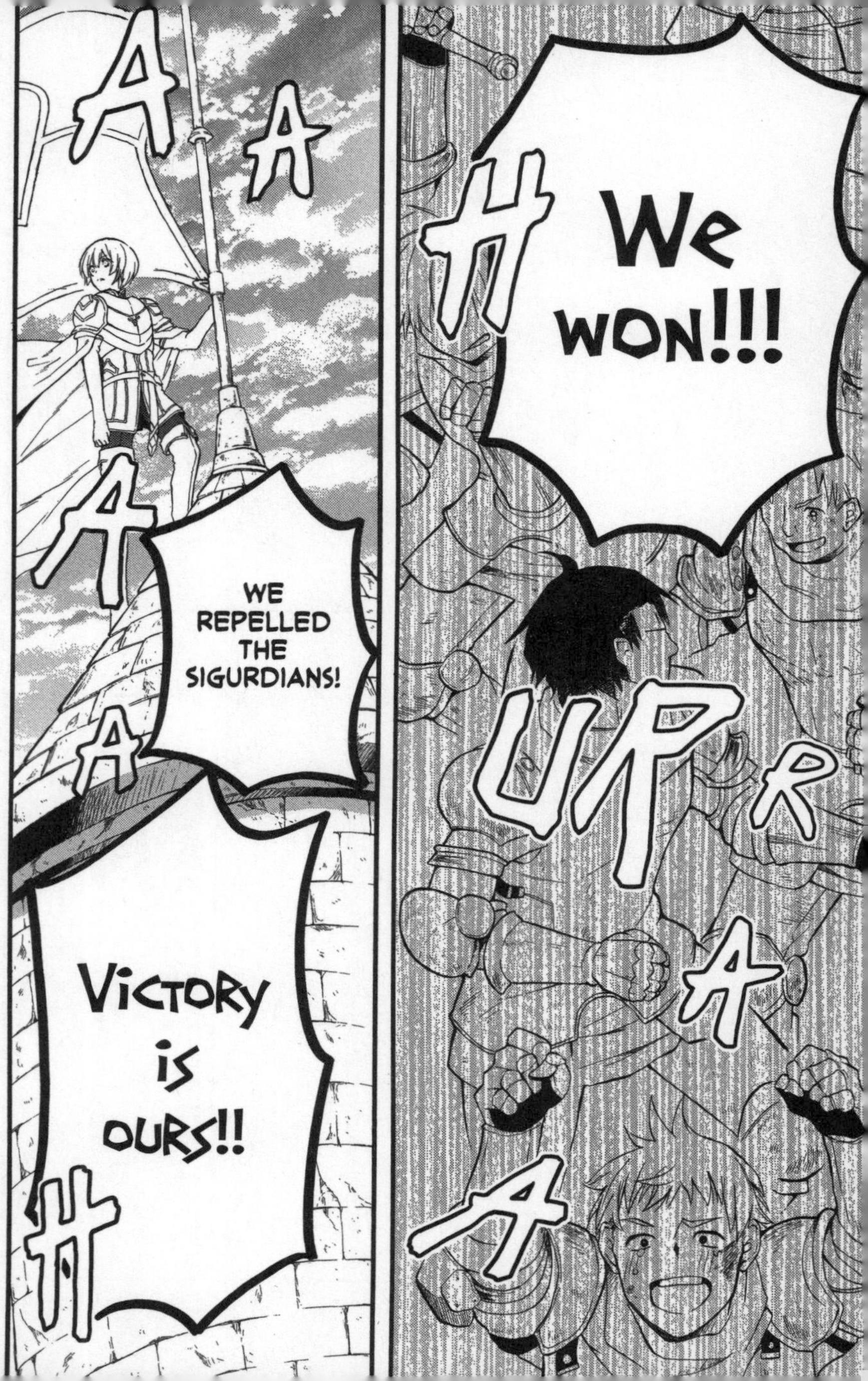
We won!!!
H
UPRAA
AAAAAH
WE REPELLED THE SIGURDIANS!
Victory is ours!!

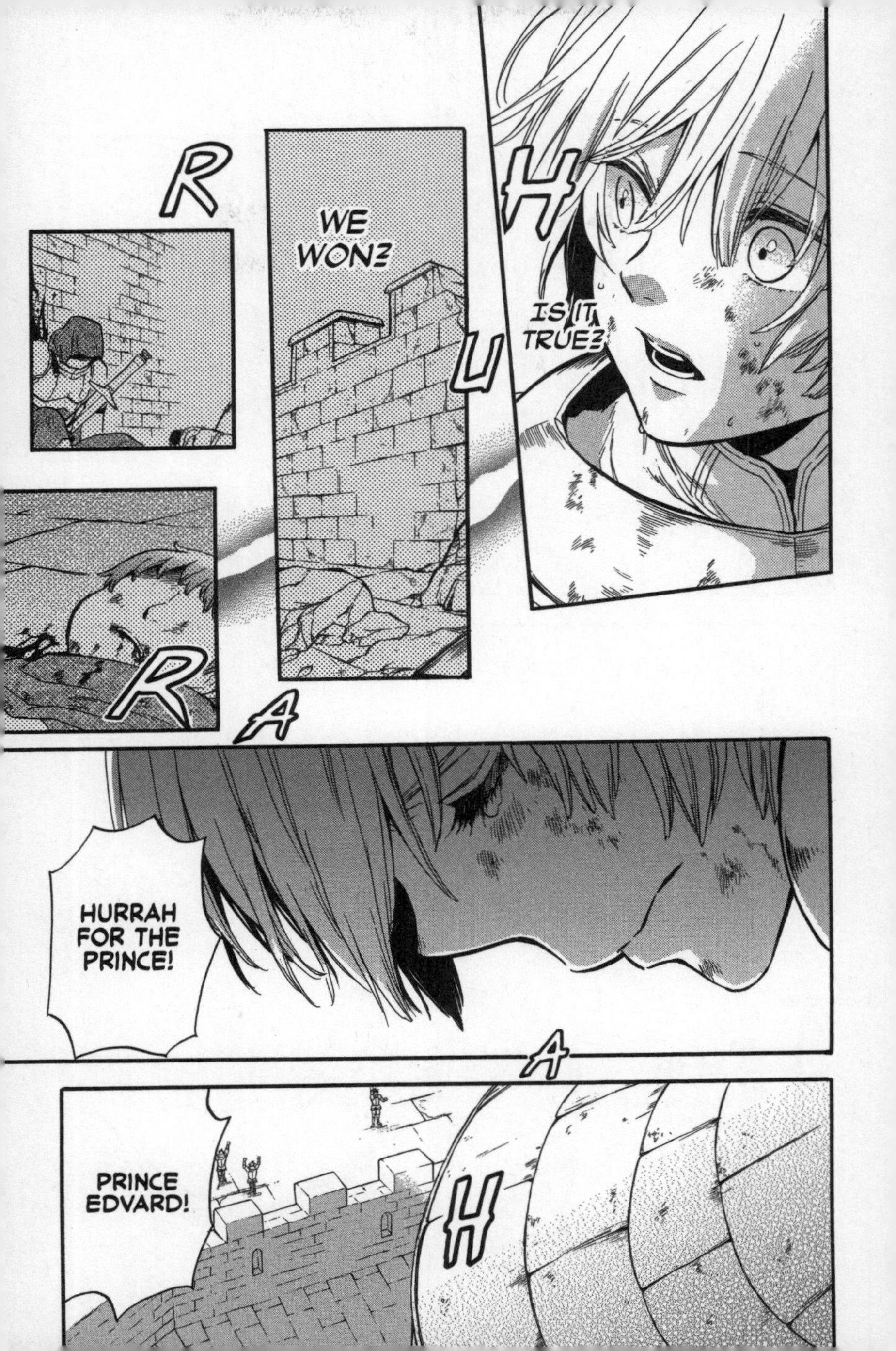
H
IS IT TRUE?
U
WE WON?
R
R
A
HURRAH FOR THE PRINCE!
A
H
PRINCE EDVARD!

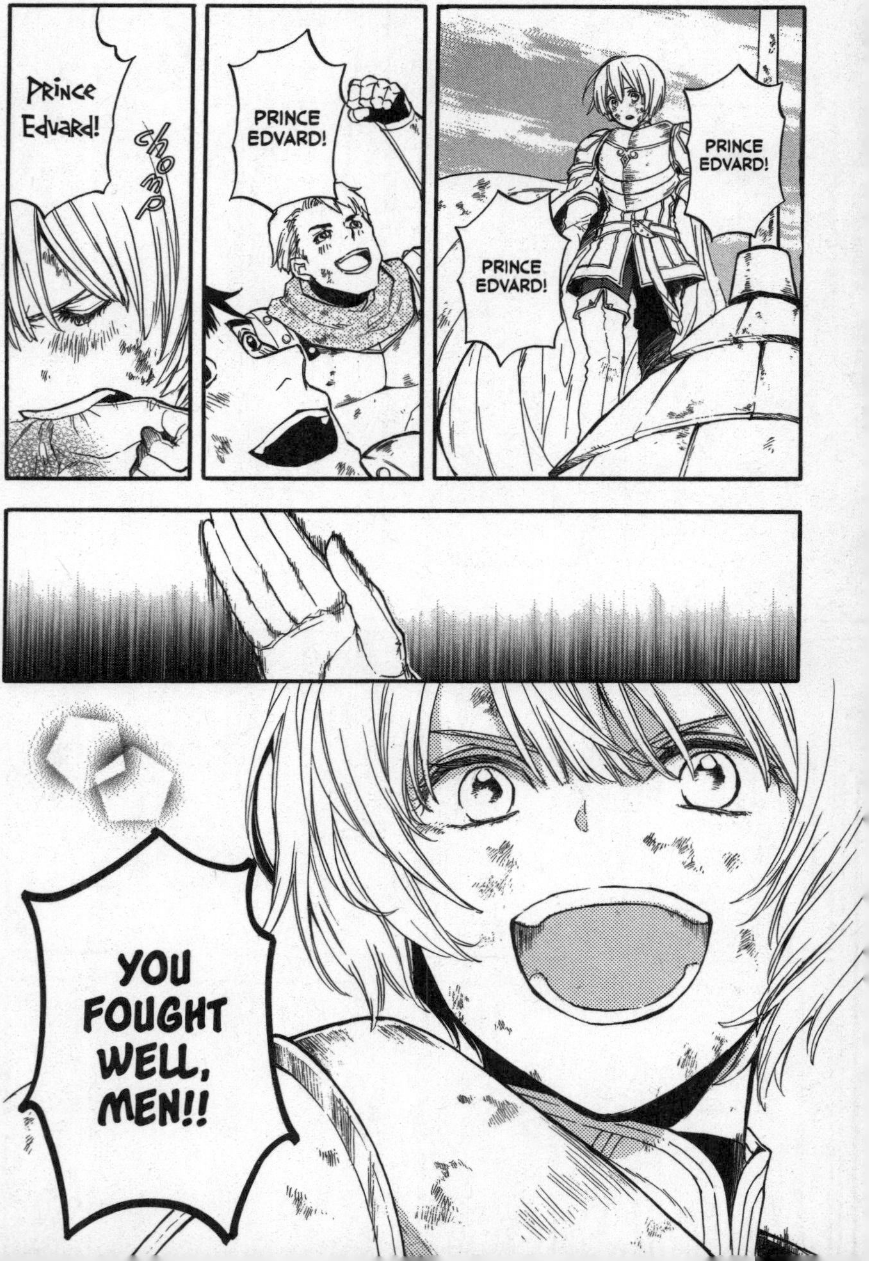
PRINCE EDVARD!
PRINCE EDVARD!
PRINCE EDVARD!
Prince Edvard!
chomp
YOU FOUGHT WELL, MEN!!

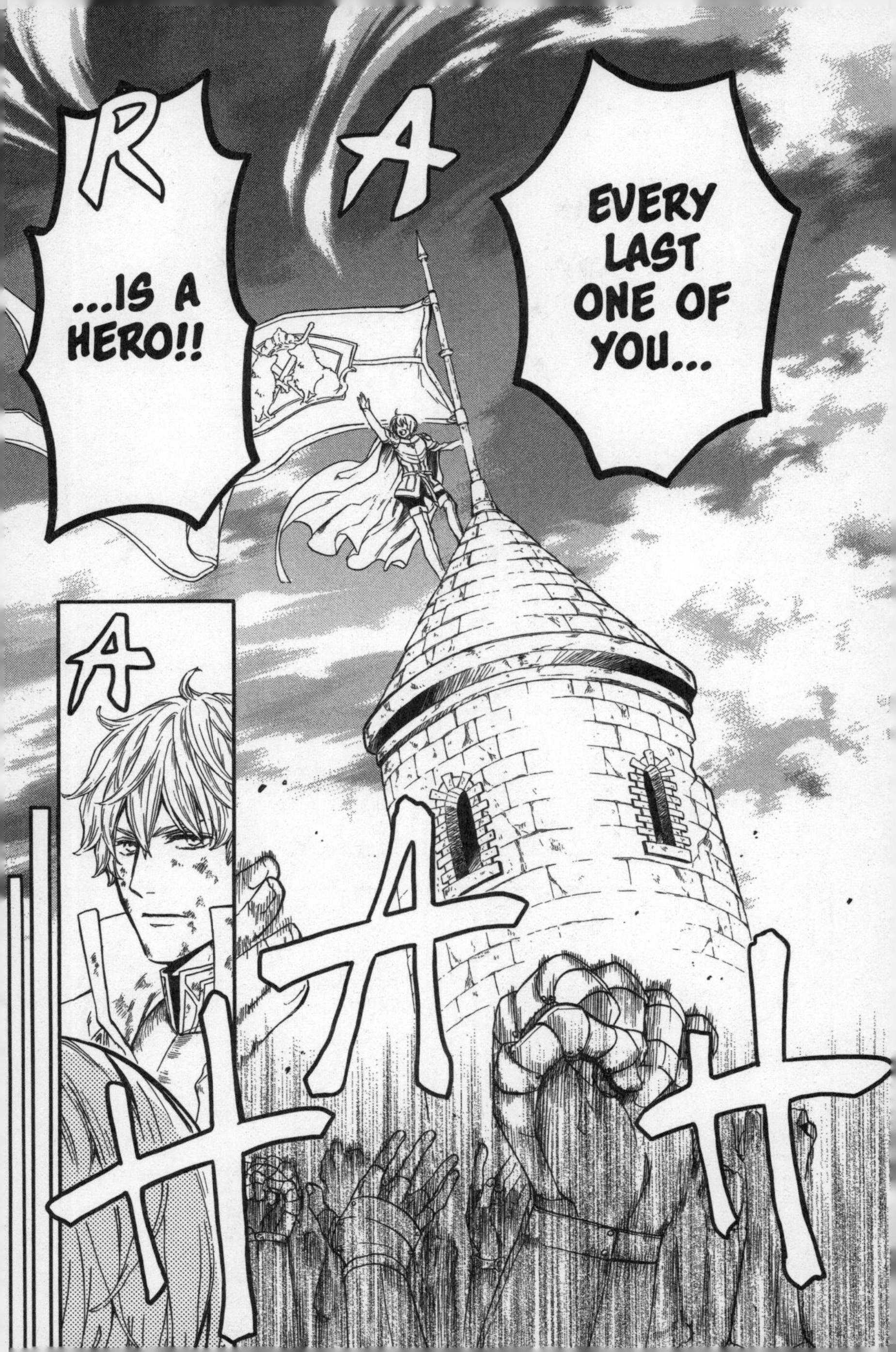
EVERY LAST ONE OF YOU...
A
R
...IS A HERO!!
A

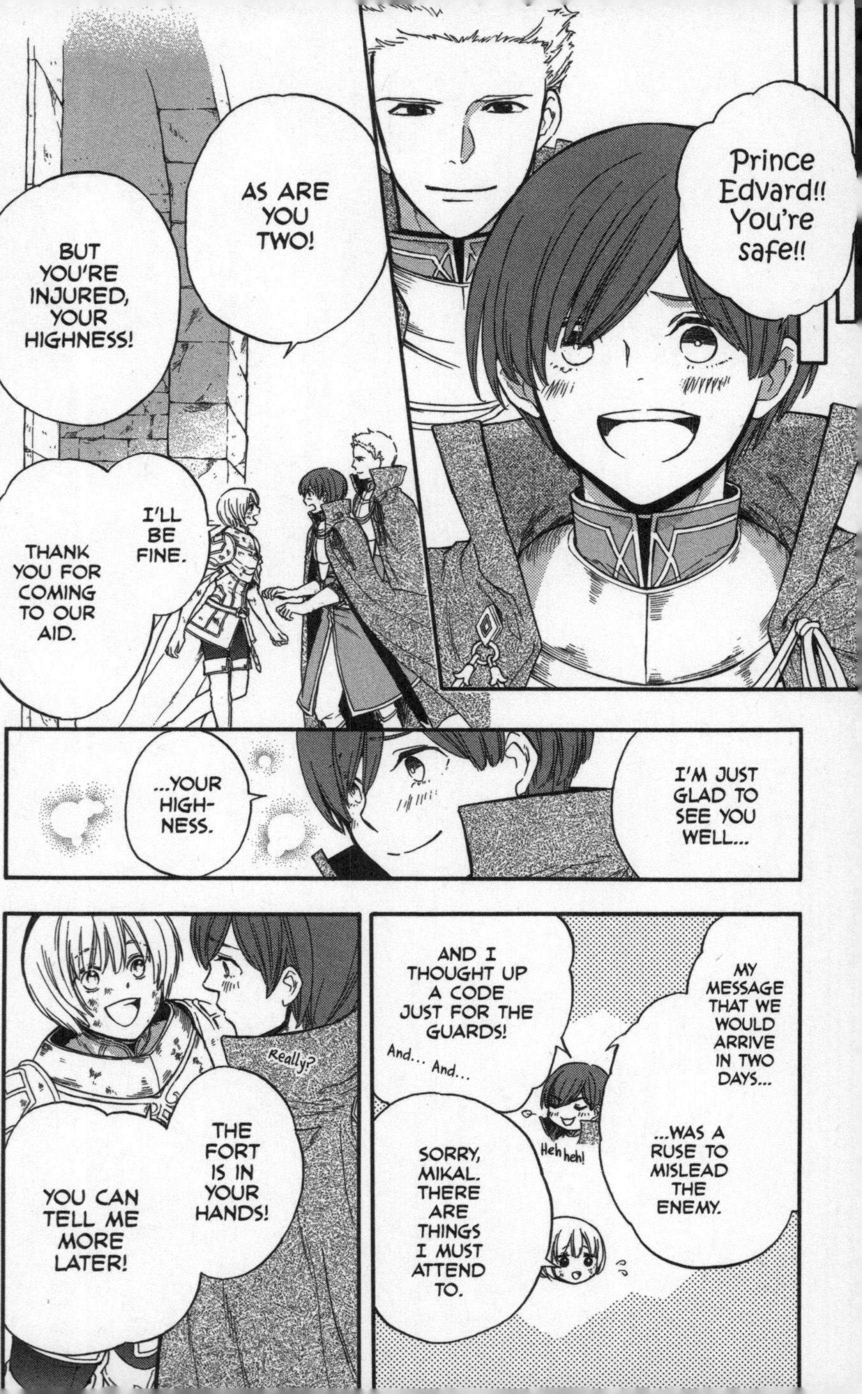

Prince Edvard!! You're safe!!
AS ARE YOU TWO!
BUT YOU'RE INJURED, YOUR HIGHNESS!
I'LL BE FINE.
THANK YOU FOR COMING TO OUR AID.
I'M JUST GLAD TO SEE YOU WELL...
...YOUR HIGHNESS.
MY MESSAGE THAT WE WOULD ARRIVE IN TWO DAYS...
AND I THOUGHT UP A CODE JUST FOR THE GUARDS!
And... And...
...WAS A RUSE TO MISLEAD THE ENEMY.
Heh heh!
SORRY, MIKAL. THERE ARE THINGS I MUST ATTEND TO.
Really?
THE FORT IS IN YOUR HANDS!
YOU CAN TELL ME MORE LATER!

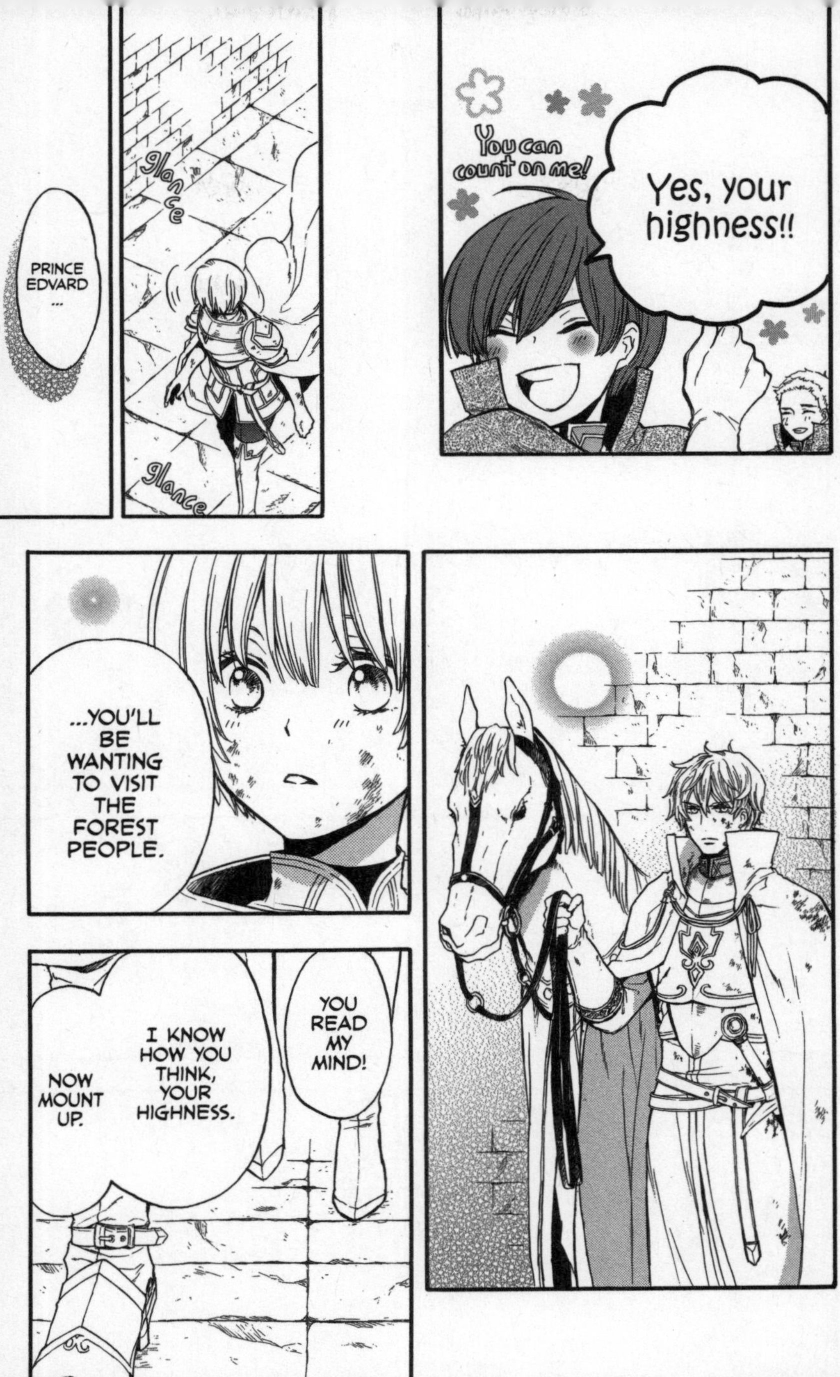
Yes, your highness!!
You can count on me!
glance
glance
PRINCE EDVARD ...
...YOU'LL BE WANTING TO VISIT THE FOREST PEOPLE.
YOU READ MY MIND!
I KNOW HOW YOU THINK, YOUR HIGHNESS.
NOW MOUNT UP.

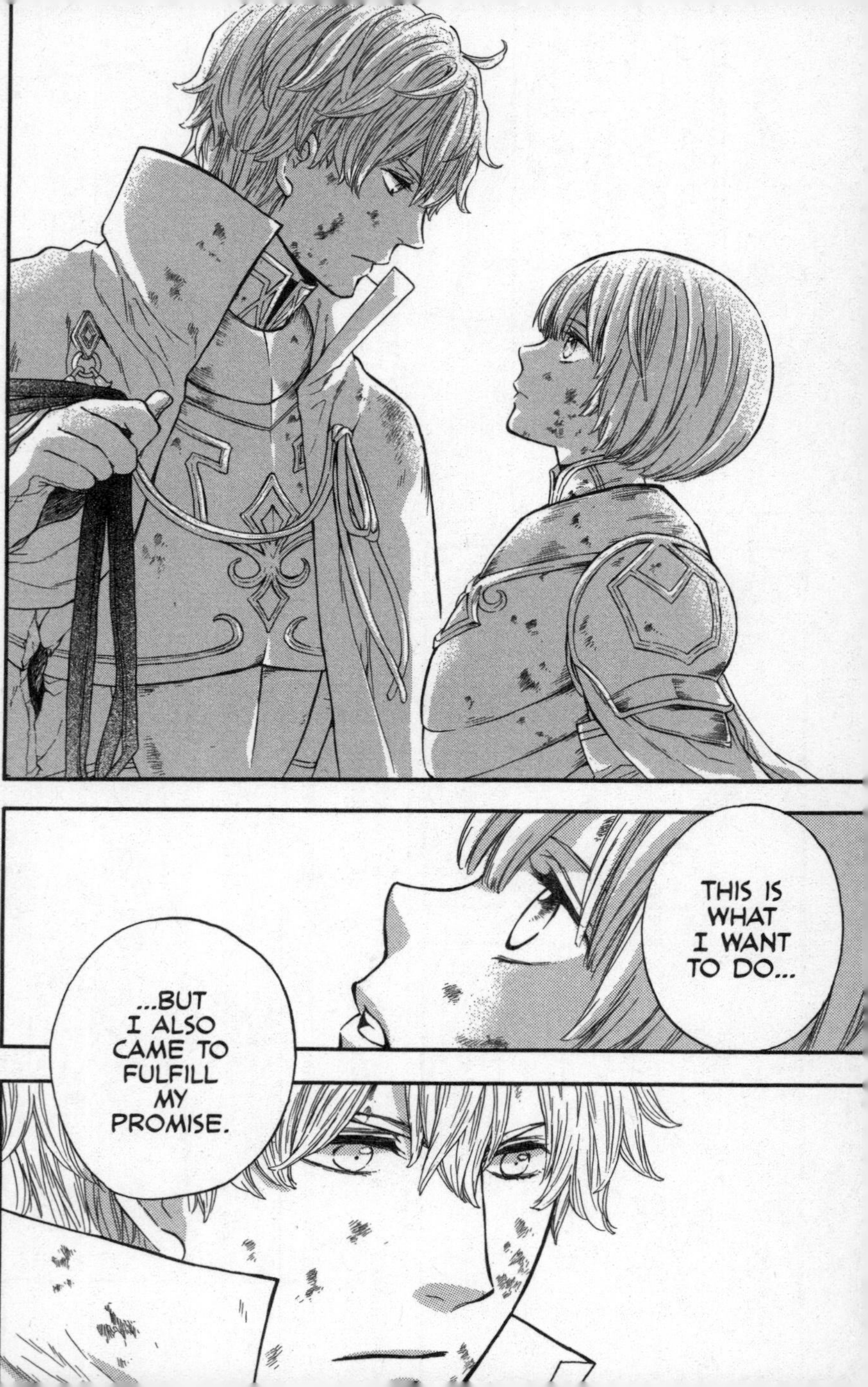
THIS IS WHAT I WANT TO DO...
...BUT I ALSO CAME TO FULFILL MY PROMISE.

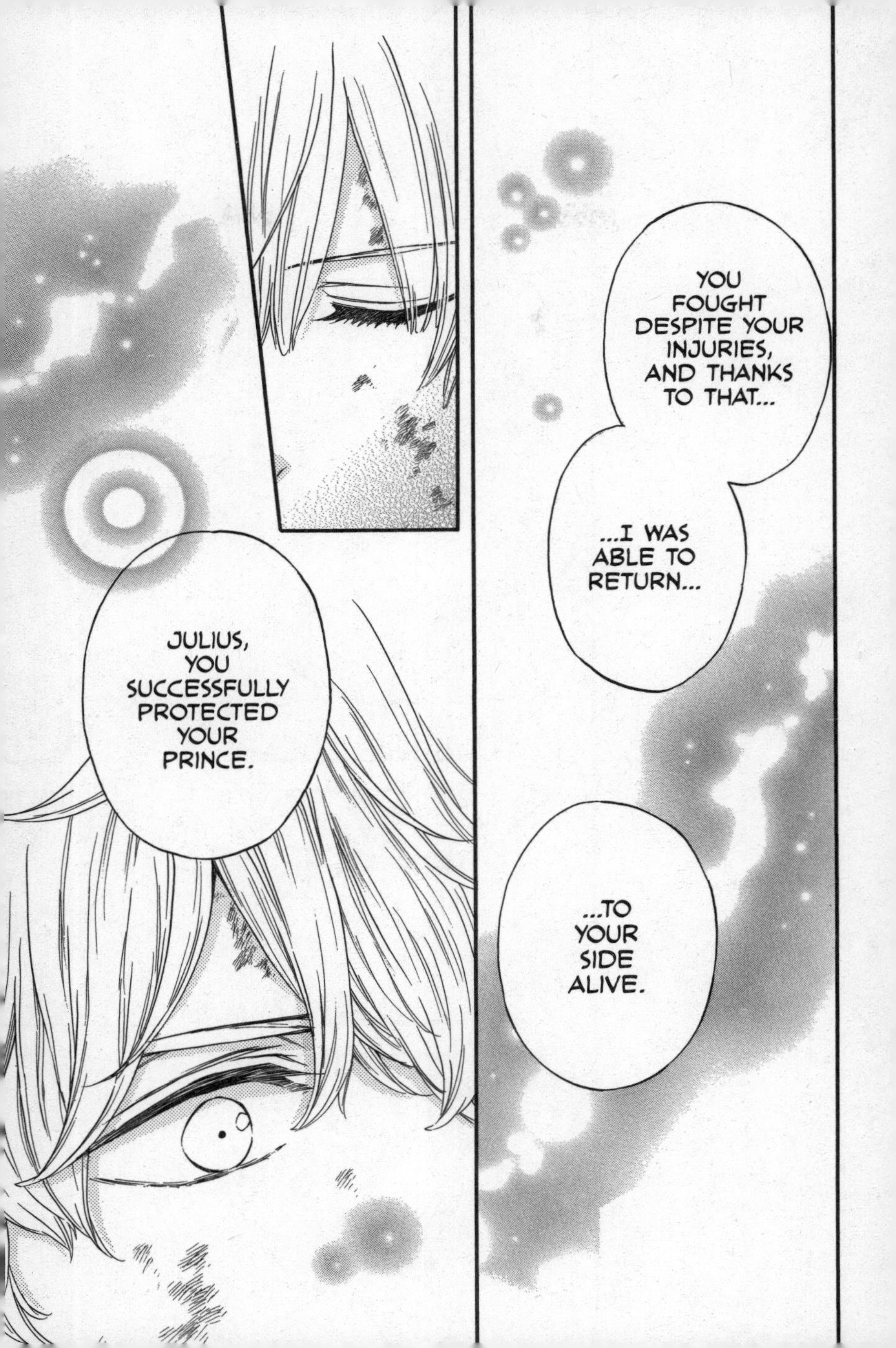
YOU FOUGHT DESPITE YOUR INJURIES, AND THANKS TO THAT...
...I WAS ABLE TO RETURN...
...TO YOUR SIDE ALIVE.
JULIUS, YOU SUCCESSFULLY PROTECTED YOUR PRINCE.

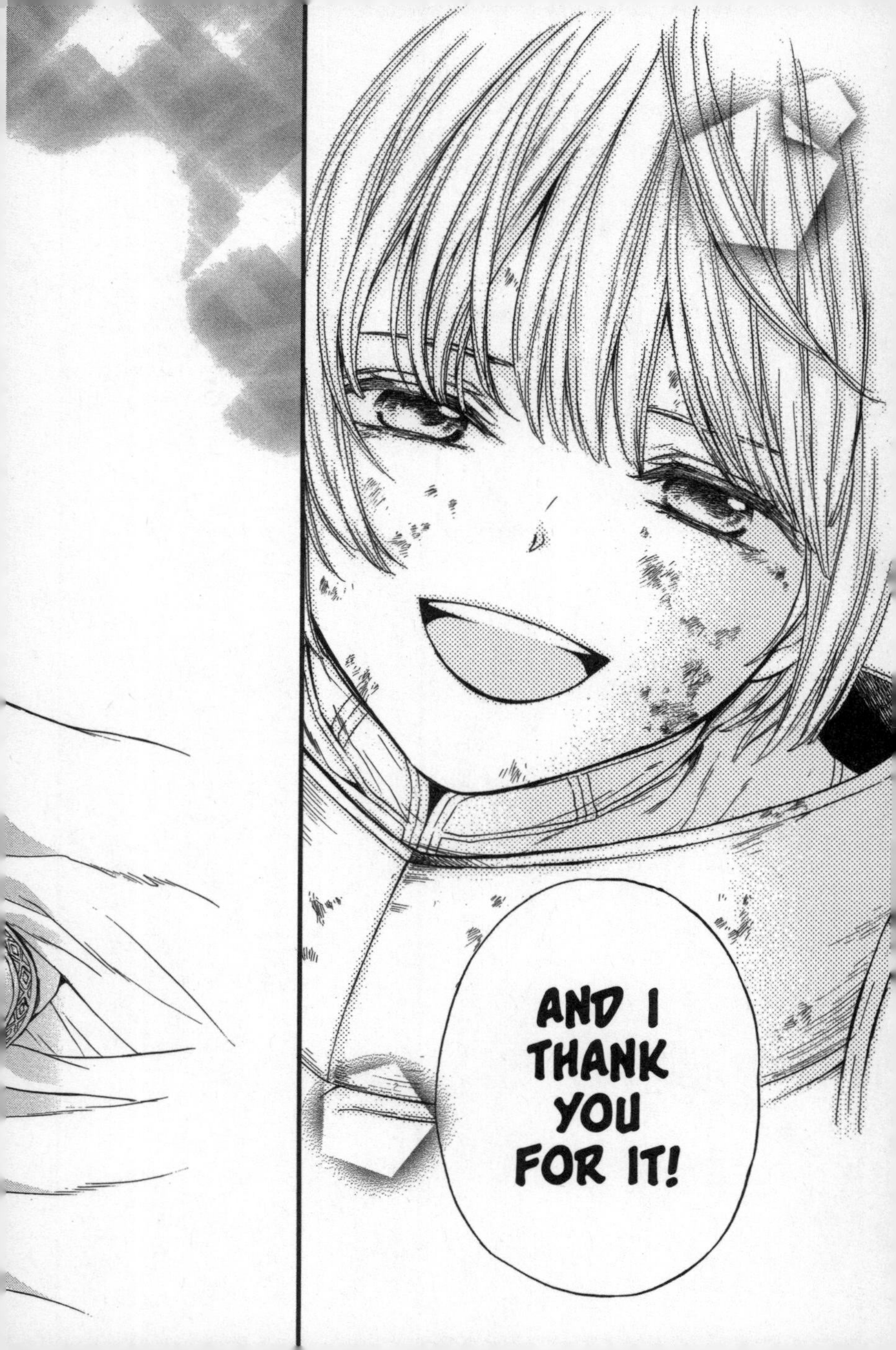
AND I THANK YOU FOR IT!

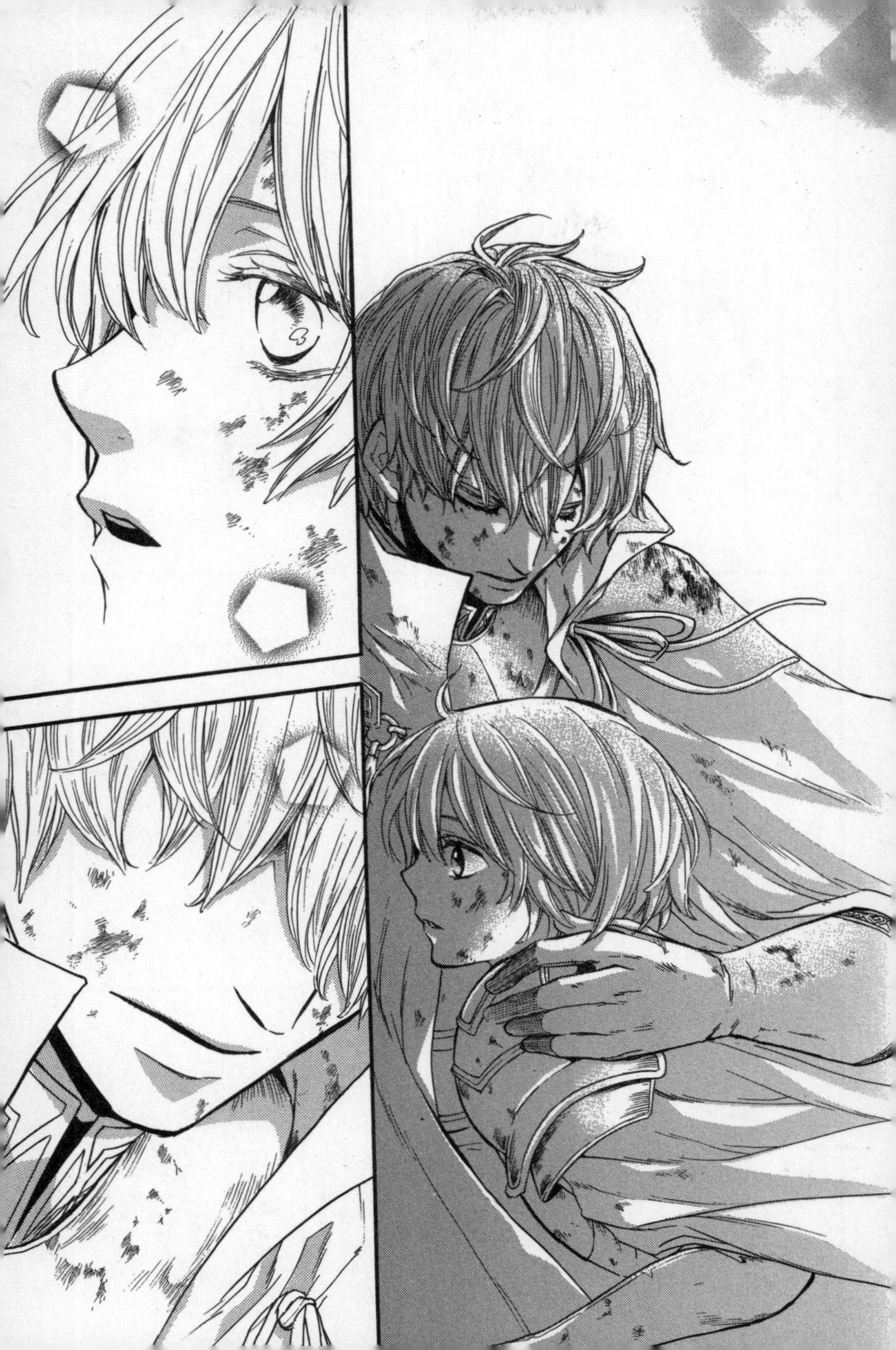

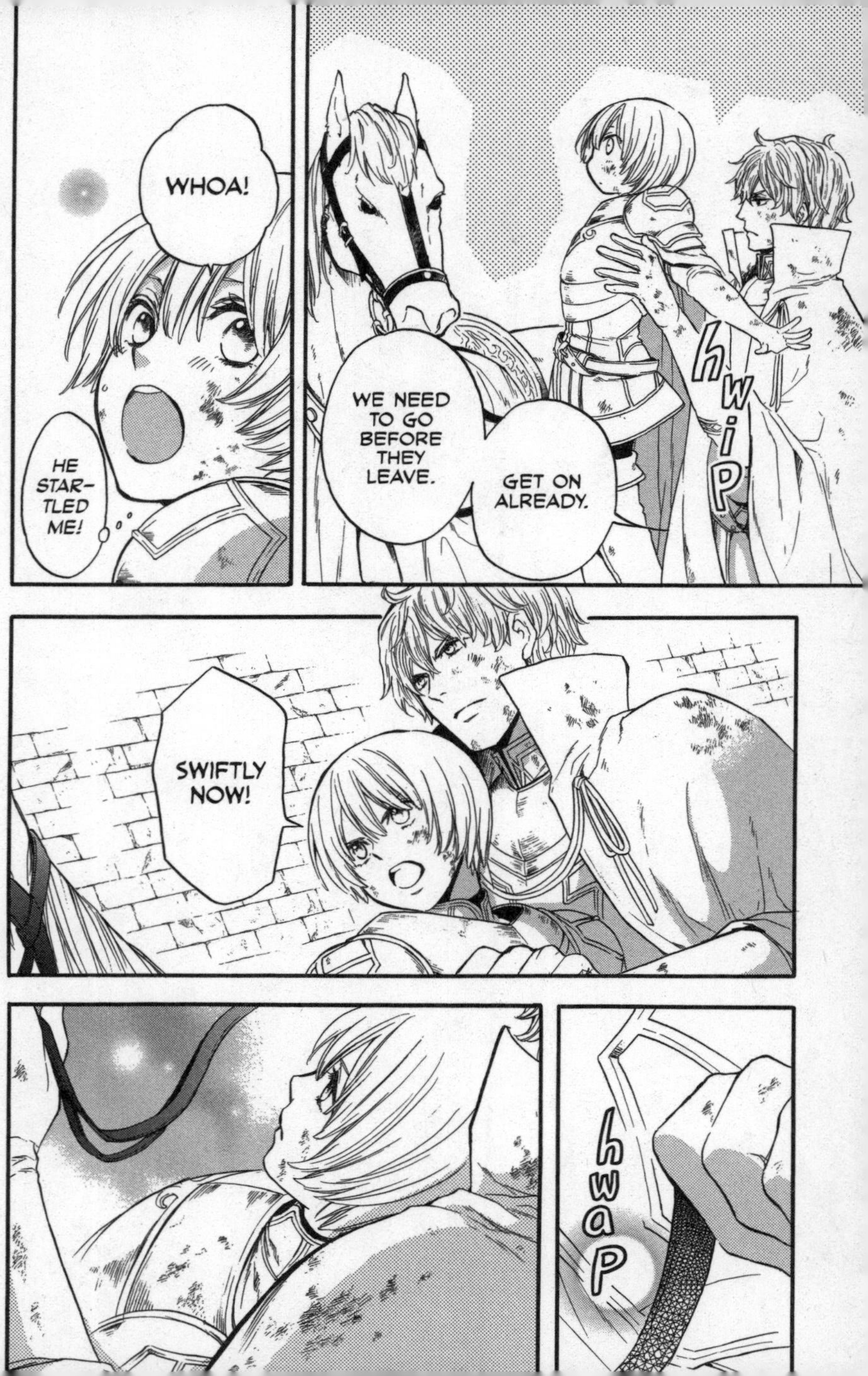hwip
WE NEED TO GO BEFORE THEY LEAVE.
GET ON ALREADY.
WHOA!
HE STARTLED ME!
SWIFTLY NOW!
hwap

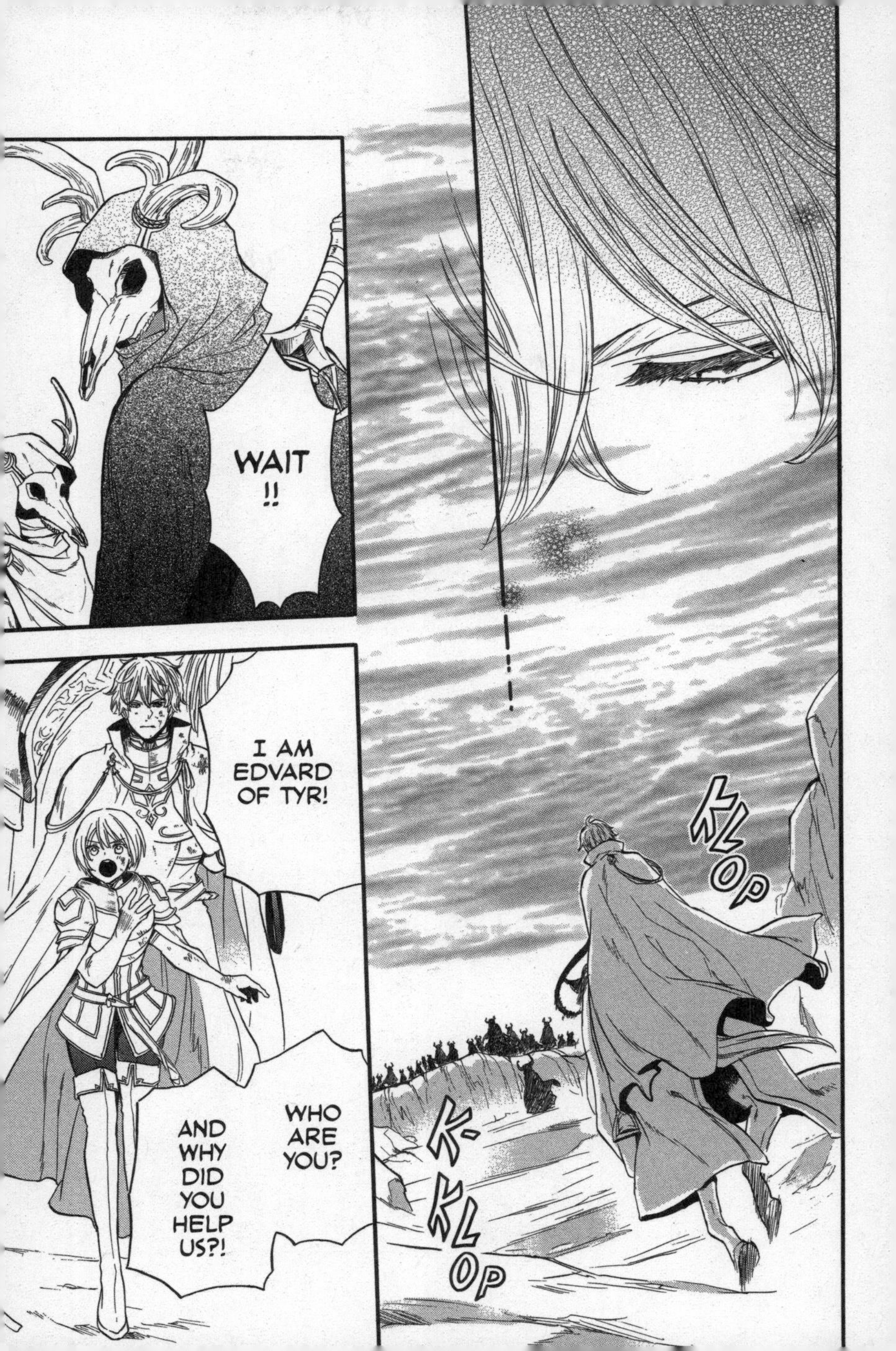
KLOP
K-KLOP
WAIT!!
I AM EDVARD OF TYR!
WHO ARE YOU?
AND WHY DID YOU HELP US?!

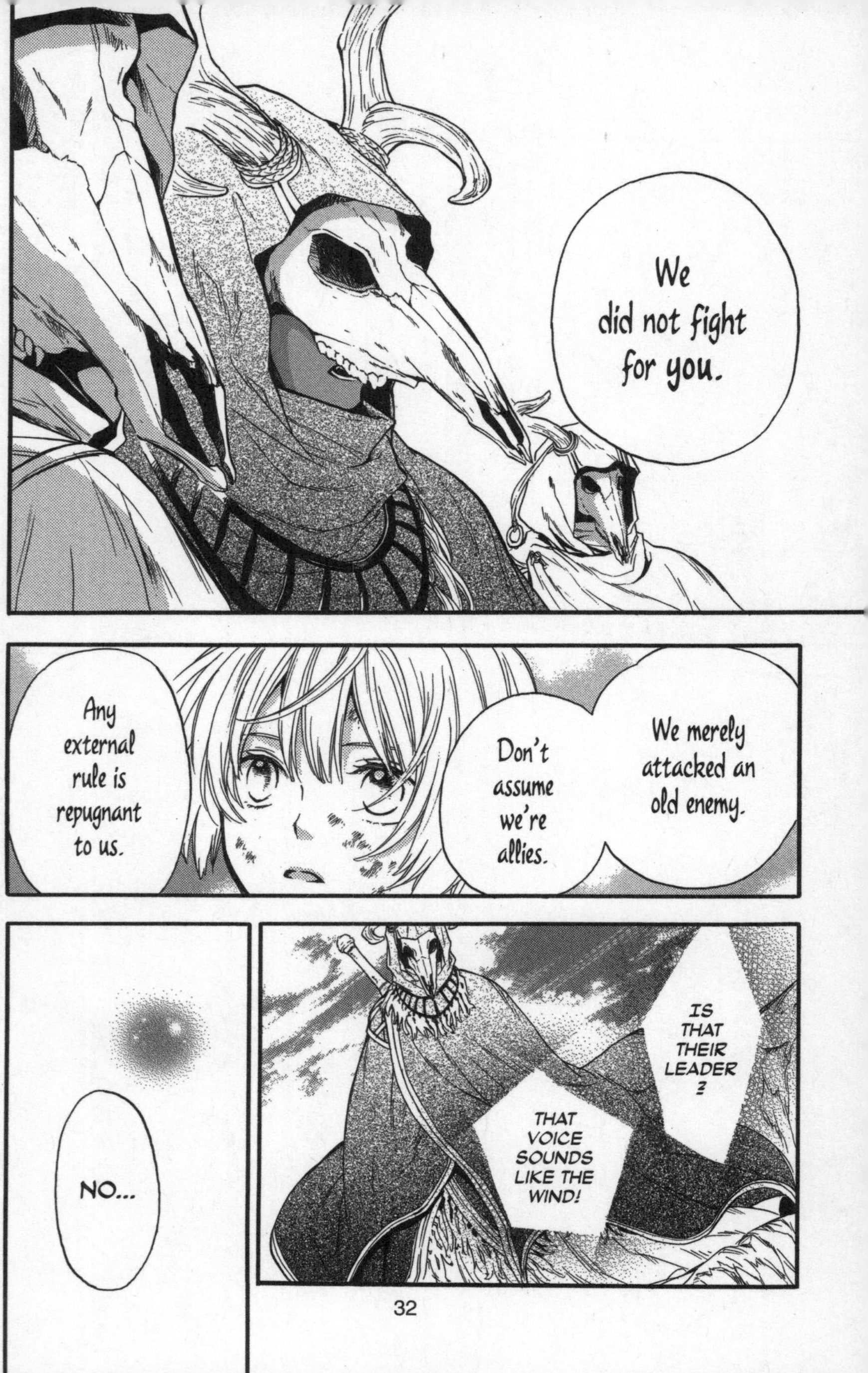
We did not fight for you.
We merely attacked an old enemy.
Don't assume we're allies.
Any external rule is repugnant to us.
IS THAT THEIR LEADER?
THAT VOICE SOUNDS LIKE THE WIND!
NO...

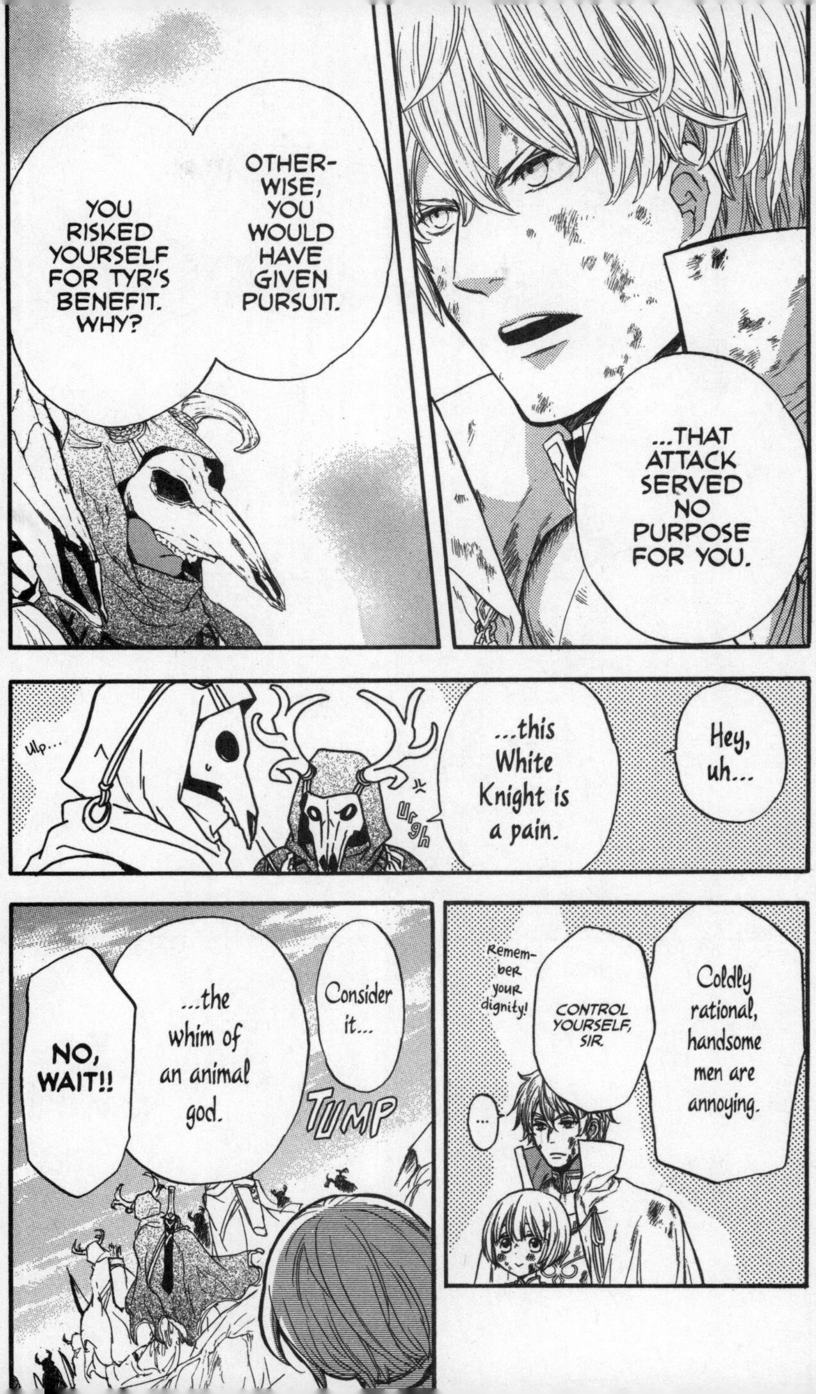
...THAT ATTACK SERVED NO PURPOSE FOR YOU.
OTHER-WISE, YOU WOULD HAVE GIVEN PURSUIT.
YOU RISKED YOURSELF FOR TYR'S BENEFIT. WHY?
Hey, uh...
...this White Knight is a pain.
urgh
Ulp...
Coldly rational, handsome men are annoying.
CONTROL YOURSELF, SIR.
Remem-ber your dignity!
...
Consider it...
...the whim of an animal god.
TUMP
NO, WAIT!!

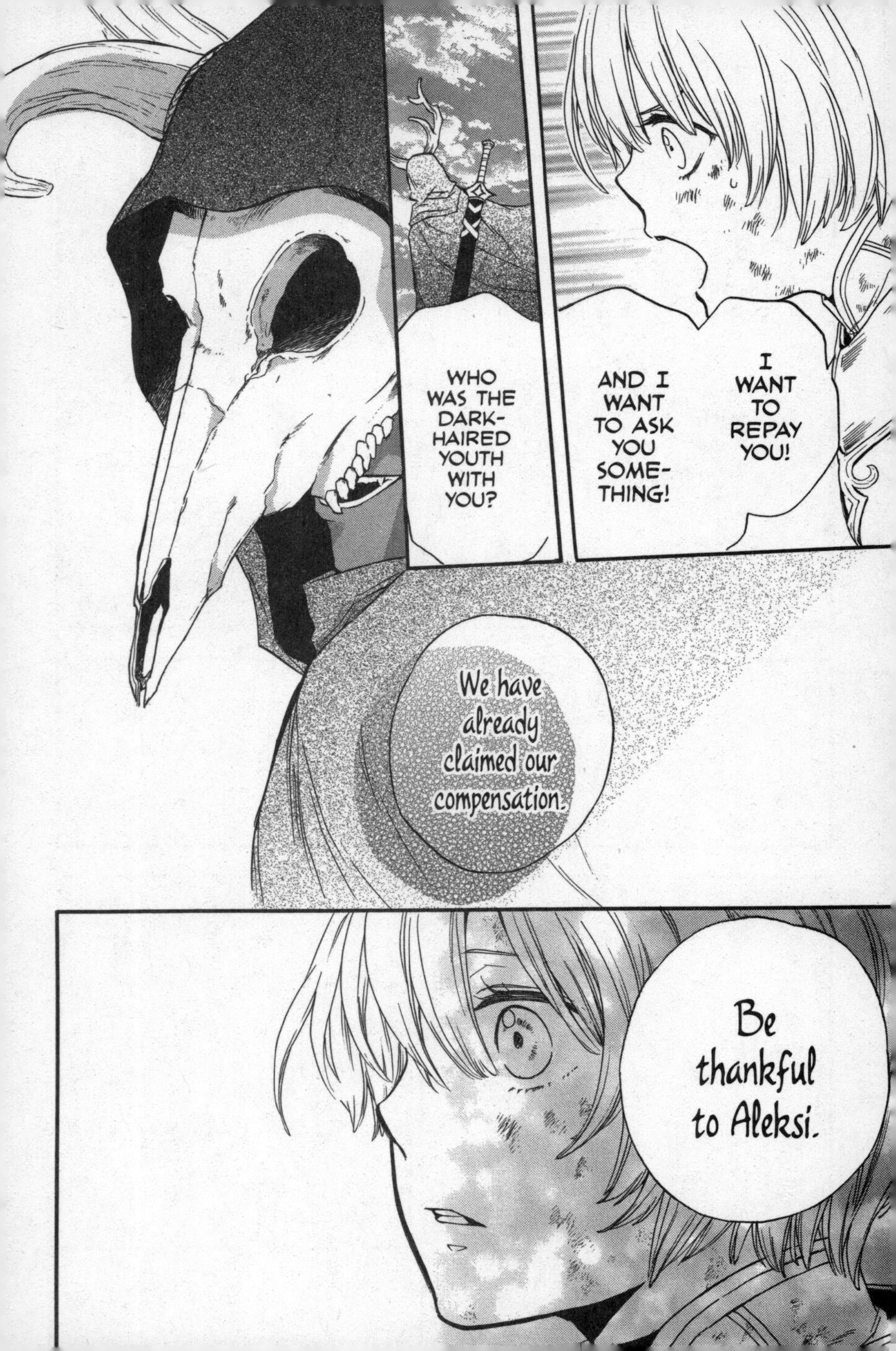
I WANT TO REPAY YOU!
AND I WANT TO ASK YOU SOMETHING!
WHO WAS THE DARK-HAIRED YOUTH WITH YOU?
We have already claimed our compensation.
Be thankful to Aleksi.

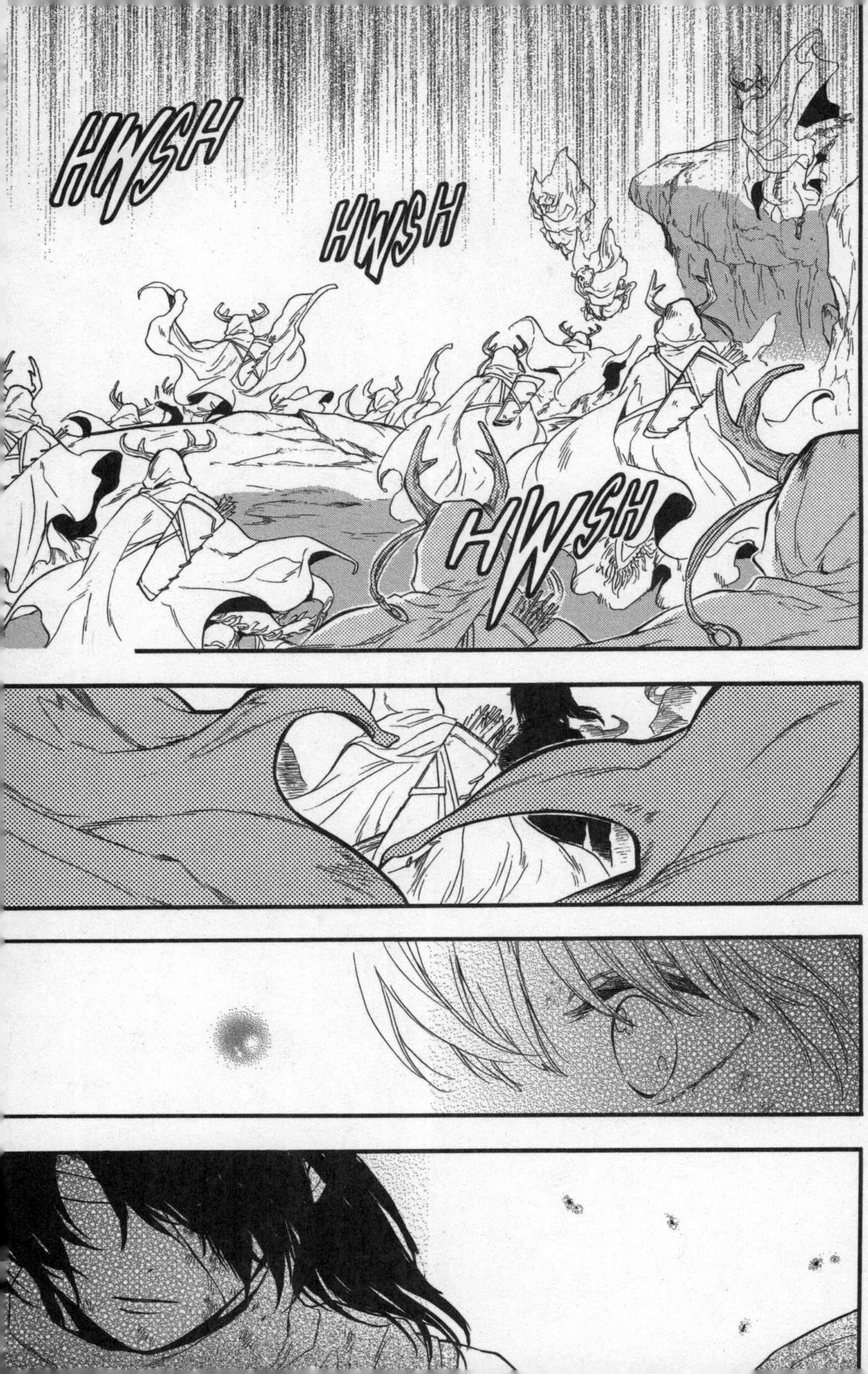
HWSH
HWSH
HWSH

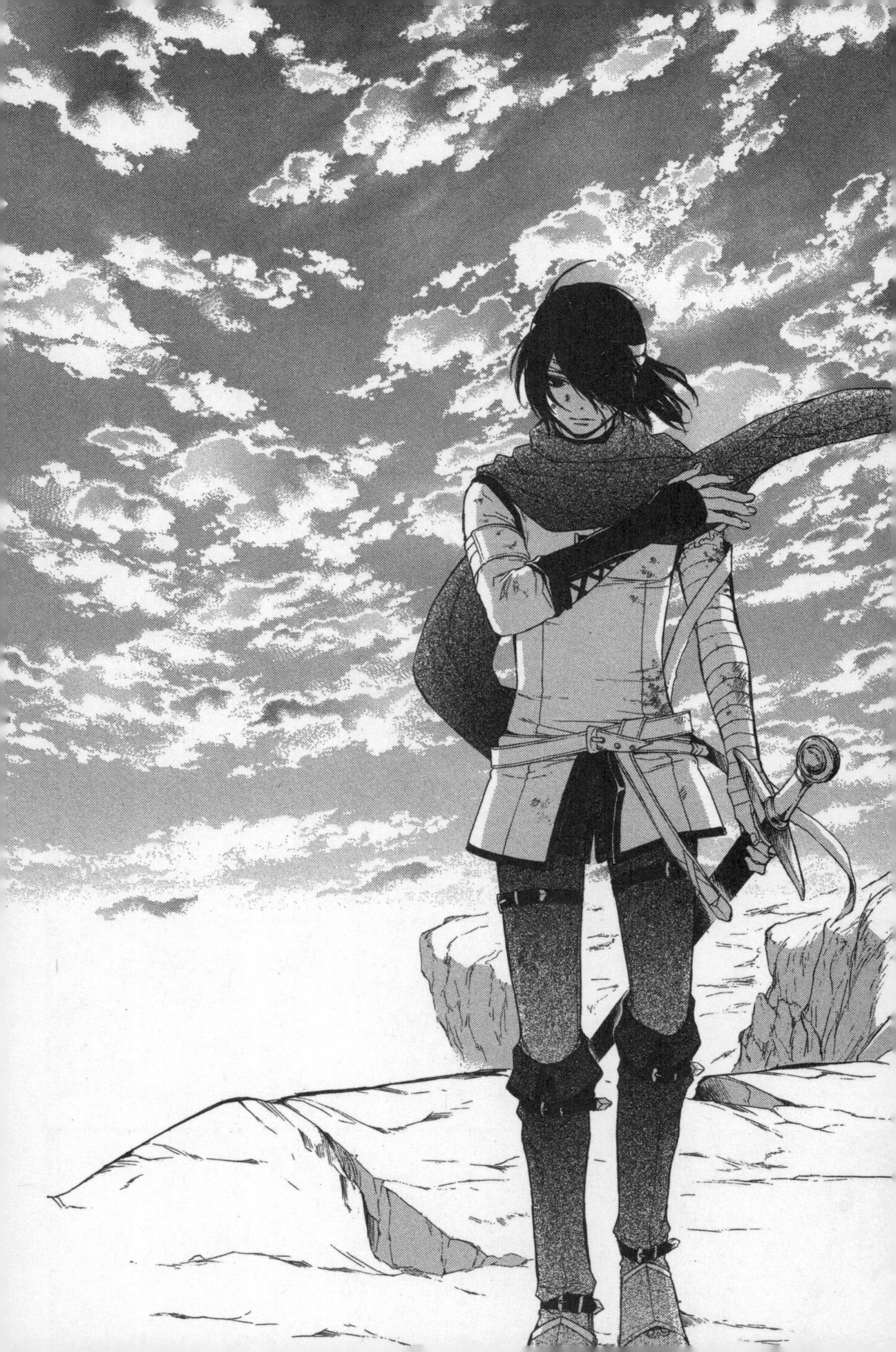

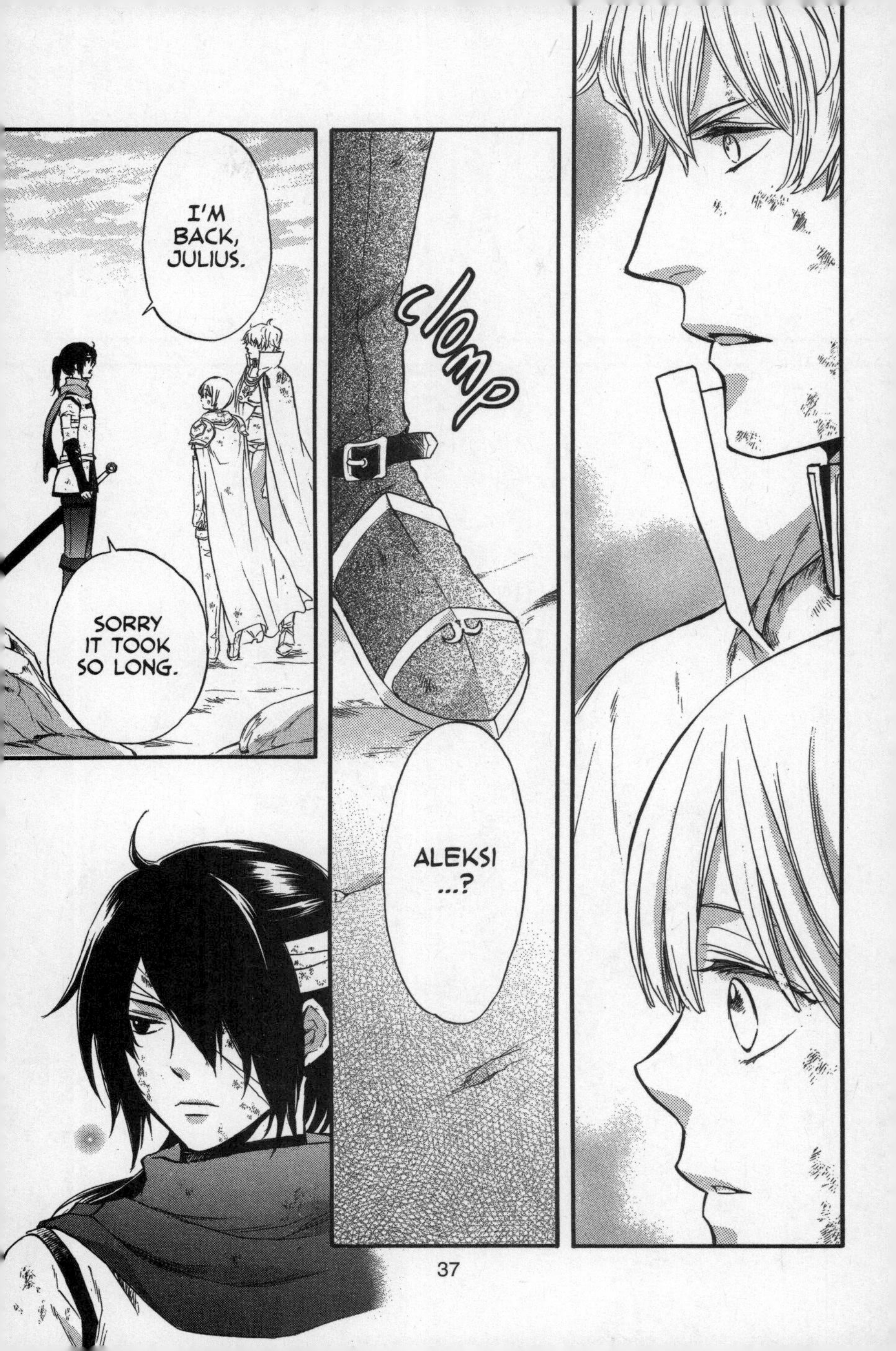
clomp
ALEKSI ...?
I'M BACK, JULIUS.
SORRY IT TOOK SO LONG.

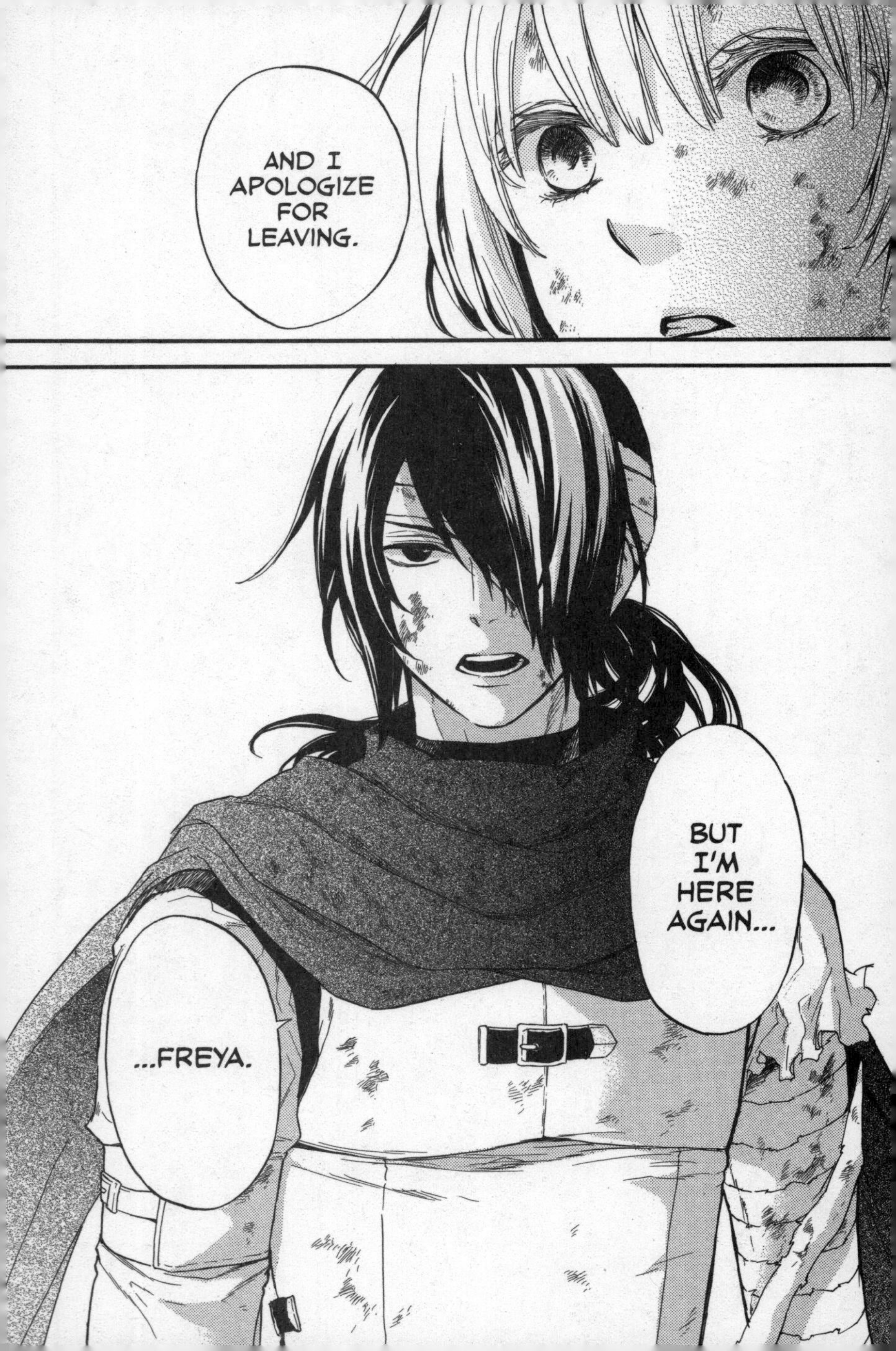
AND I APOLOGIZE FOR LEAVING.
BUT I'M HERE AGAIN...
...FREYA.

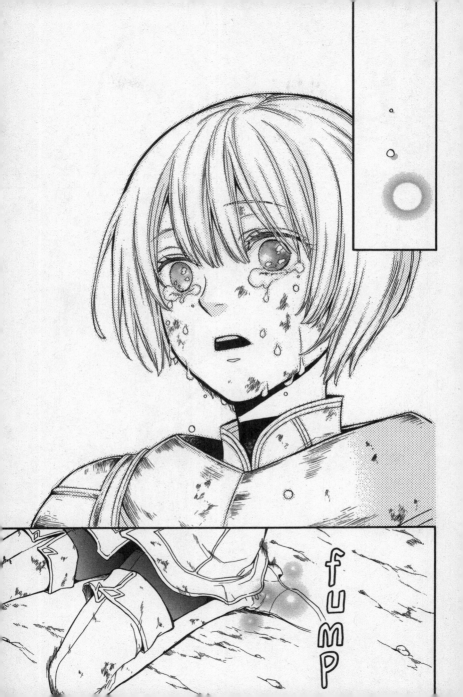

fuMP

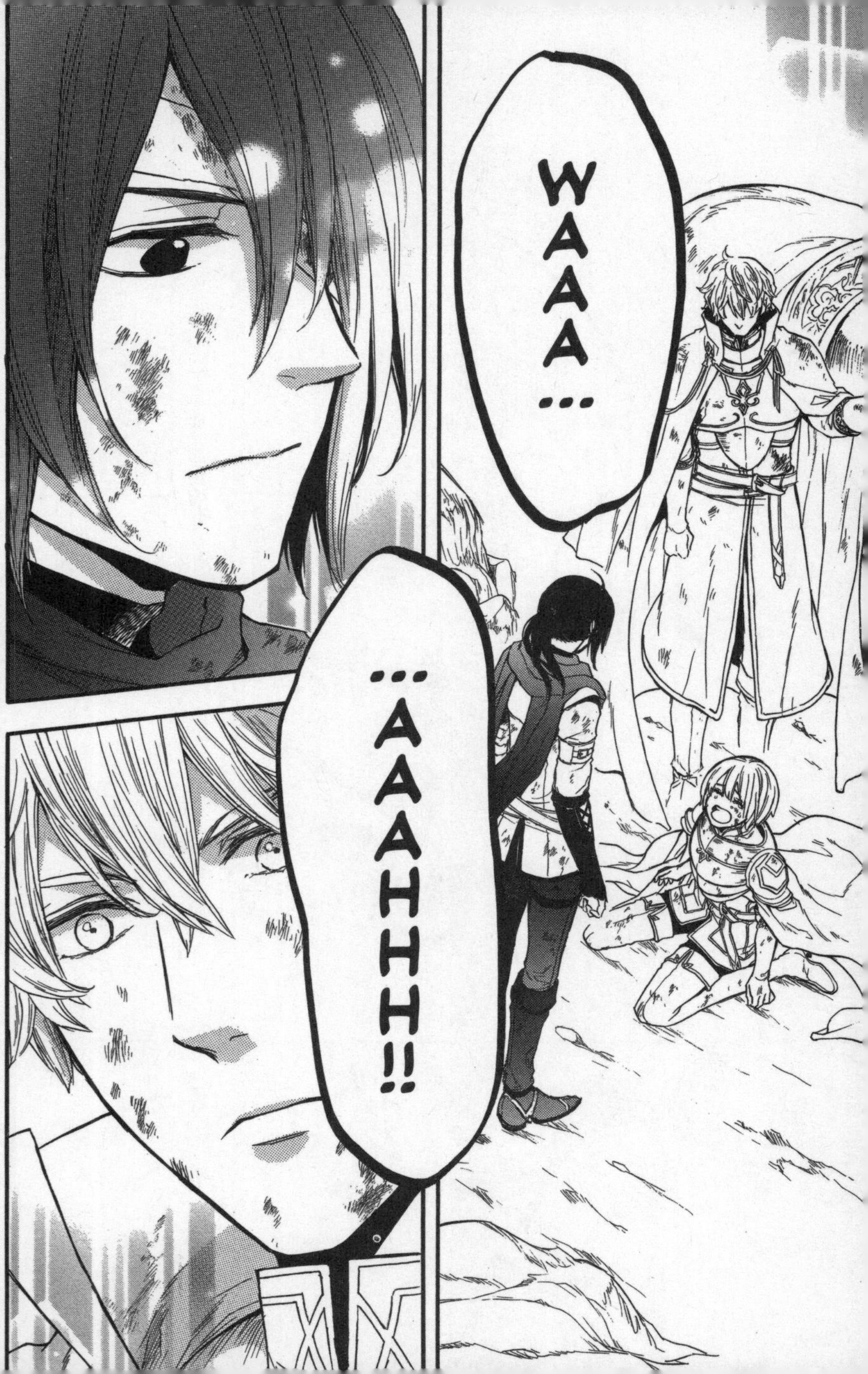
WAAA...
...AAAHHH!!

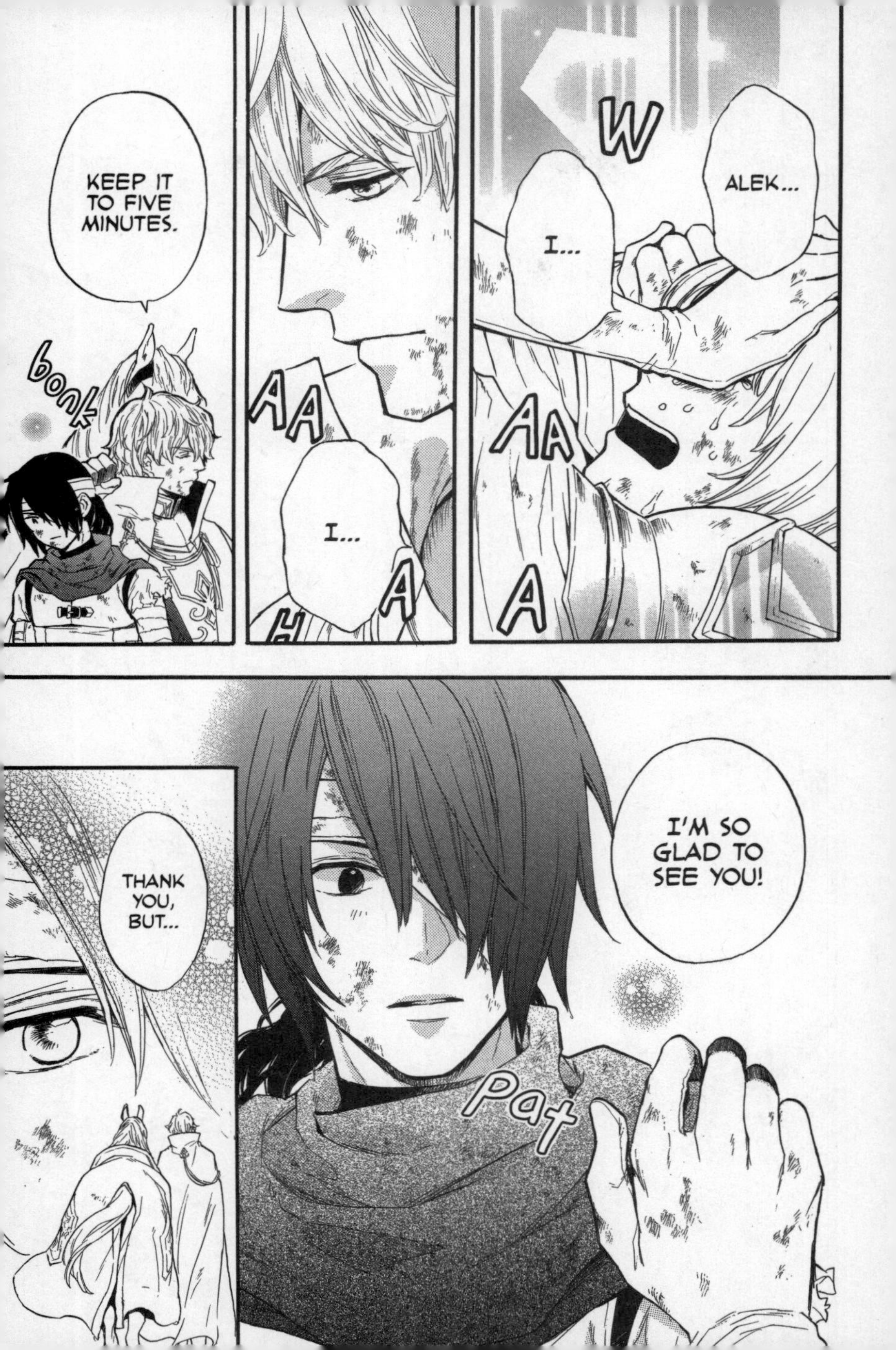
W
ALEK...
I...
AA
A
AA
I...
A
H
KEEP IT TO FIVE MINUTES.
bonk
I'M SO GLAD TO SEE YOU!
pat
THANK YOU, BUT...

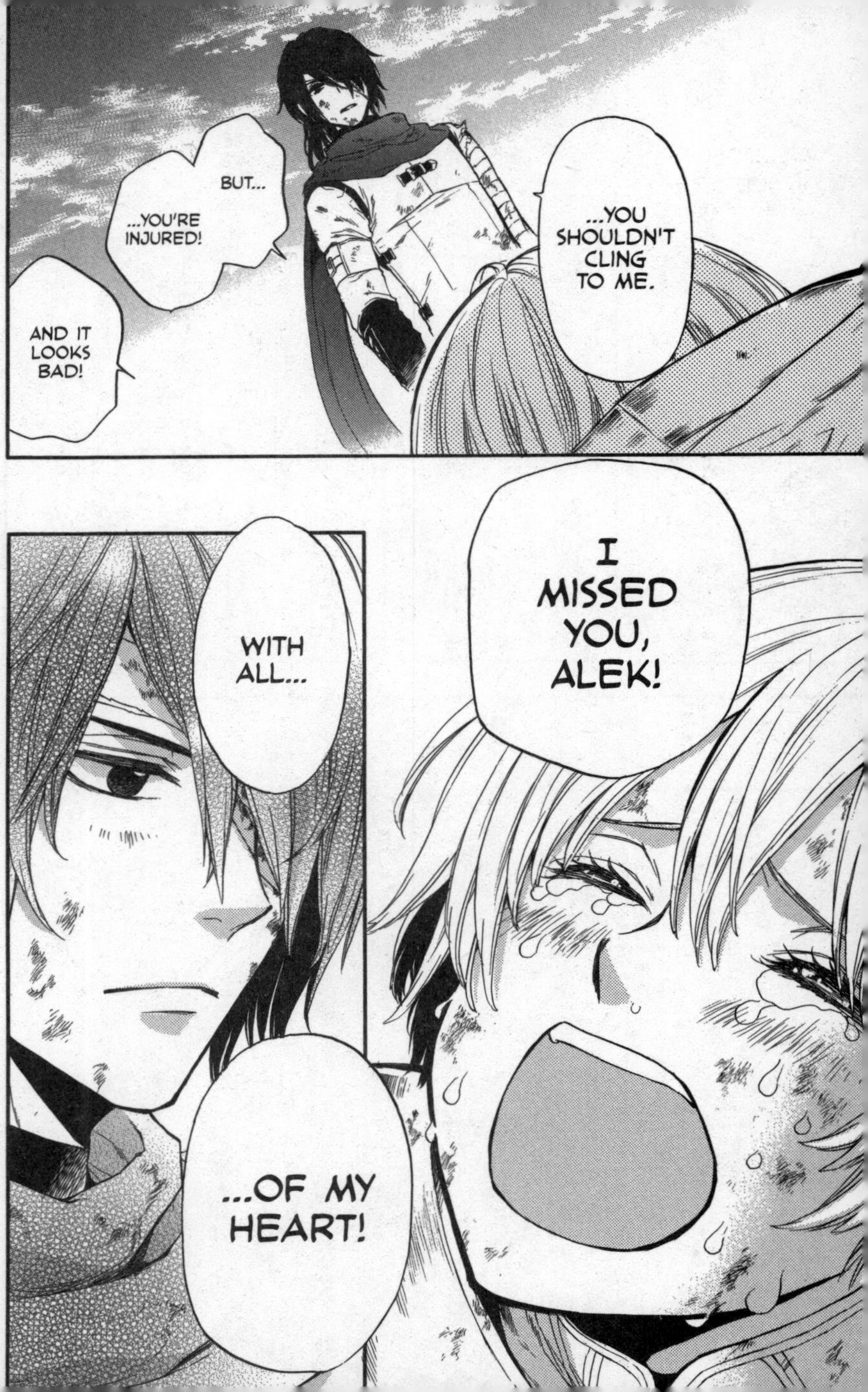
...YOU SHOULDN'T CLING TO ME.
BUT...
...YOU'RE INJURED!
AND IT LOOKS BAD!
I MISSED YOU, ALEK!
WITH ALL...
...OF MY HEART!

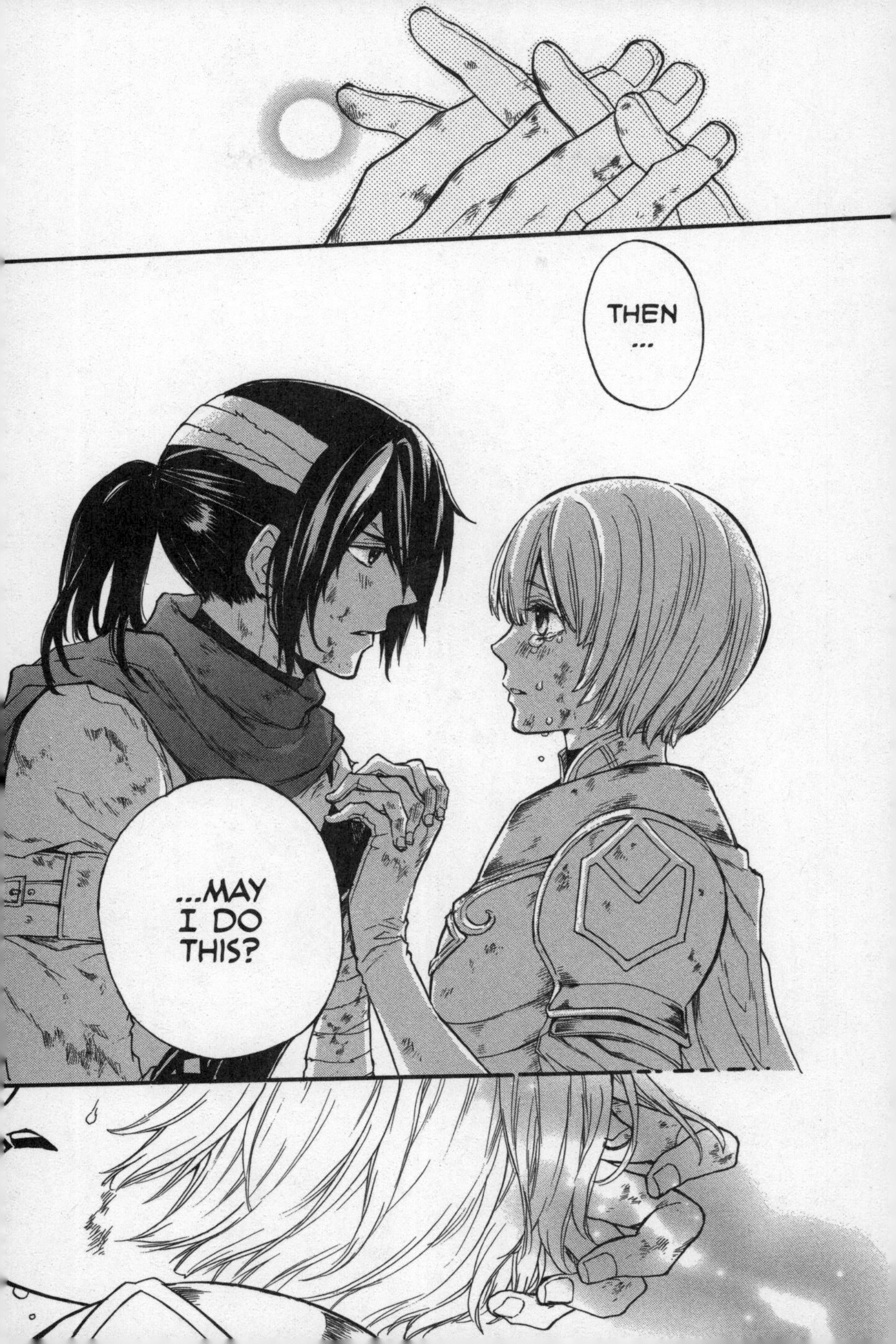
THEN ...
...MAY I DO THIS?

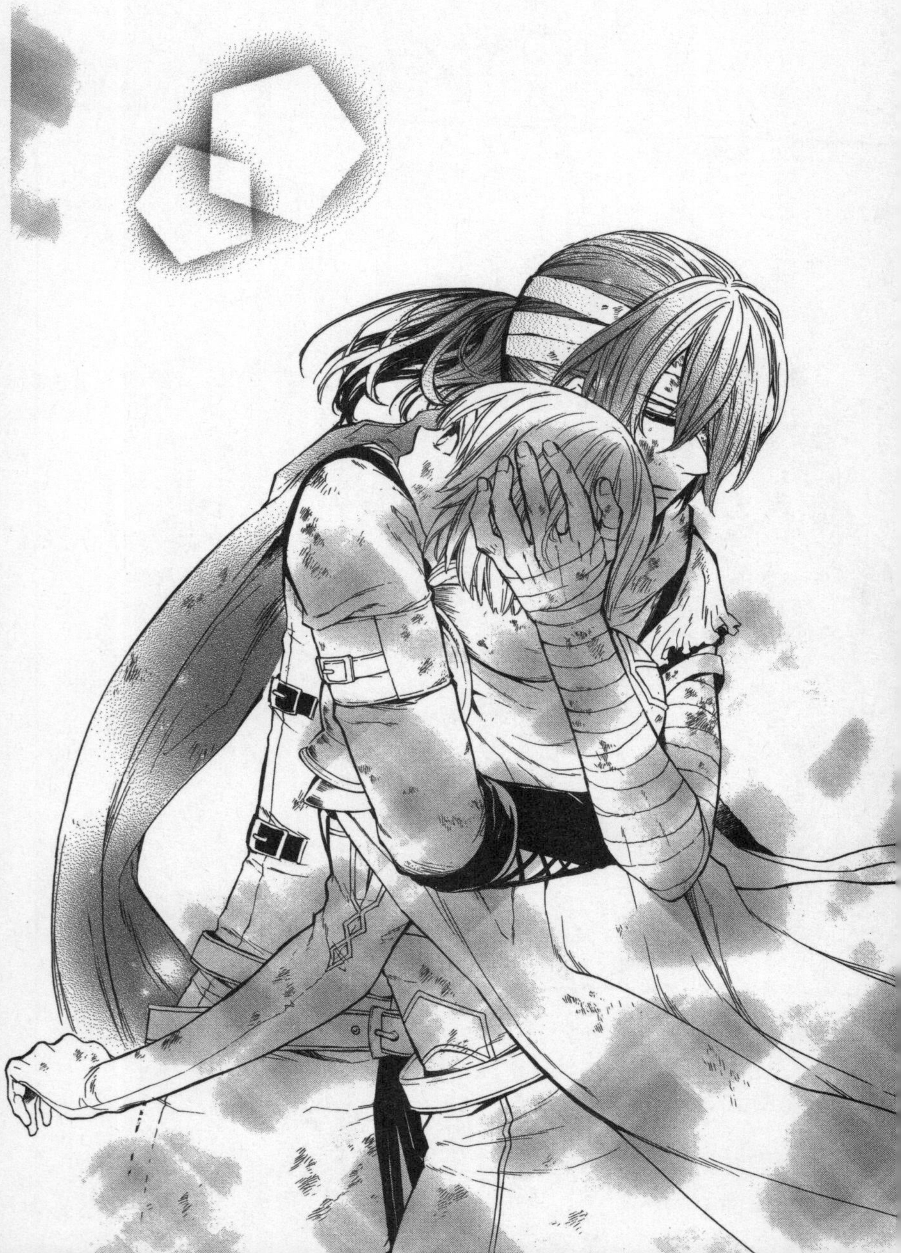

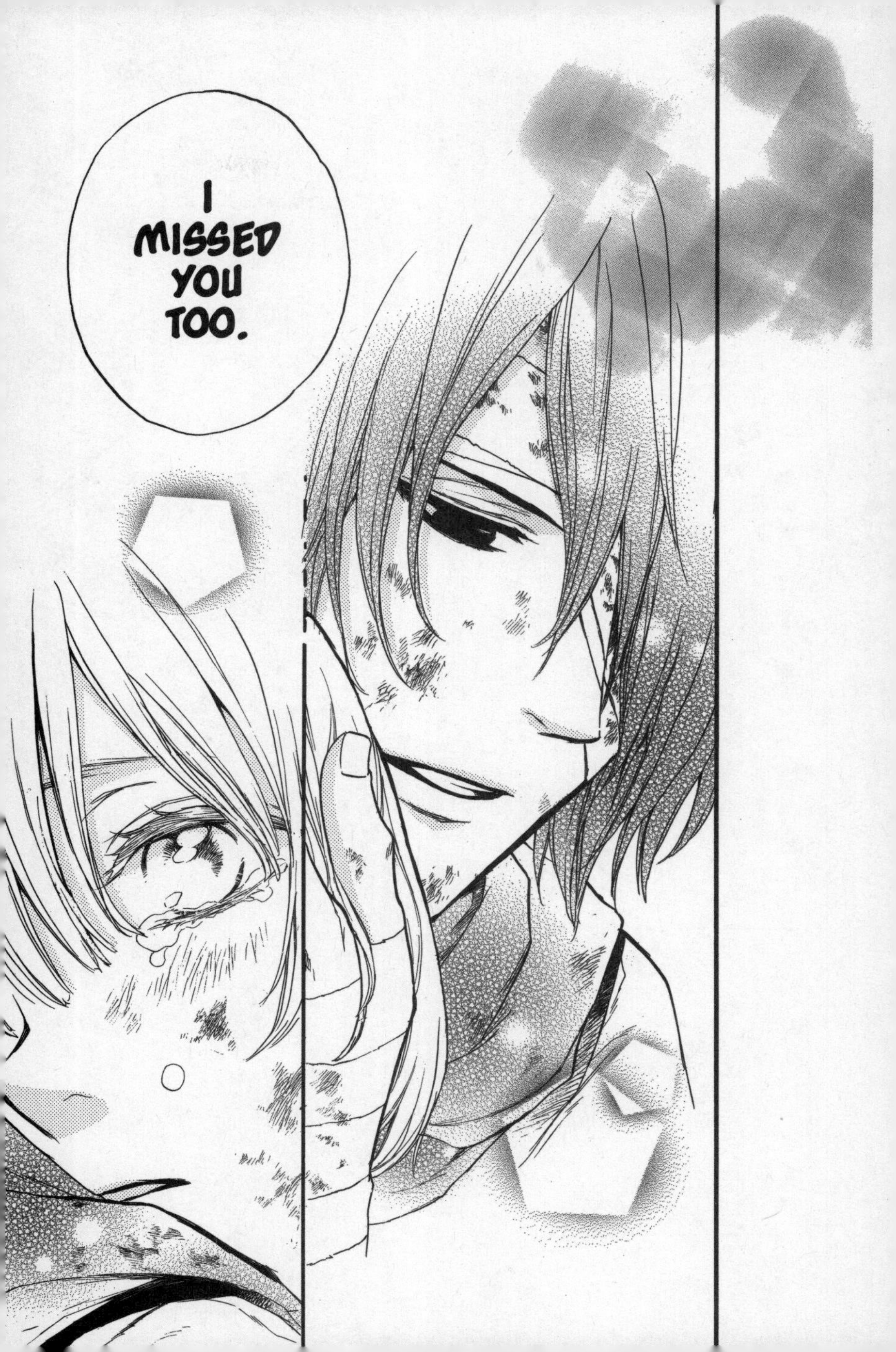
I MISSED YOU TOO.

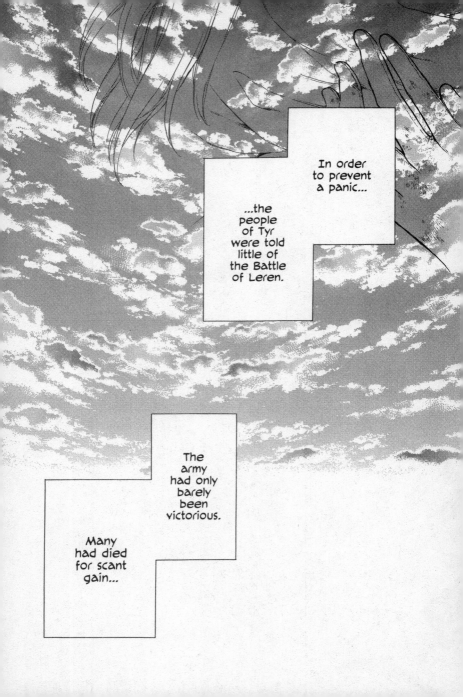

In order
to prevent
a panic...

...the
people
of Tyr
were told
little of
the Battle
of Leren.

The
army
had only
barely
been
victorious.

Many
had died
for scant
gain...

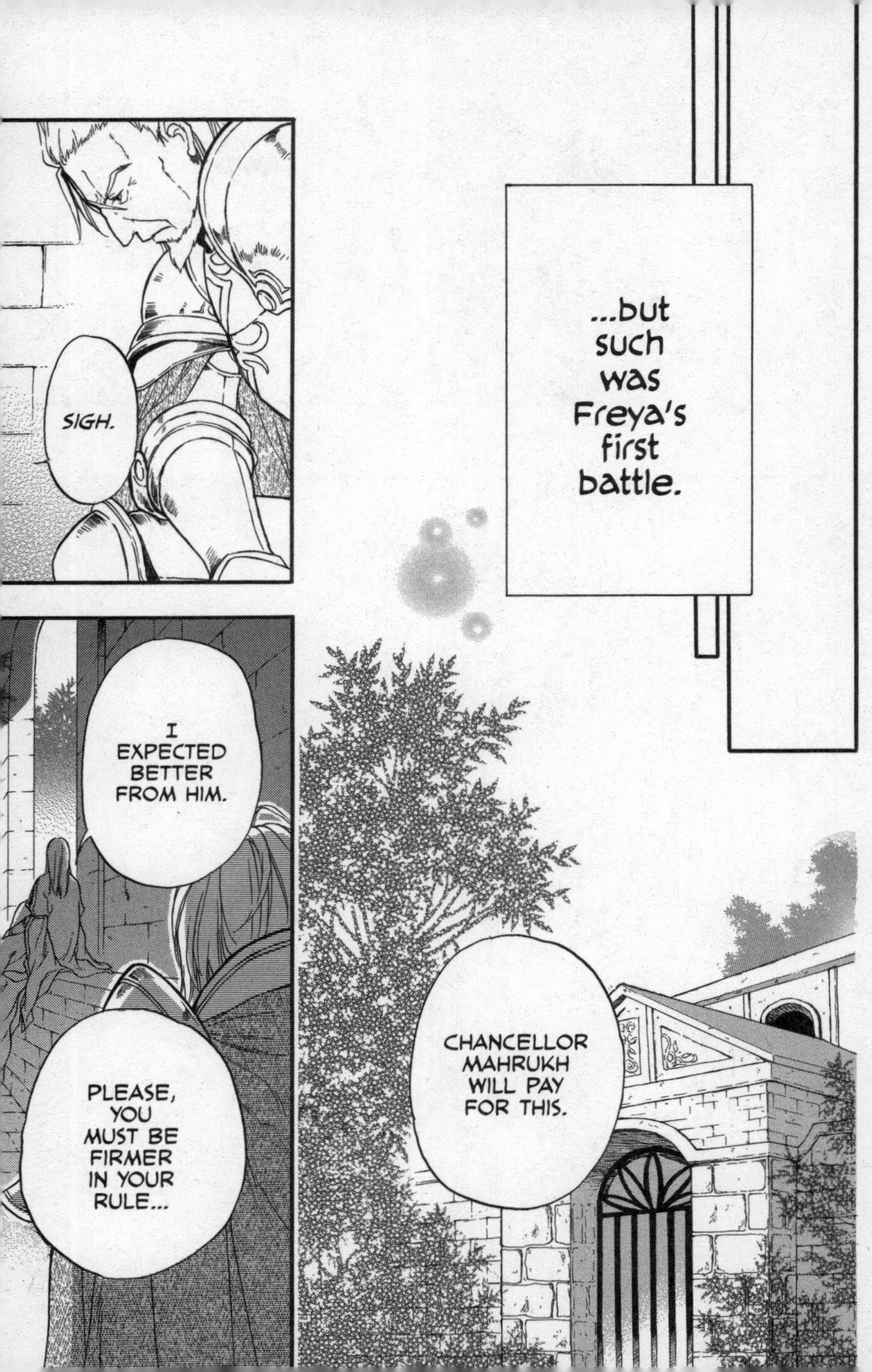
...but such was Freya's first battle.
SIGH.
CHANCELLOR MAHRUKH WILL PAY FOR THIS.
I EXPECTED BETTER FROM HIM.
PLEASE, YOU MUST BE FIRMER IN YOUR RULE...

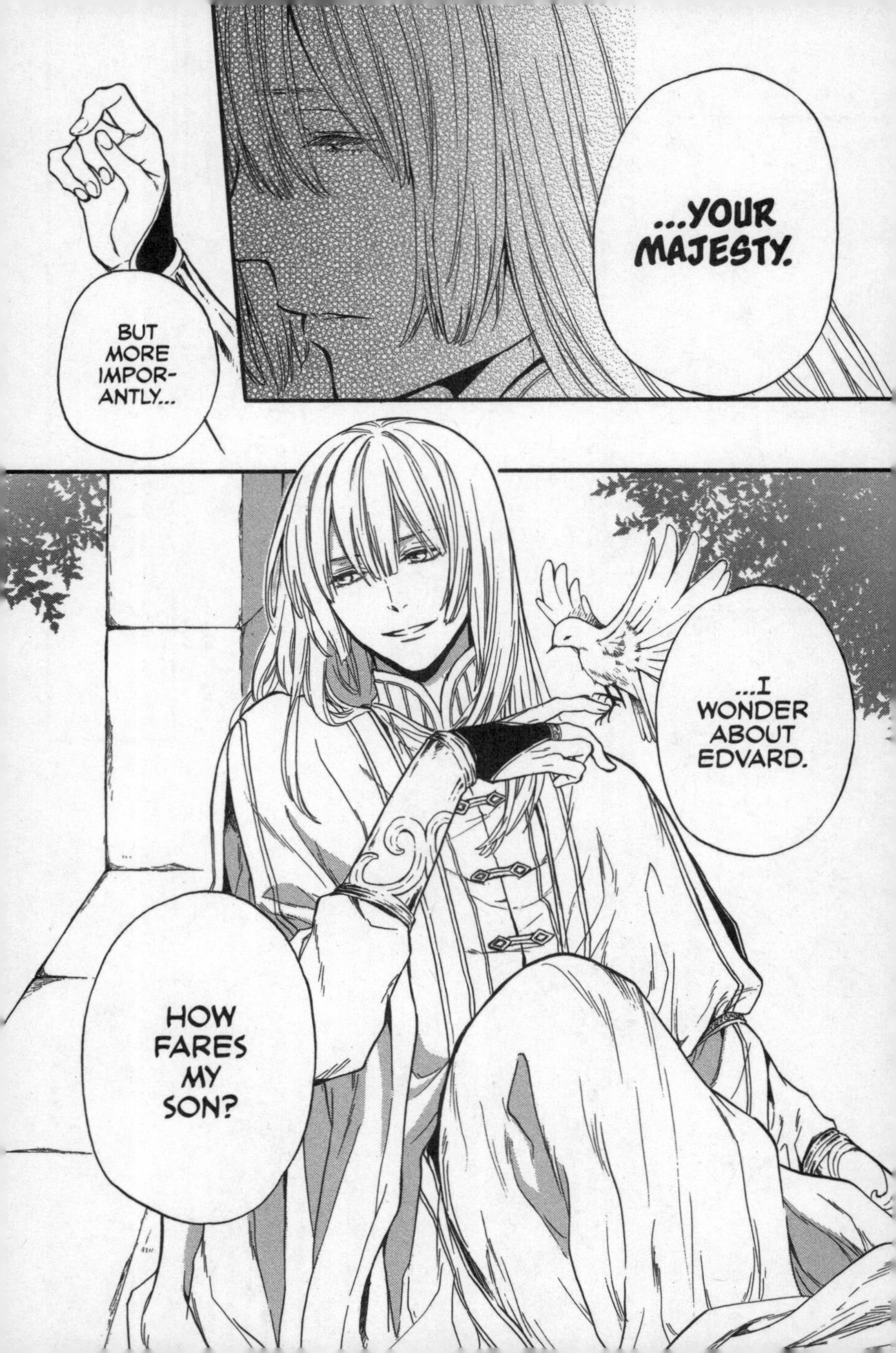
...YOUR MAJESTY.
BUT MORE IMPOR-ANTLY...
...I WONDER ABOUT EDVARD.
HOW FARES MY SON?

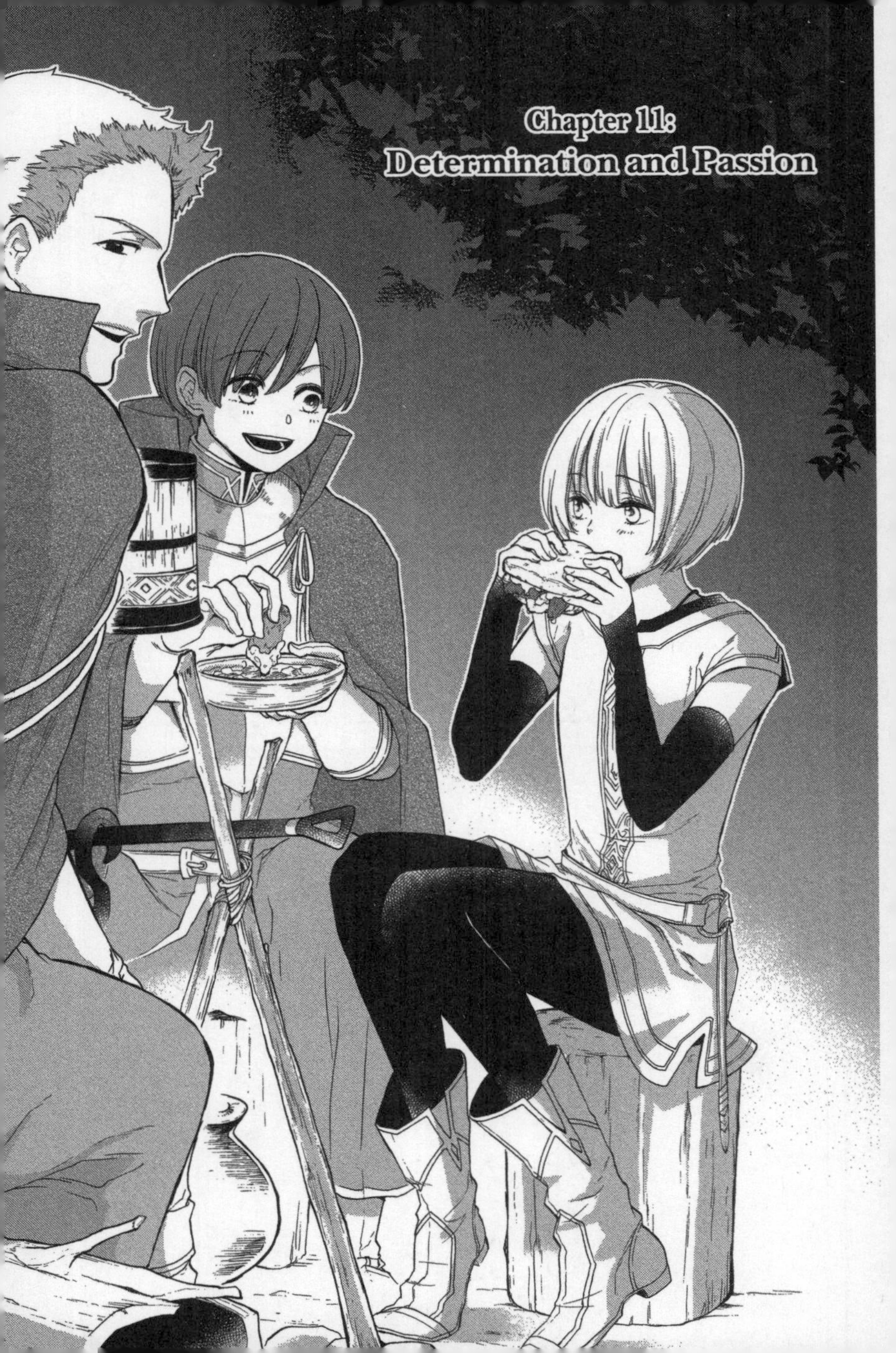
Chapter 11:
Determination and Passion

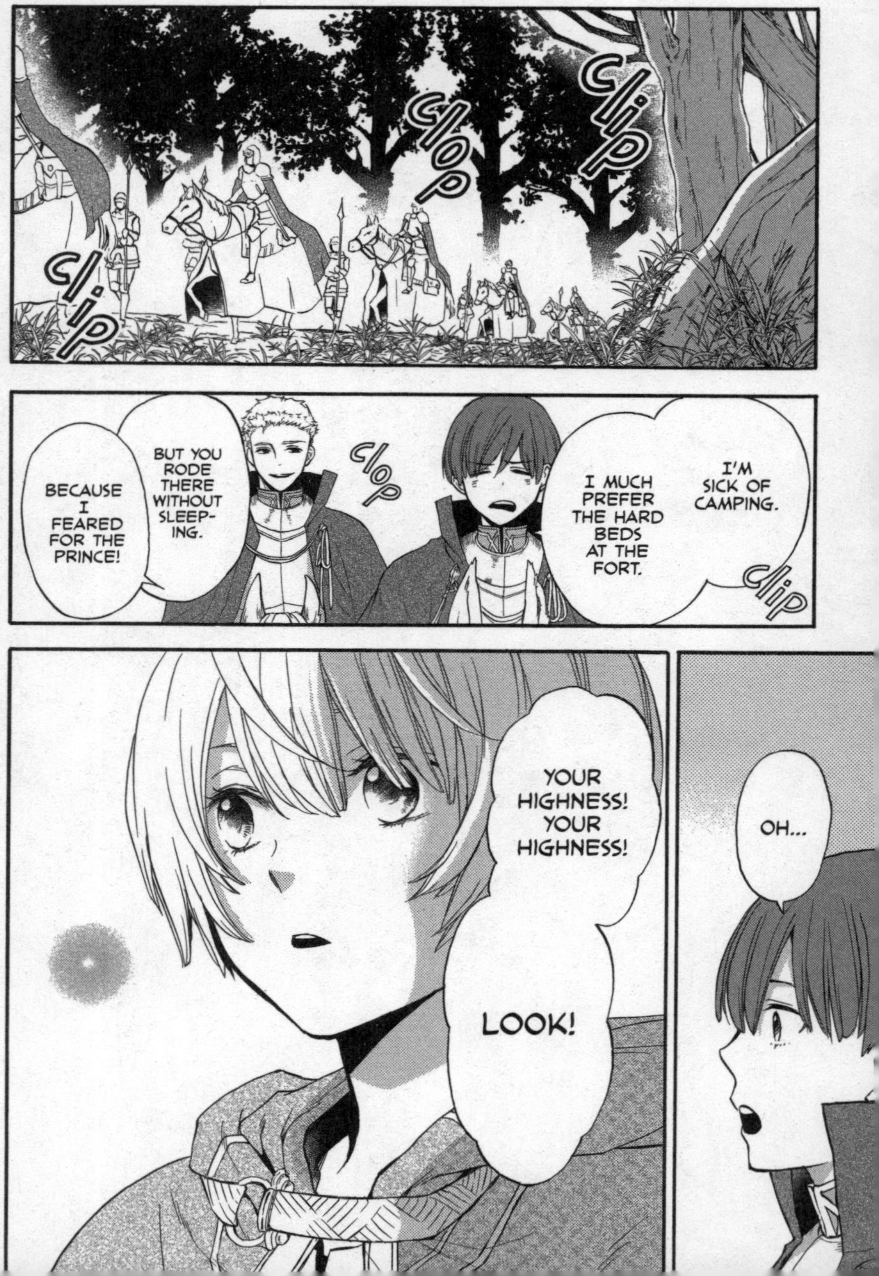
clip
clop
clip
I'M SICK OF CAMPING.
I MUCH PREFER THE HARD BEDS AT THE FORT.
clip
clop
BUT YOU RODE THERE WITHOUT SLEEP-ING.
BECAUSE I FEARED FOR THE PRINCE!
OH...
YOUR HIGHNESS! YOUR HIGHNESS!
LOOK!

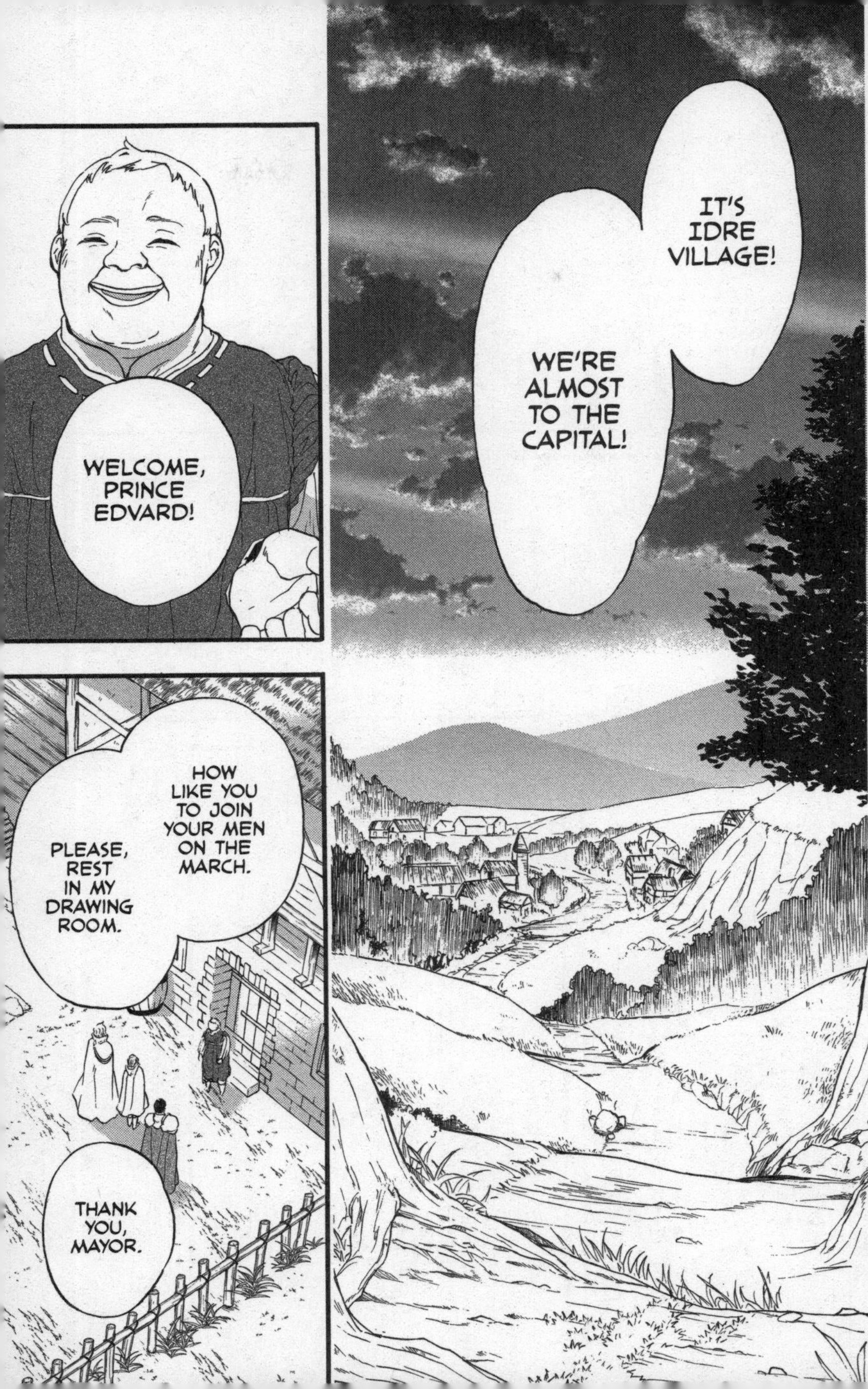
IT'S IDRE VILLAGE!
WE'RE ALMOST TO THE CAPITAL!
WELCOME, PRINCE EDVARD!
HOW LIKE YOU TO JOIN YOUR MEN ON THE MARCH.
PLEASE, REST IN MY DRAWING ROOM.
THANK YOU, MAYOR.

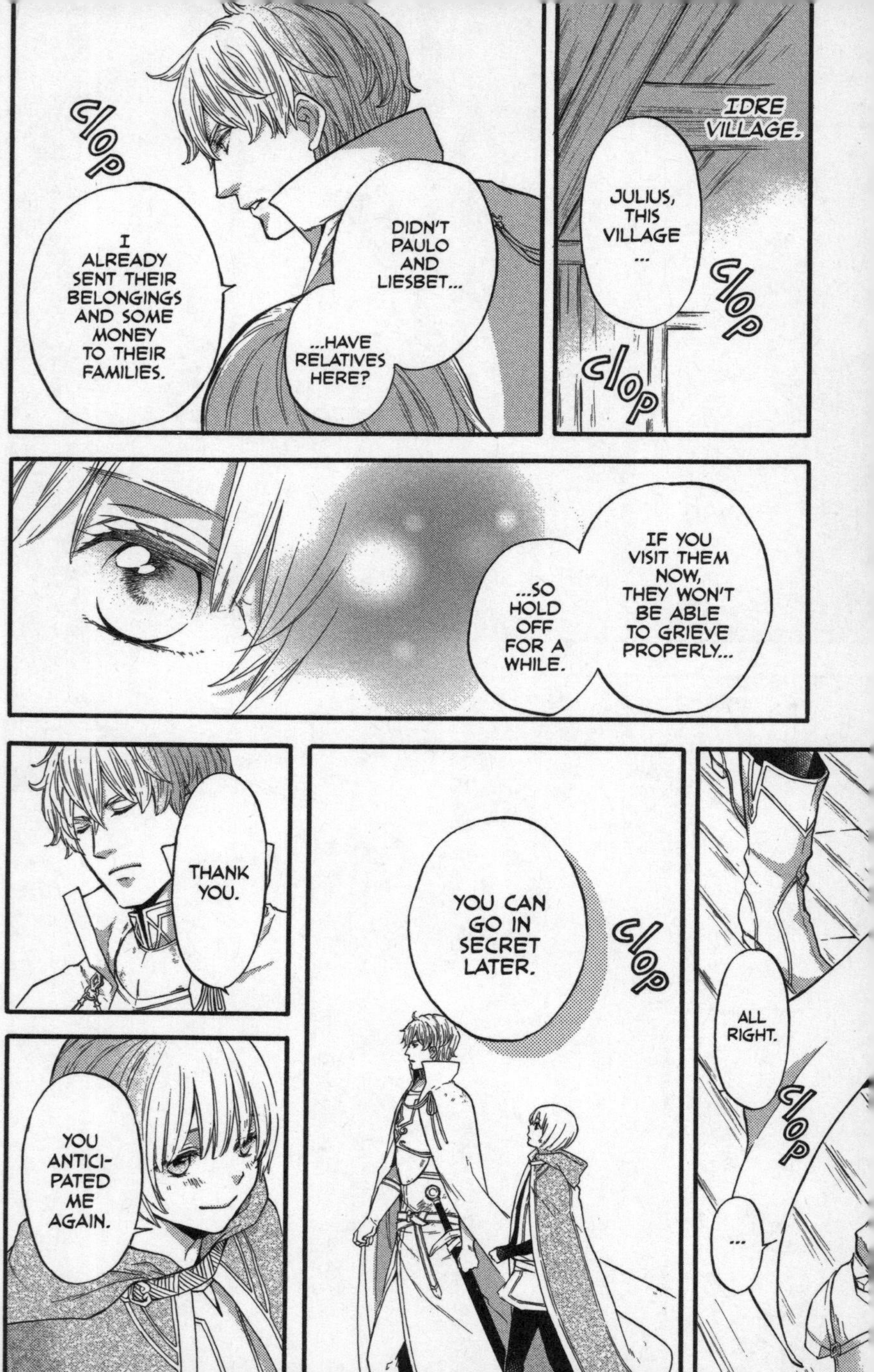
IDRE VILLAGE.
JULIUS, THIS VILLAGE ...
CLOP
CLOP
CLOP
DIDN'T PAULO AND LIESBET...
...HAVE RELATIVES HERE?
I ALREADY SENT THEIR BELONGINGS AND SOME MONEY TO THEIR FAMILIES.
IF YOU VISIT THEM NOW, THEY WON'T BE ABLE TO GRIEVE PROPERLY...
...SO HOLD OFF FOR A WHILE.
ALL RIGHT.
CLOP
...
YOU CAN GO IN SECRET LATER.
CLOP
THANK YOU.
YOU ANTICI-PATED ME AGAIN.

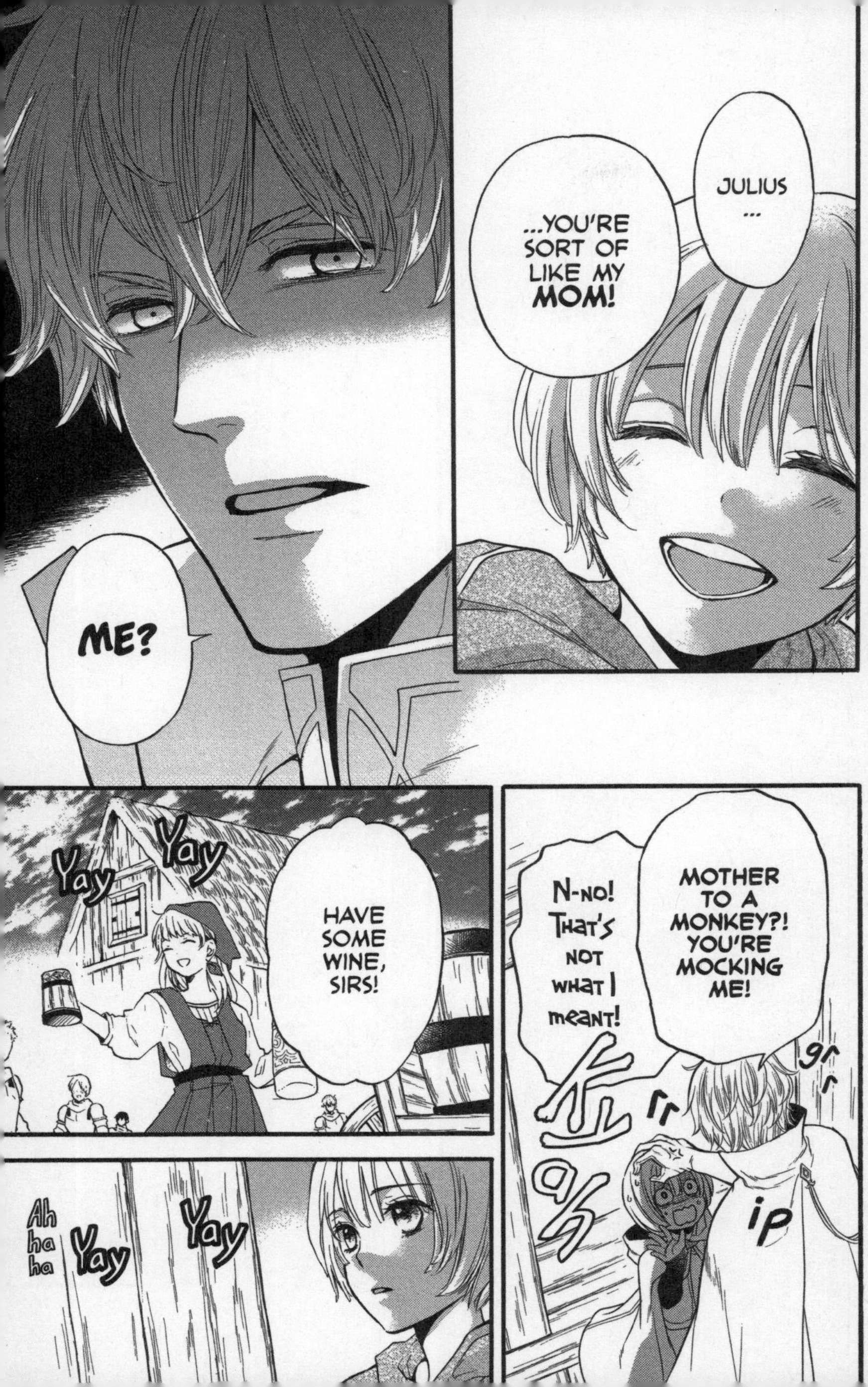
JULIUS ...
...YOU'RE SORT OF LIKE MY MOM!
ME?
MOTHER TO A MONKEY?! YOU'RE MOCKING ME!
N-no! That's not what I meant!
Yay
Yay
HAVE SOME WINE, SIRS!
Yay
Yay
Ah ha ha

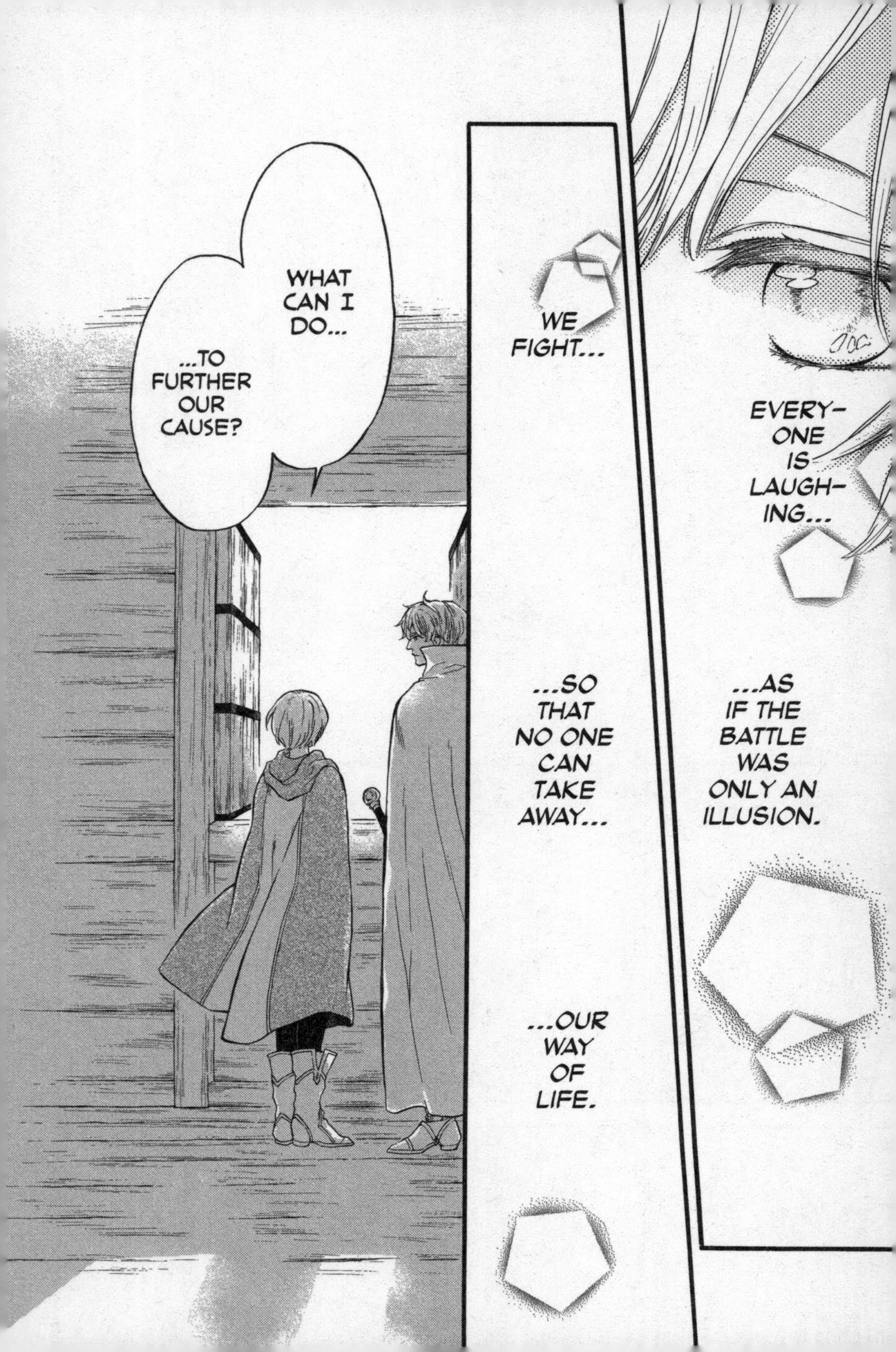
EVERYONE IS LAUGHING...
...AS IF THE BATTLE WAS ONLY AN ILLUSION.
WE FIGHT...
...SO THAT NO ONE CAN TAKE AWAY...
...OUR WAY OF LIFE.
WHAT CAN I DO...
...TO FURTHER OUR CAUSE?

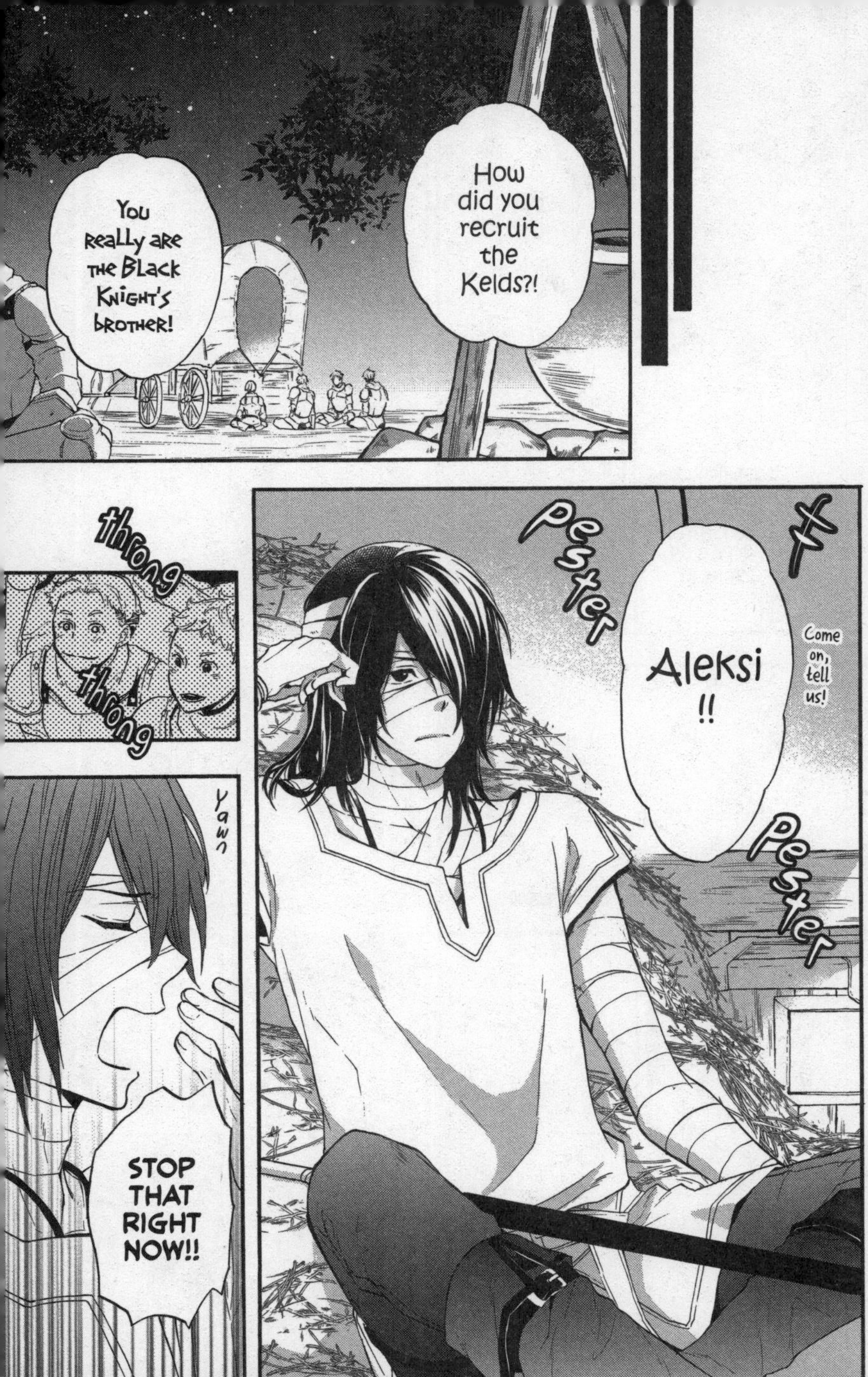
How did you recruit the Kelds?!
You really are the Black Knight's brother!
Aleksi!!
Come on, tell us!
pester
pester
throng
throng
Yawn
STOP THAT RIGHT NOW!!

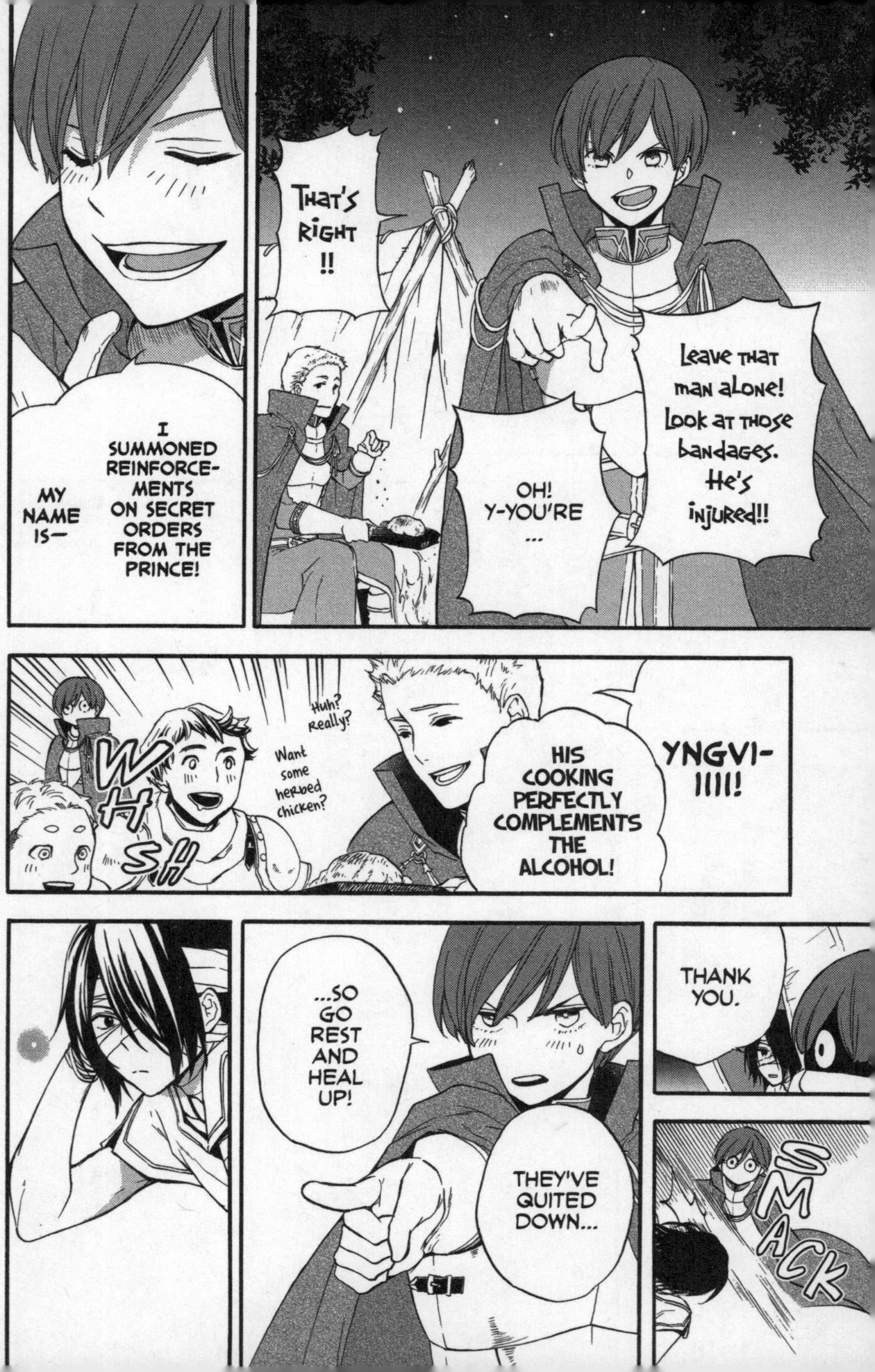
Leave that man alone! Look at those bandages. He's injured!!
OH! Y-YOU'RE ...
THAT'S RIGHT !!
I SUMMONED REINFORCE-MENTS ON SECRET ORDERS FROM THE PRINCE!
MY NAME IS—
YNGVI-IIII!
HIS COOKING PERFECTLY COMPLEMENTS THE ALCOHOL!
Huh? Really?
Want some herbed chicken?
WHSH
THANK YOU.
SMACK
...SO GO REST AND HEAL UP!
THEY'VE QUITED DOWN...

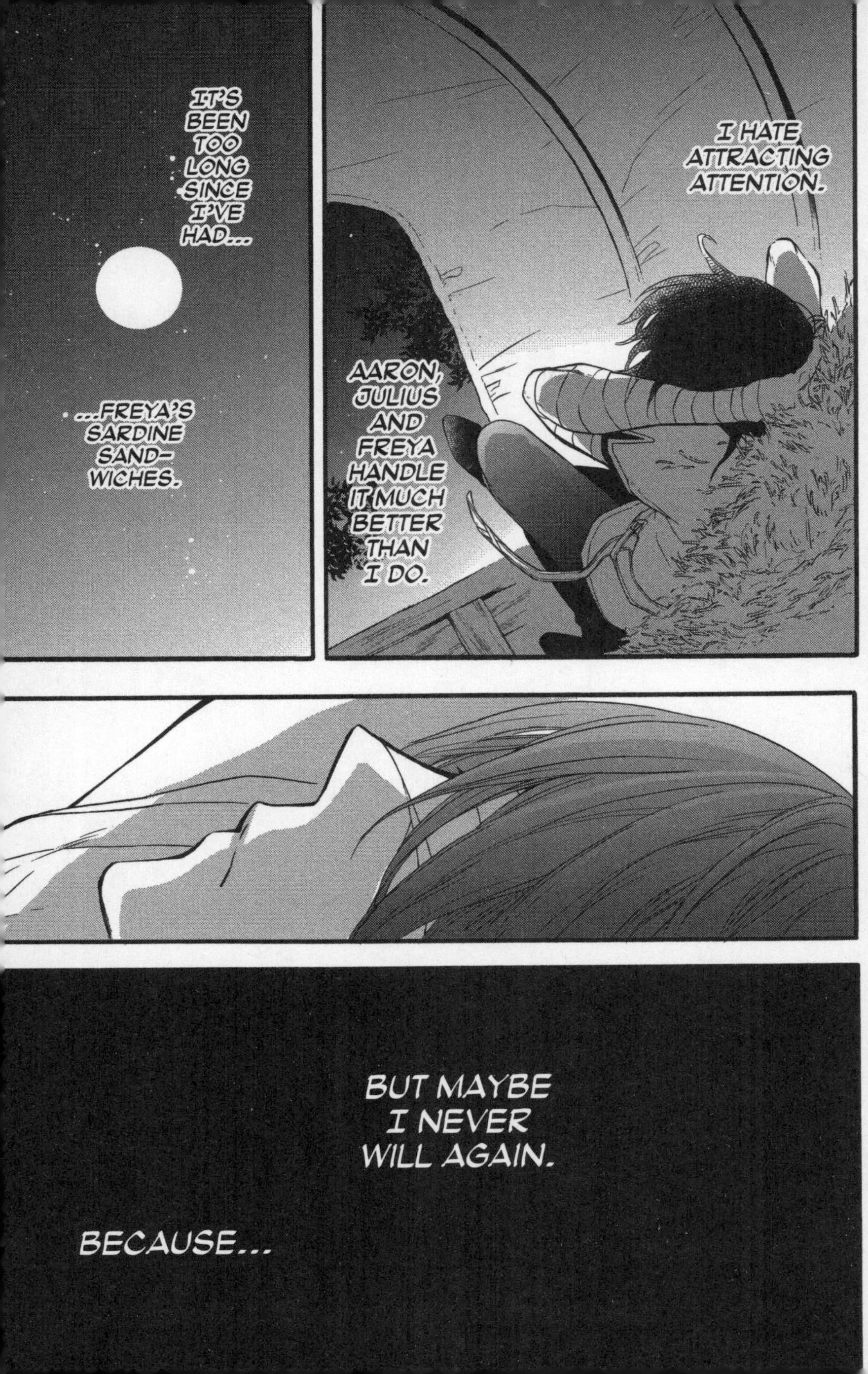
I HATE ATTRACTING ATTENTION.
AARON, JULIUS AND FREYA HANDLE IT MUCH BETTER THAN I DO.
IT'S BEEN TOO LONG SINCE I'VE HAD...
...FREYA'S SARDINE SAND-WICHES.
BUT MAYBE I NEVER WILL AGAIN.
BECAUSE...

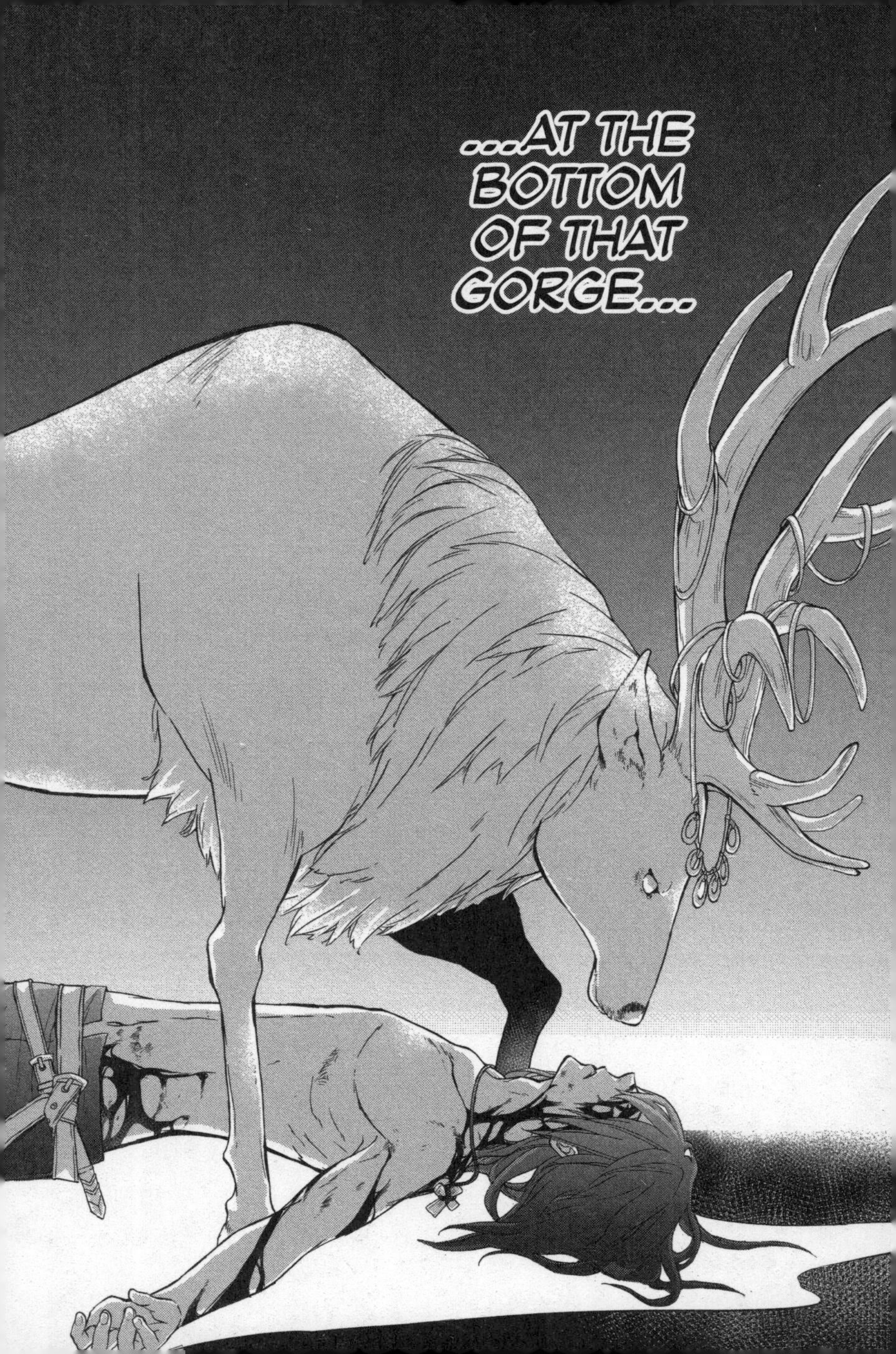
...AT THE BOTTOM OF THAT GORGE...

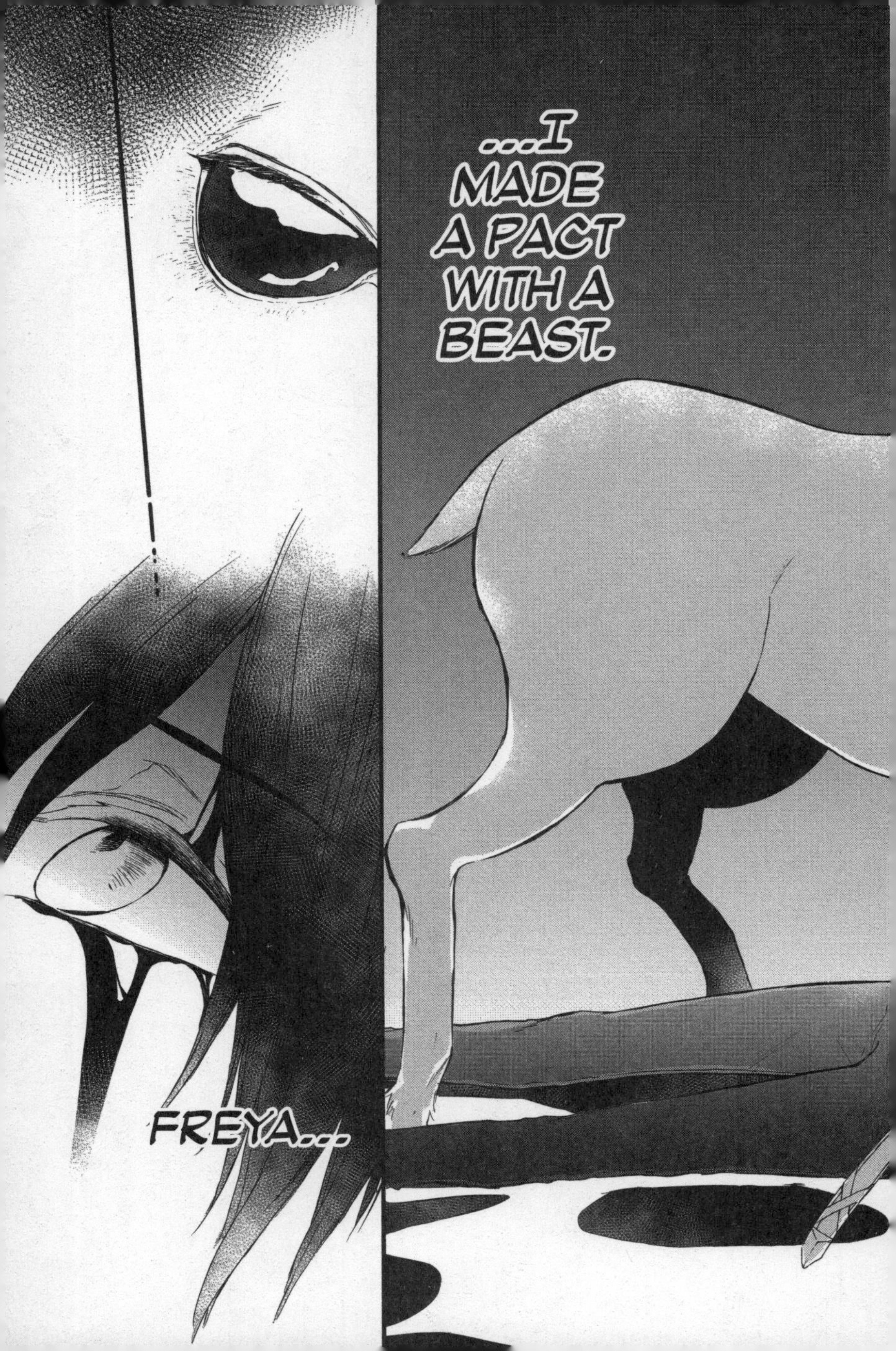
...I MADE A PACT WITH A BEAST.
FREYA...

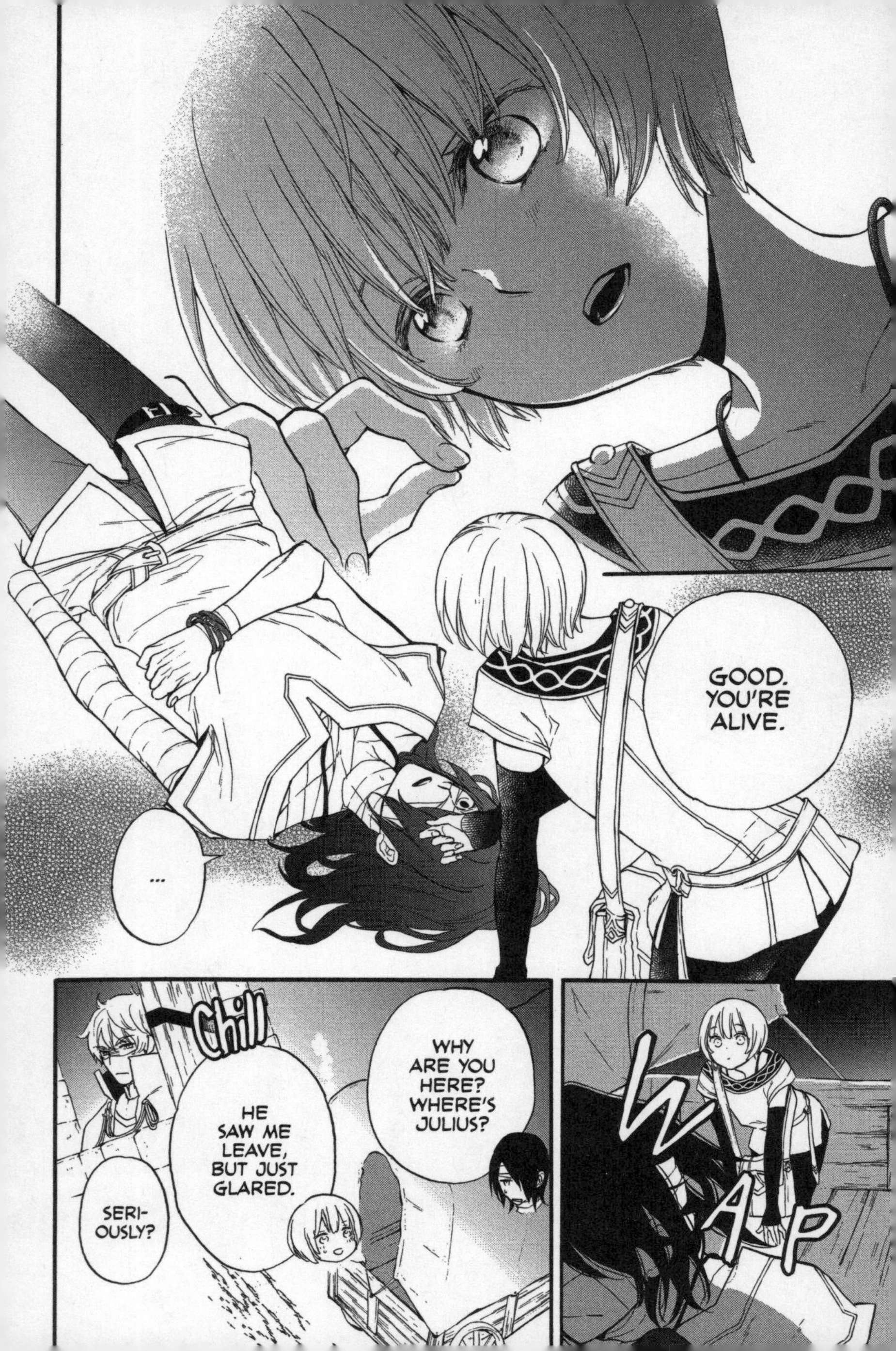
GOOD. YOU'RE ALIVE.
...
WAP
WHY ARE YOU HERE? WHERE'S JULIUS?
Chill
HE SAW ME LEAVE, BUT JUST GLARED.
SERI-OUSLY?

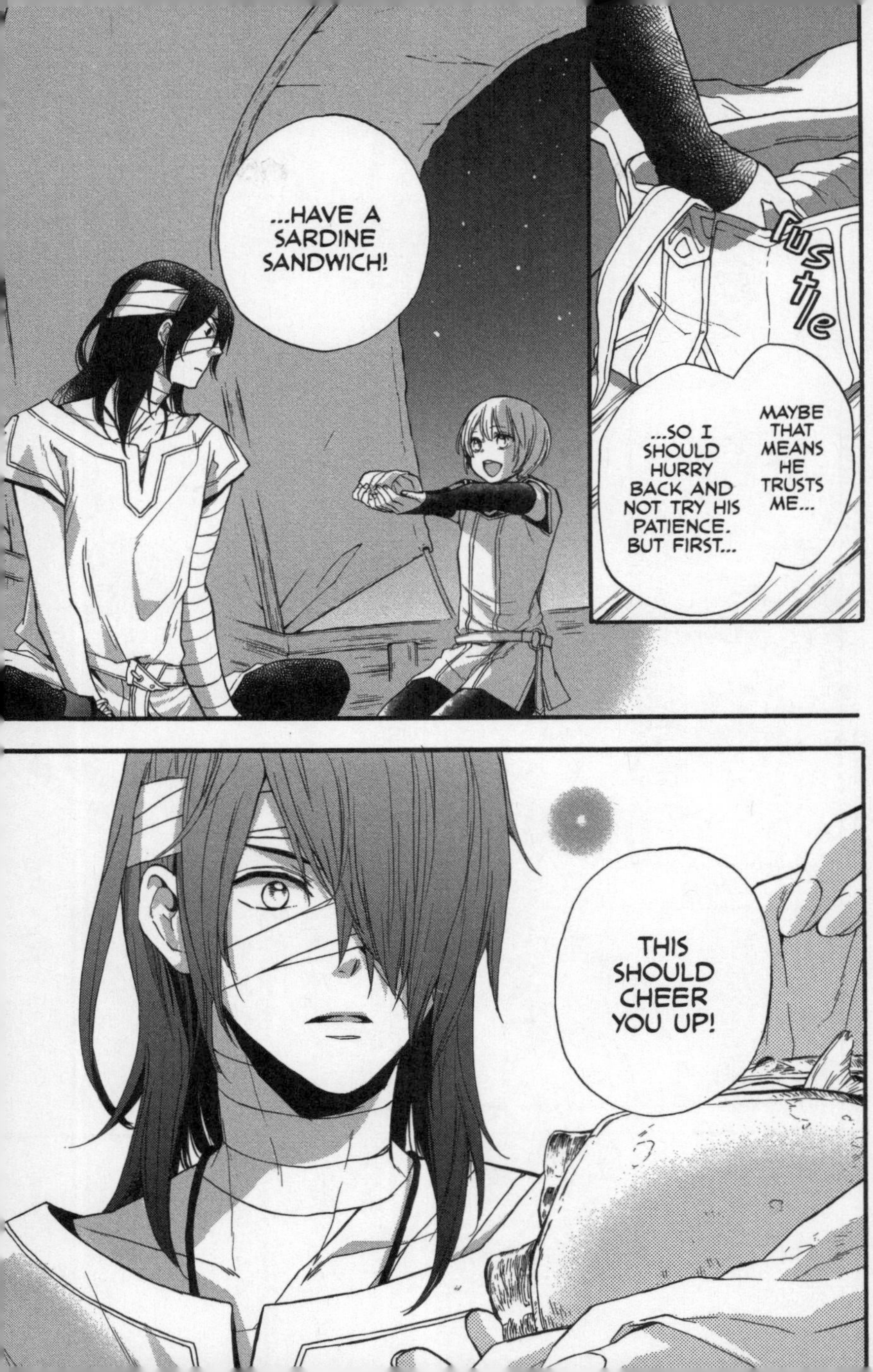
rustle
MAYBE THAT MEANS HE TRUSTS ME...
...SO I SHOULD HURRY BACK AND NOT TRY HIS PATIENCE. BUT FIRST...
...HAVE A SARDINE SANDWICH!
THIS SHOULD CHEER YOU UP!

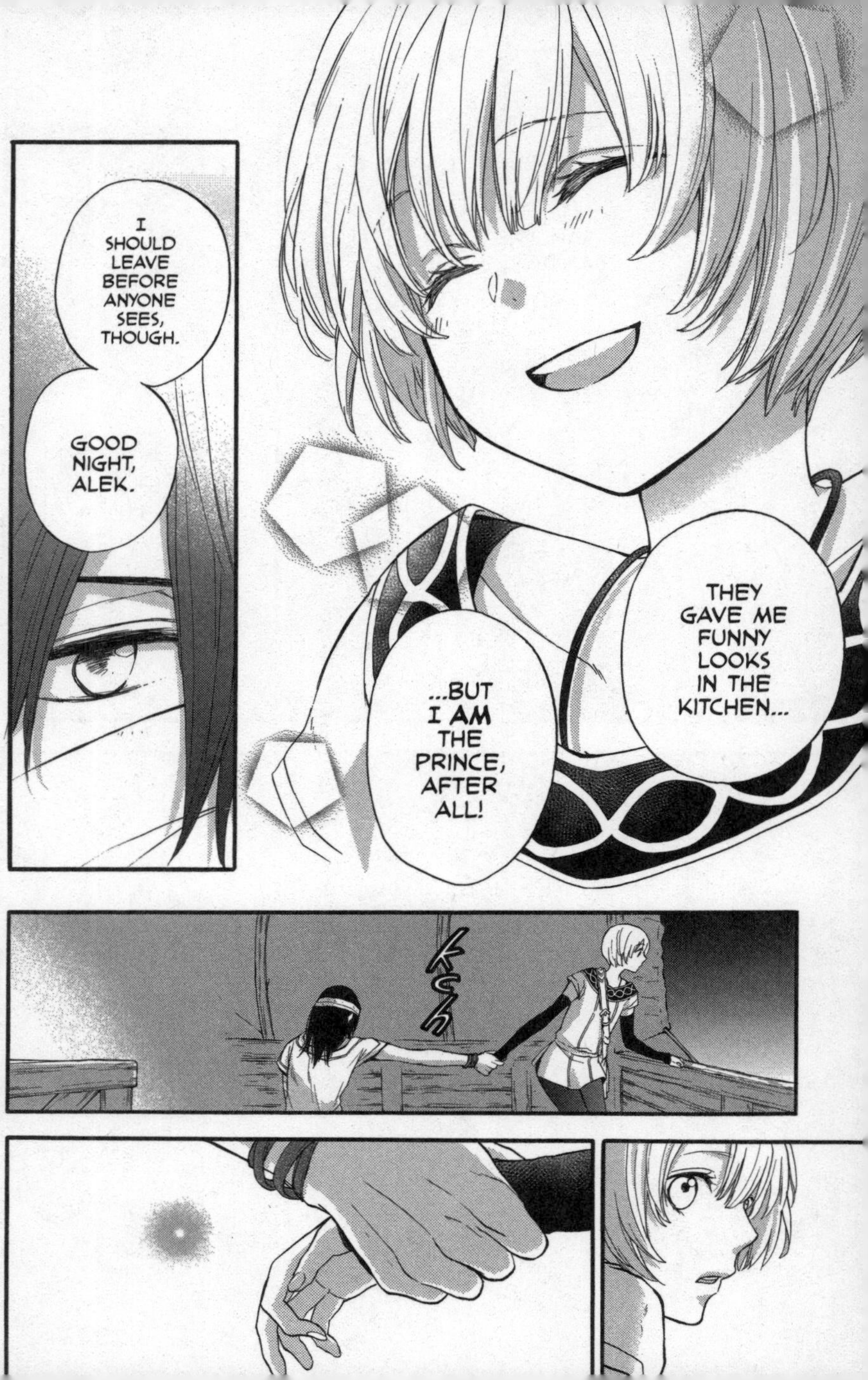
THEY GAVE ME FUNNY LOOKS IN THE KITCHEN...
...BUT **I AM** THE PRINCE, AFTER ALL!
I SHOULD LEAVE BEFORE ANYONE SEES, THOUGH.
GOOD NIGHT, ALEK.
kch

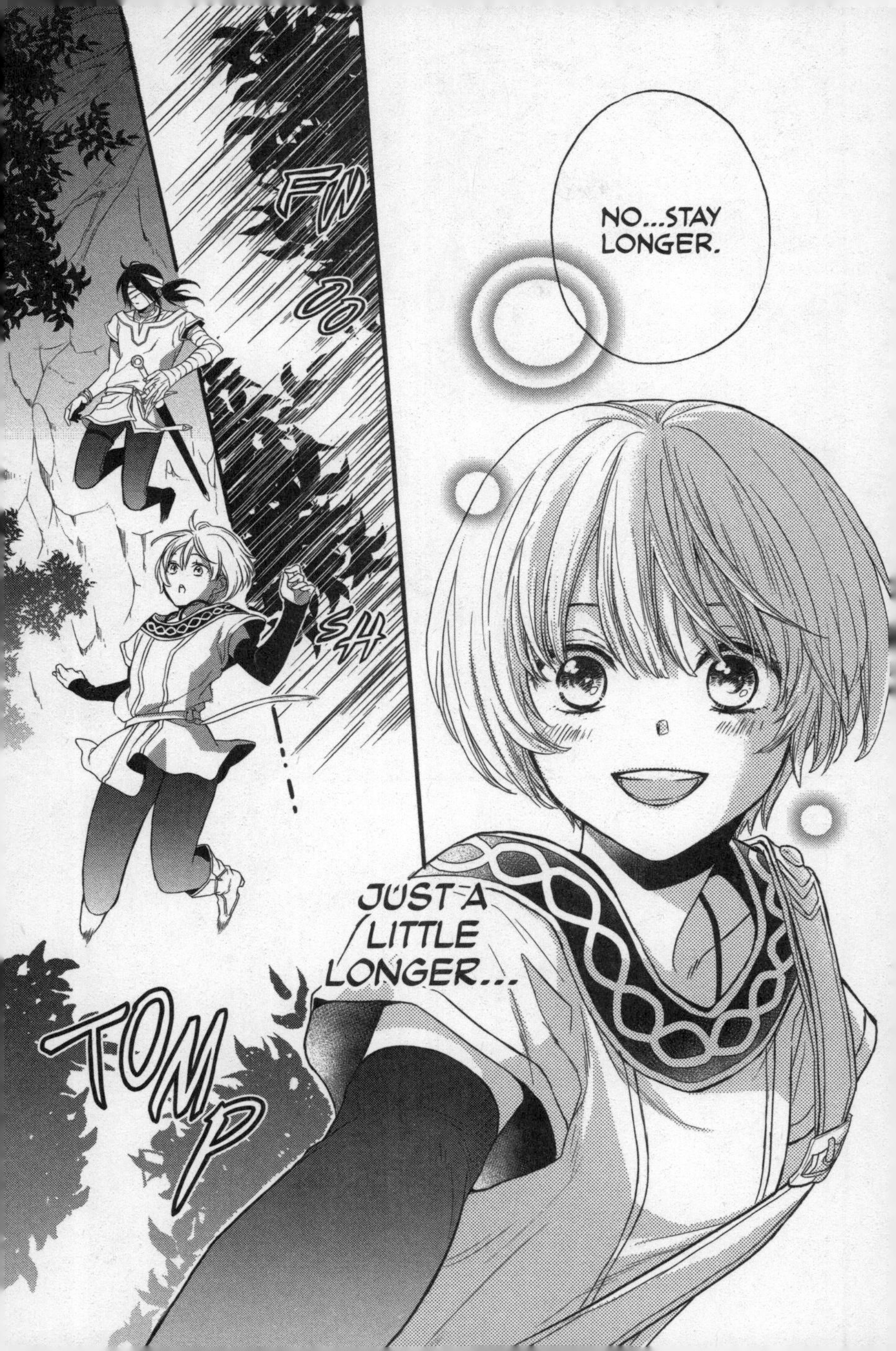
NO...STAY LONGER.
JUST A LITTLE LONGER...
FWOOSH
TOMP

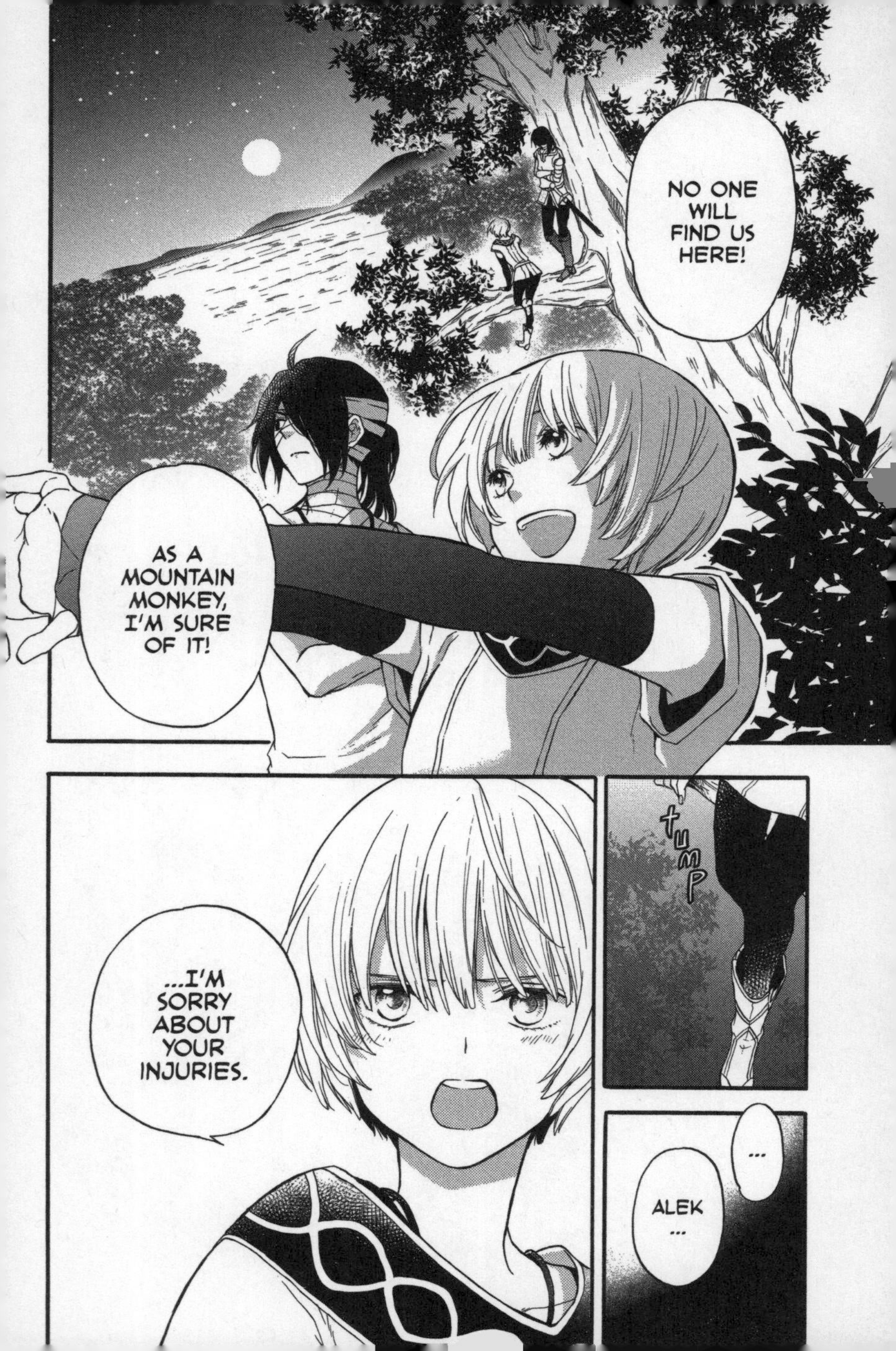
NO ONE WILL FIND US HERE!
AS A MOUNTAIN MONKEY, I'M SURE OF IT!
TUMP
...
ALEK ...
...I'M SORRY ABOUT YOUR INJURIES.

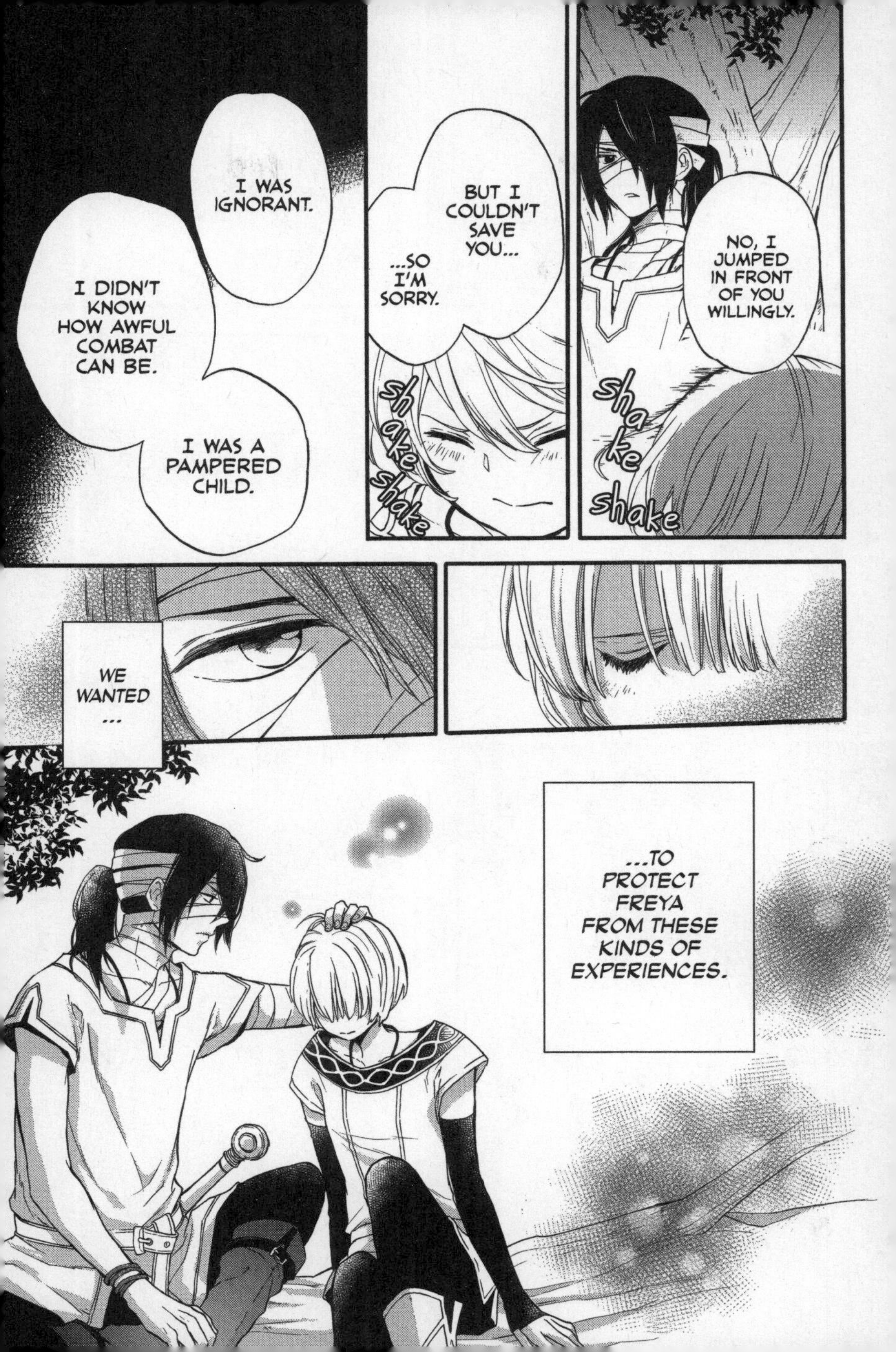
NO, I JUMPED IN FRONT OF YOU WILLINGLY.
shake shake
BUT I COULDN'T SAVE YOU...
...SO I'M SORRY.
shake shake
I WAS IGNORANT.
I DIDN'T KNOW HOW AWFUL COMBAT CAN BE.
I WAS A PAMPERED CHILD.
WE WANTED ...
...TO PROTECT FREYA FROM THESE KINDS OF EXPERIENCES.

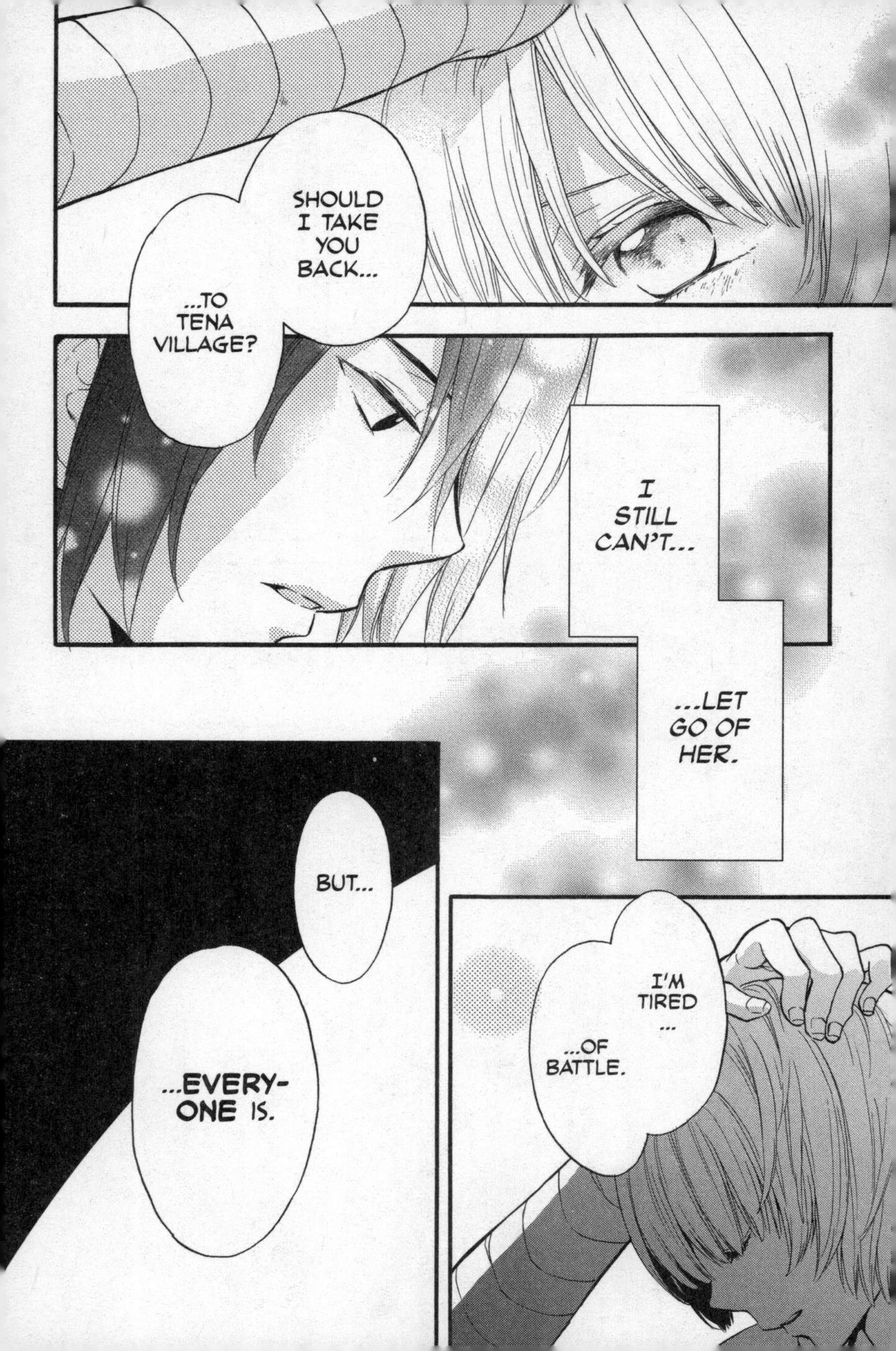
SHOULD I TAKE YOU BACK...
...TO TENA VILLAGE?
I STILL CAN'T...
...LET GO OF HER.
I'M TIRED ...
...OF BATTLE.
BUT...
...EVERY-ONE IS.

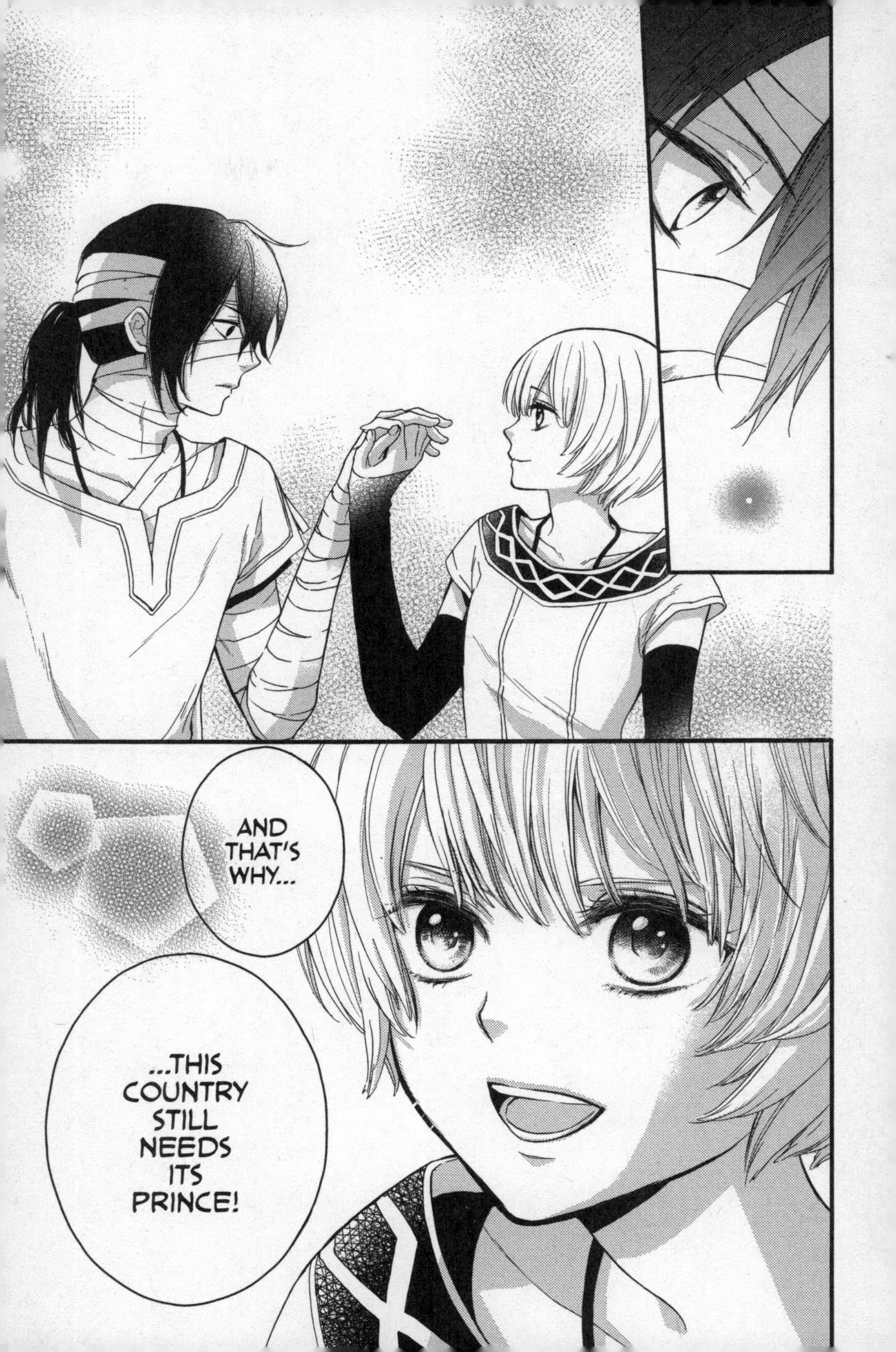
AND THAT'S WHY...
...THIS COUNTRY STILL NEEDS ITS PRINCE!

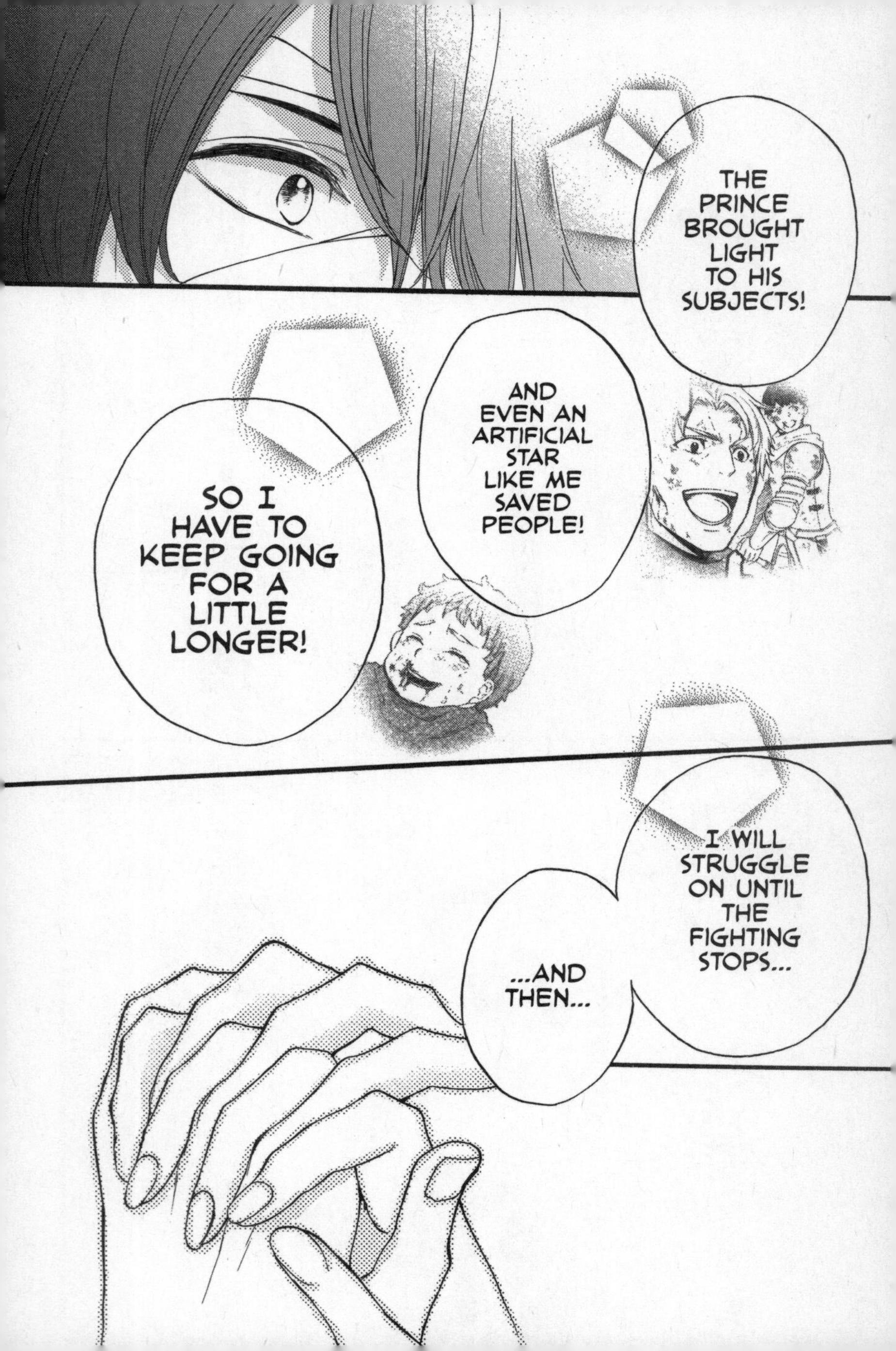
THE PRINCE BROUGHT LIGHT TO HIS SUBJECTS!
AND EVEN AN ARTIFICIAL STAR LIKE ME SAVED PEOPLE!
SO I HAVE TO KEEP GOING FOR A LITTLE LONGER!
I WILL STRUGGLE ON UNTIL THE FIGHTING STOPS...
...AND THEN...

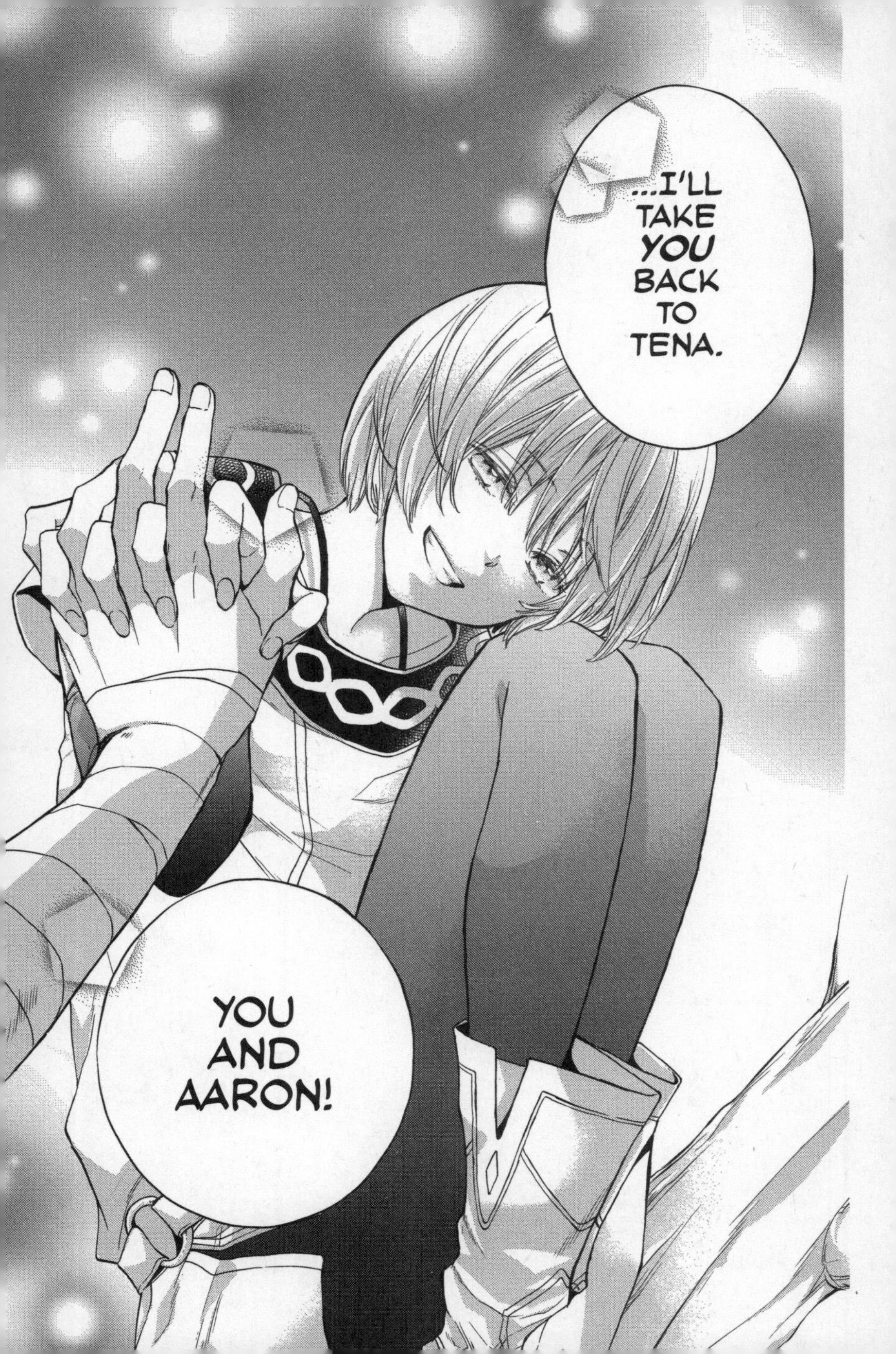
...I'LL TAKE YOU BACK TO TENA.
YOU AND AARON!

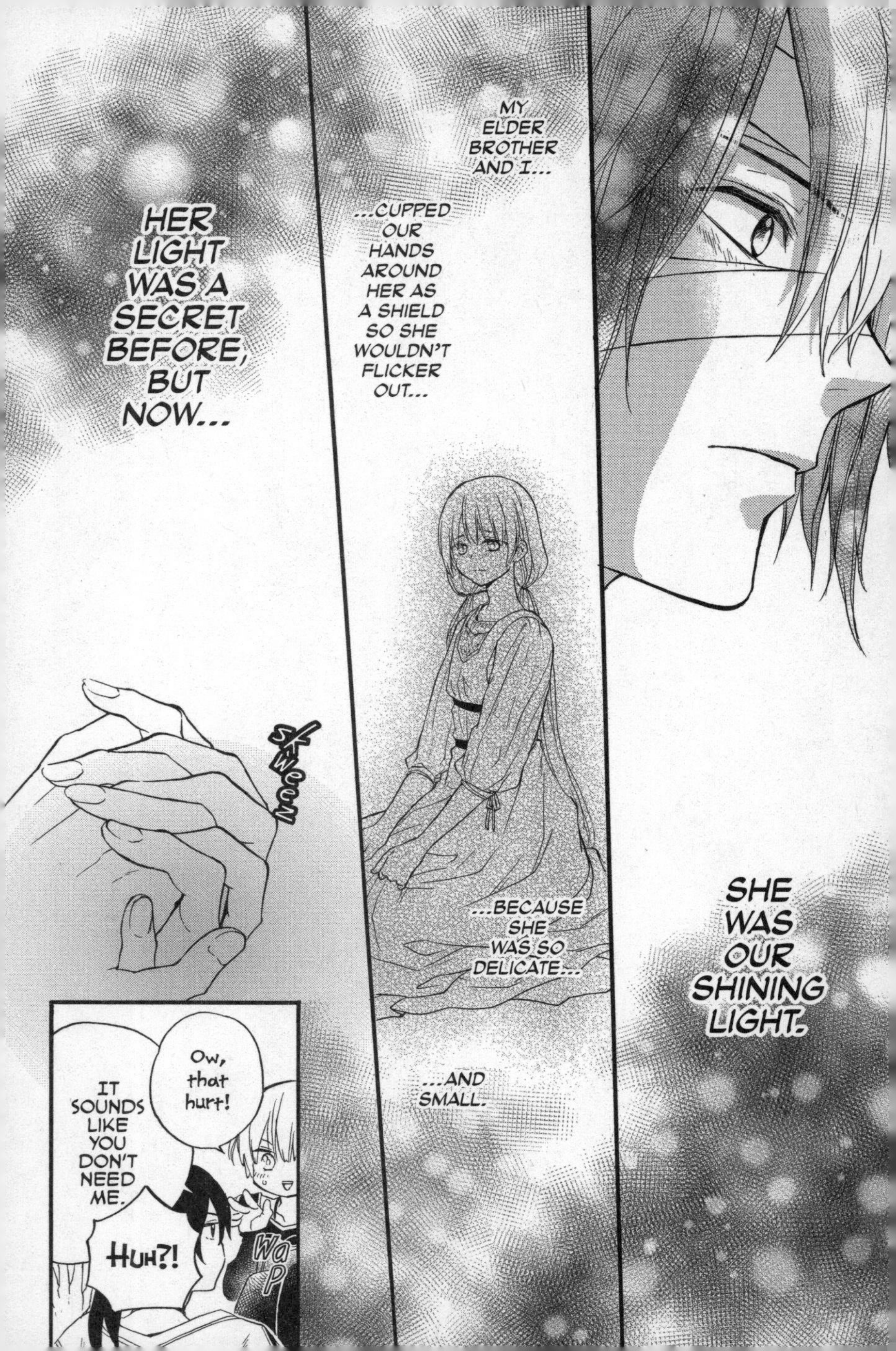
SHE WAS OUR SHINING LIGHT.
MY ELDER BROTHER AND I...
...CUPPED OUR HANDS AROUND HER AS A SHIELD SO SHE WOULDN'T FLICKER OUT...
...BECAUSE SHE WAS SO DELICATE...
...AND SMALL.
HER LIGHT WAS A SECRET BEFORE, BUT NOW...
skween
Ow, that hurt!
IT SOUNDS LIKE YOU DON'T NEED ME.
Wap
Huh?!

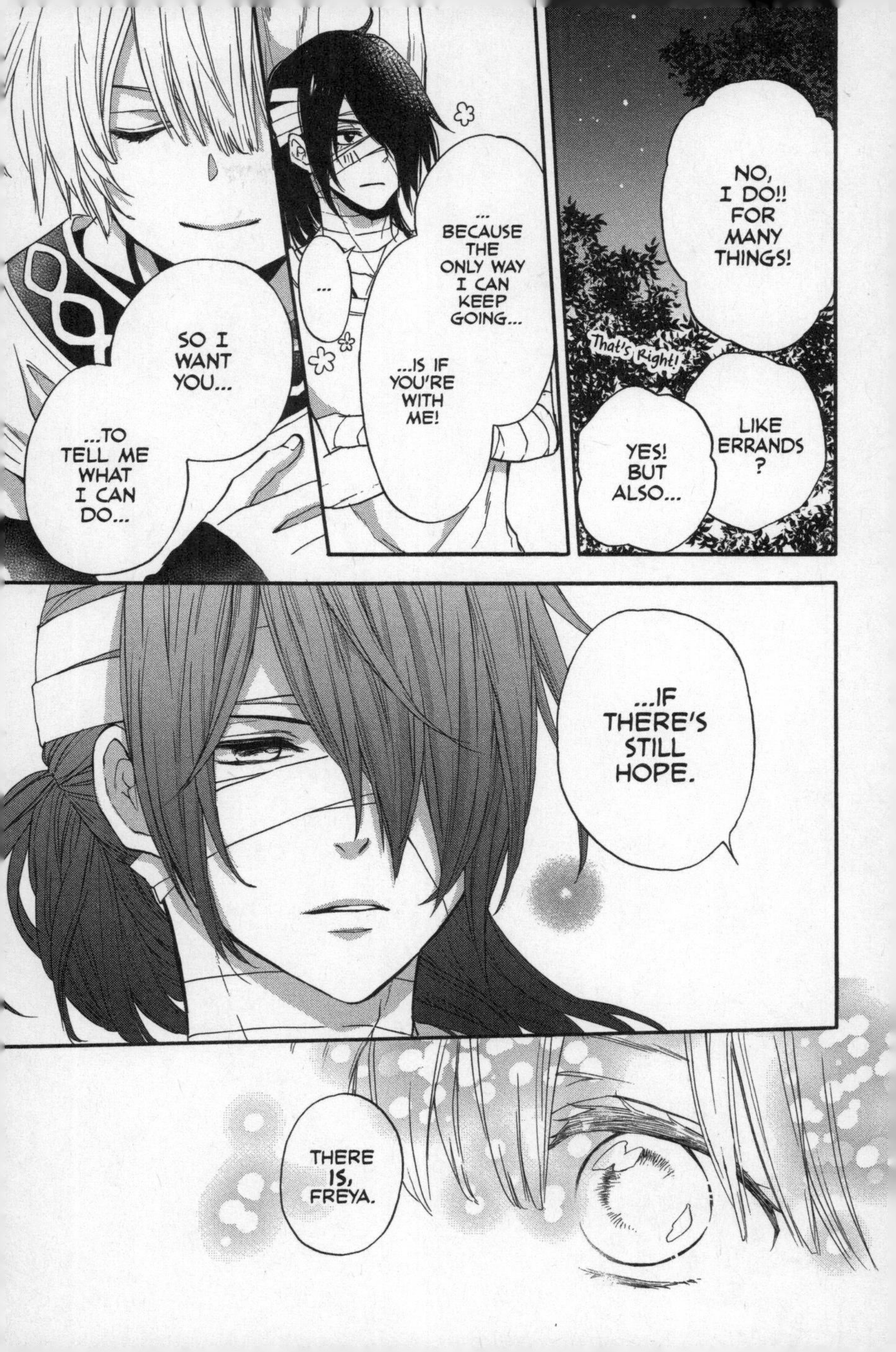
NO, I DO!! FOR MANY THINGS!
That's Right!
LIKE ERRANDS?
YES! BUT ALSO...
... BECAUSE THE ONLY WAY I CAN KEEP GOING...
...IS IF YOU'RE WITH ME!
...
SO I WANT YOU...
...TO TELL ME WHAT I CAN DO...
...IF THERE'S STILL HOPE.
THERE IS, FREYA.

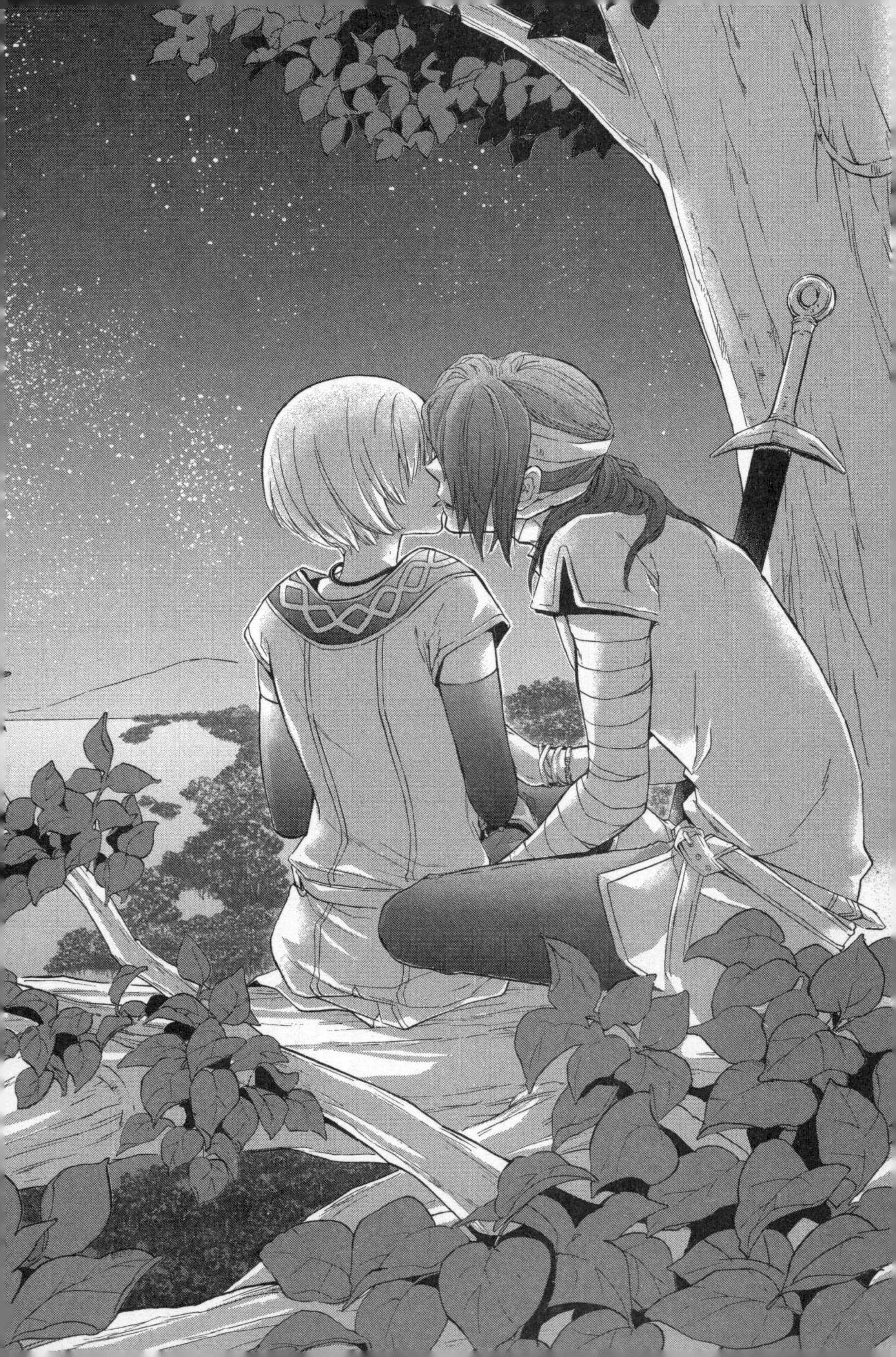

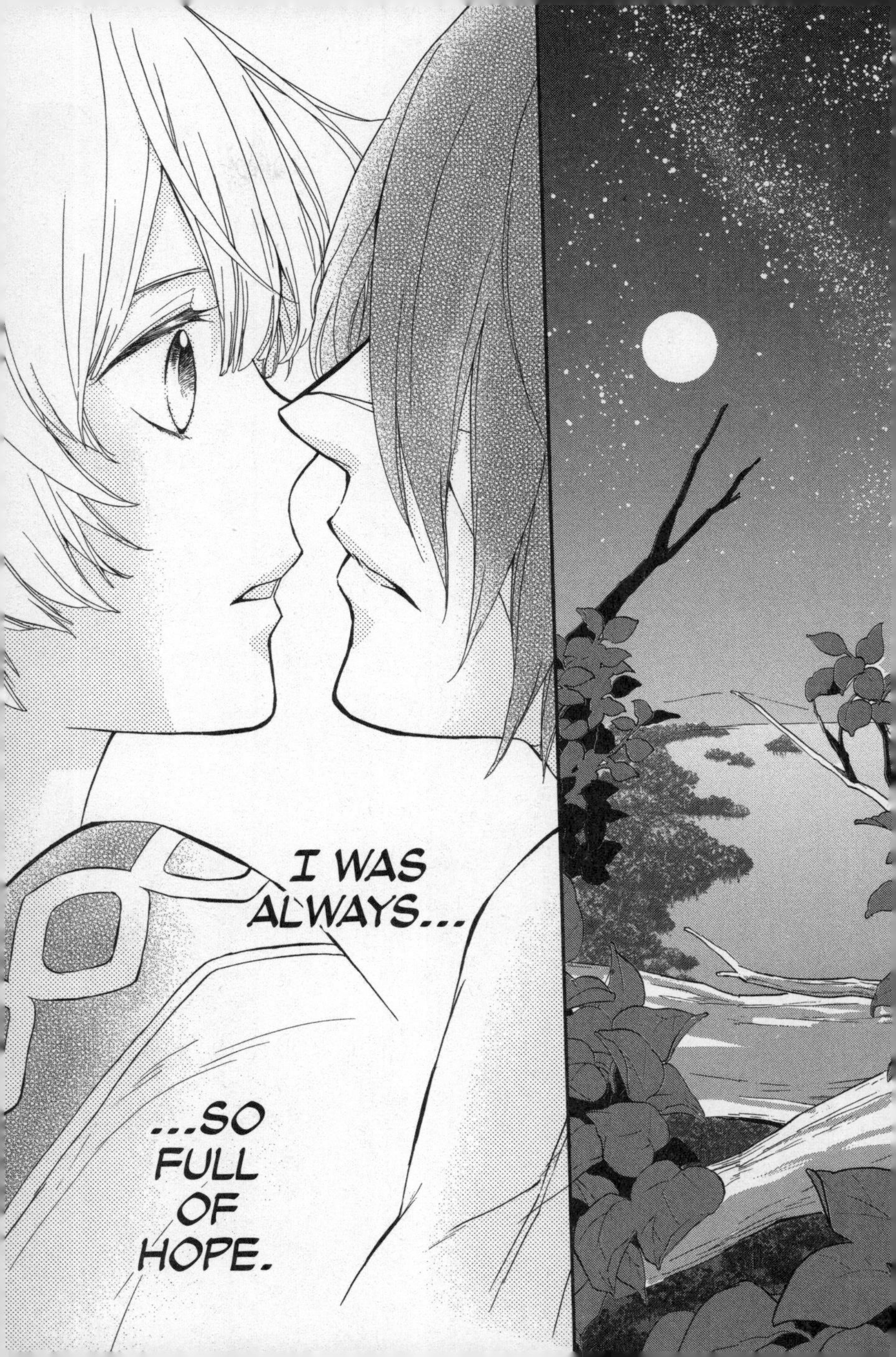
I WAS ALWAYS...
...SO FULL OF HOPE.

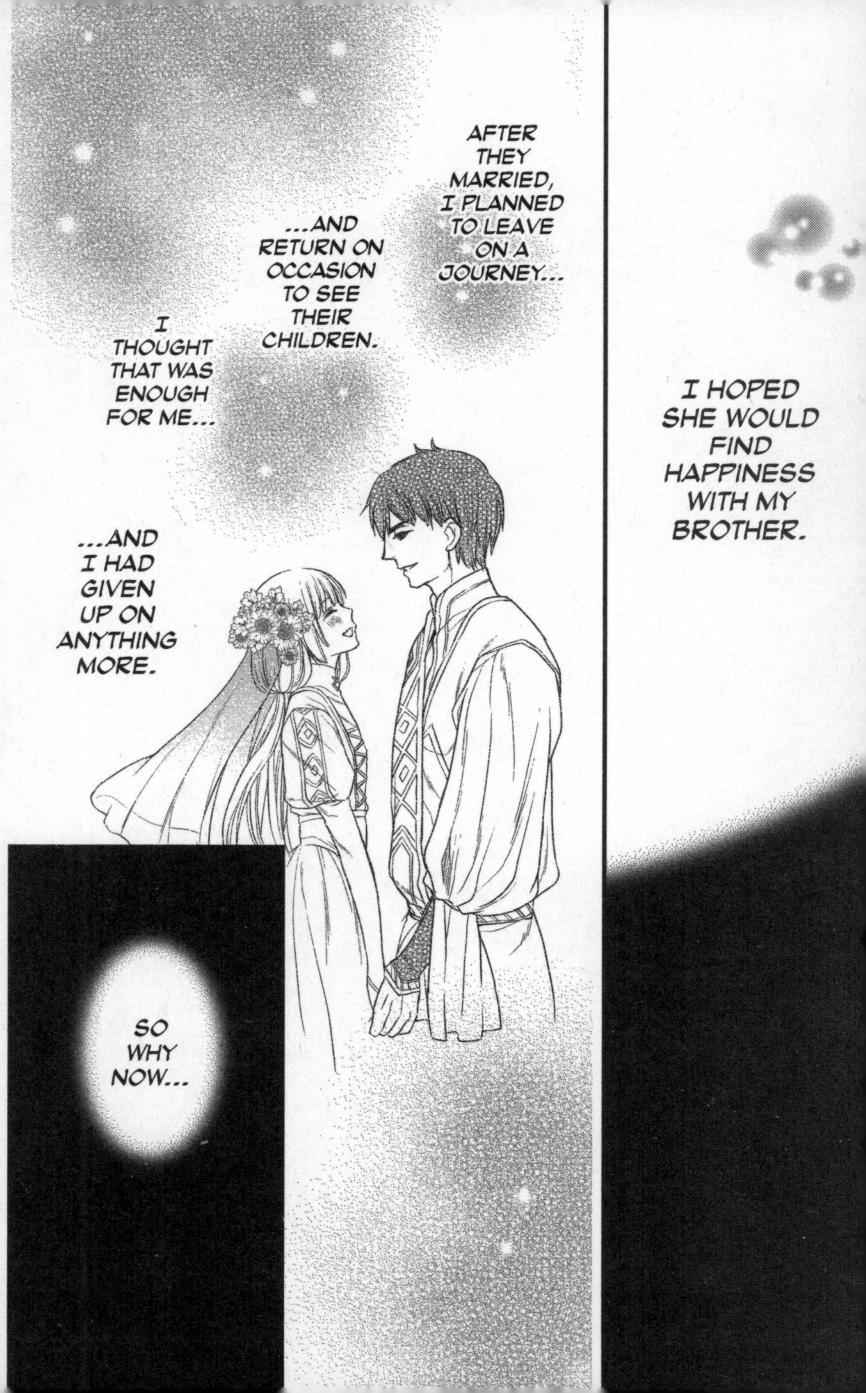
I HOPED SHE WOULD FIND HAPPINESS WITH MY BROTHER.
AFTER THEY MARRIED, I PLANNED TO LEAVE ON A JOURNEY...
...AND RETURN ON OCCASION TO SEE THEIR CHILDREN.
I THOUGHT THAT WAS ENOUGH FOR ME...
...AND I HAD GIVEN UP ON ANYTHING MORE.
SO WHY NOW...

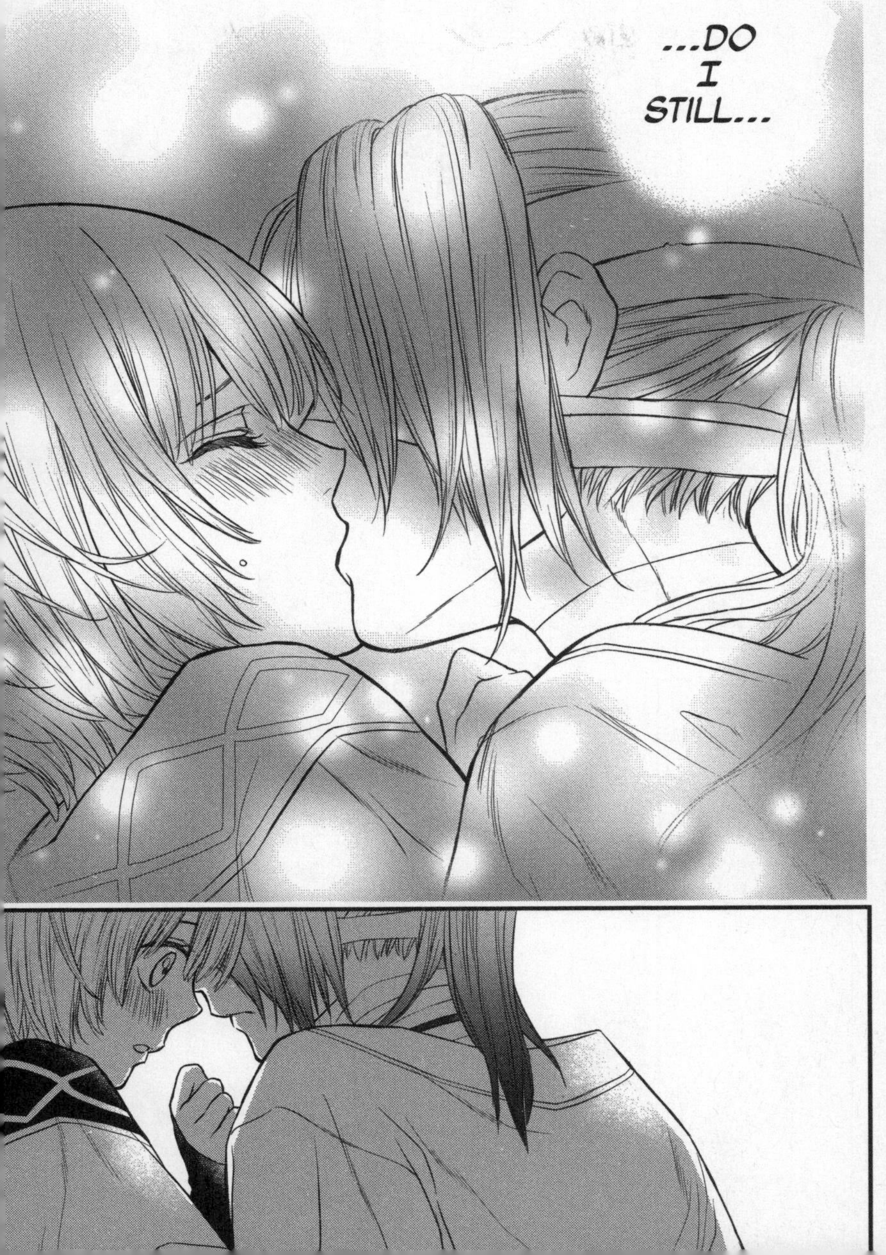
...DO
I
STILL...

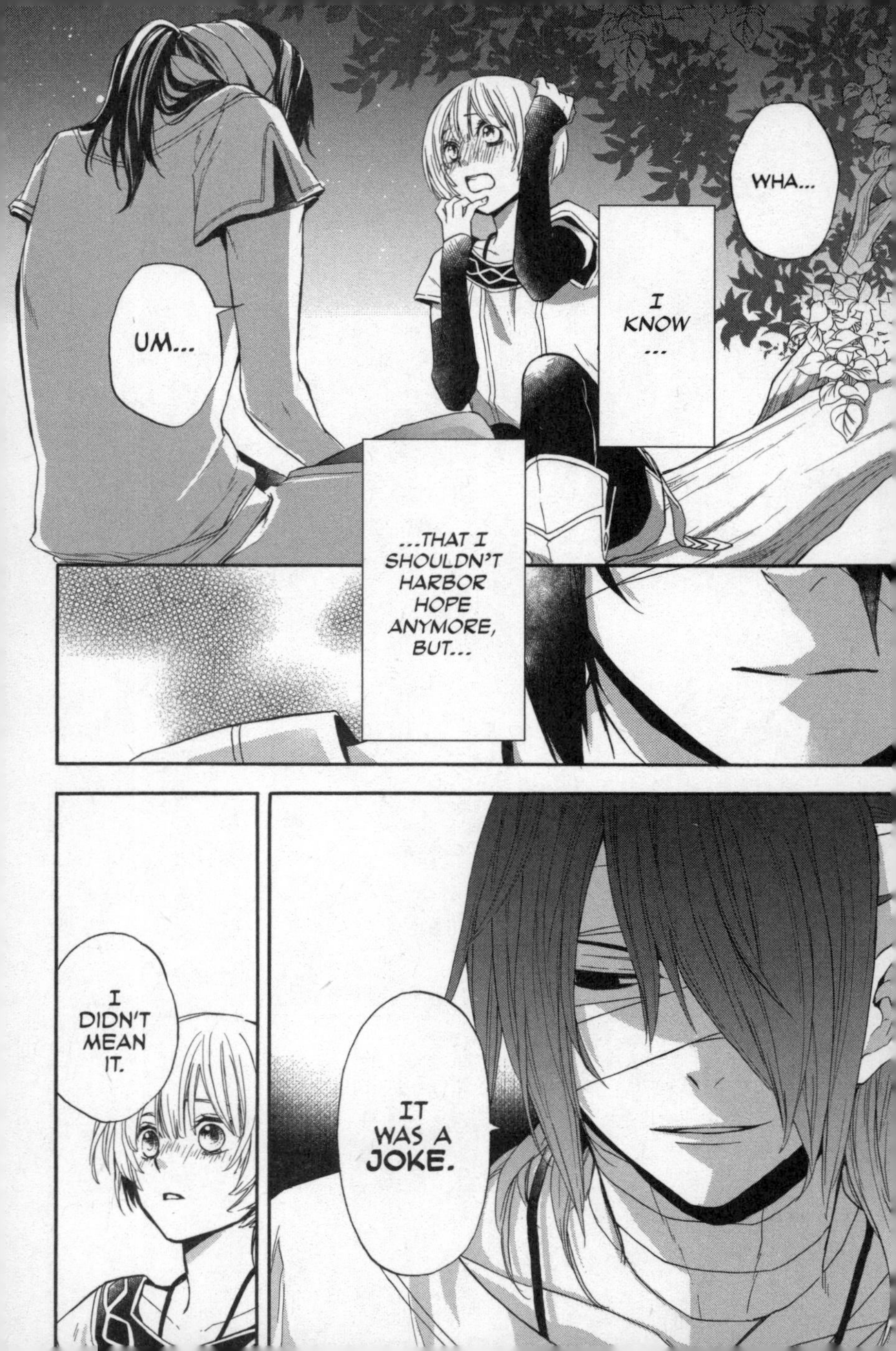
WHA...
I KNOW ...
UM...
...THAT I SHOULDN'T HARBOR HOPE ANYMORE, BUT...
IT WAS A JOKE.
I DIDN'T MEAN IT.

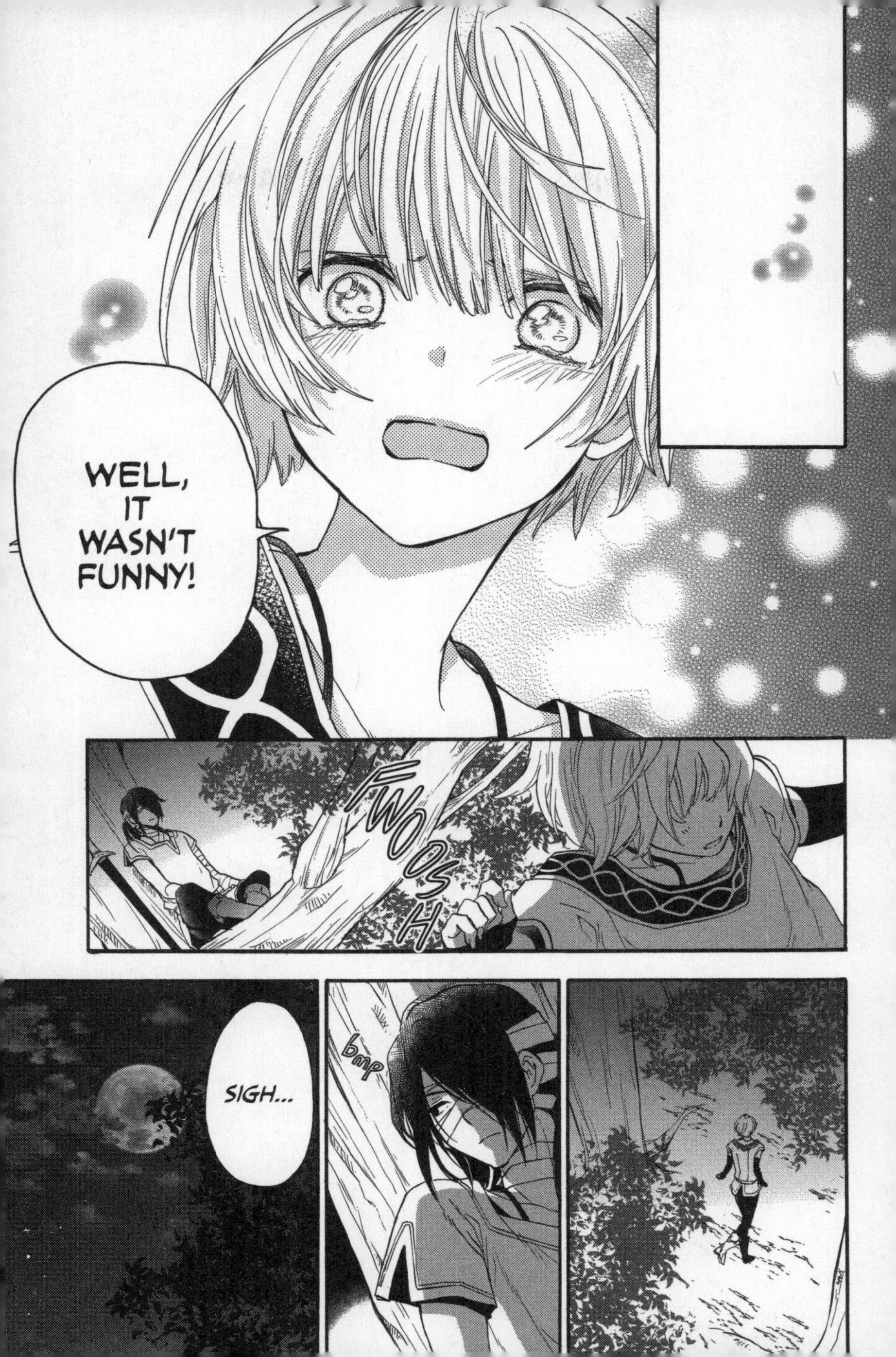
WELL, IT WASN'T FUNNY!
FWOOSH
bmp
SIGH...

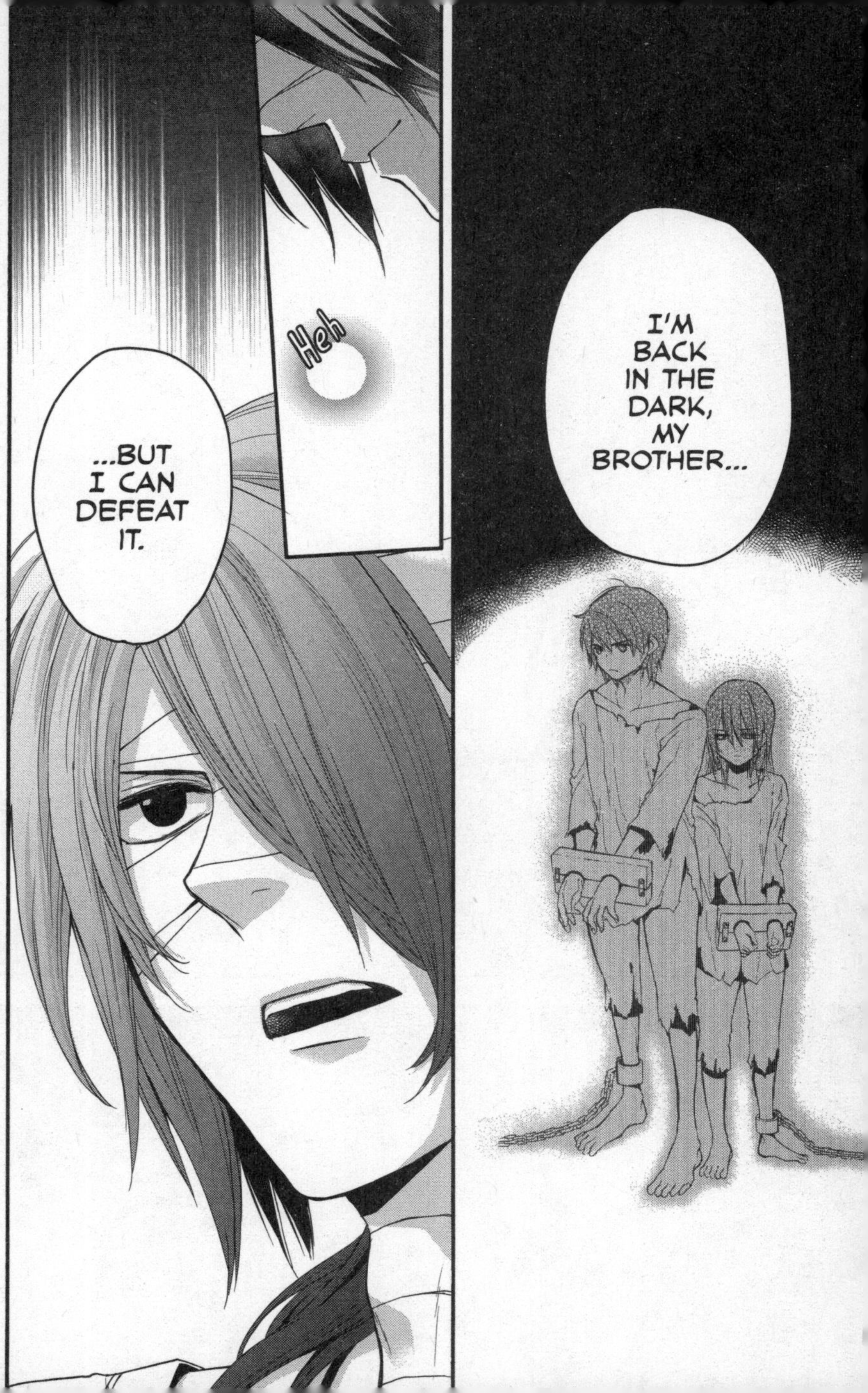
I'M BACK IN THE DARK, MY BROTHER...
Heh
...BUT I CAN DEFEAT IT.

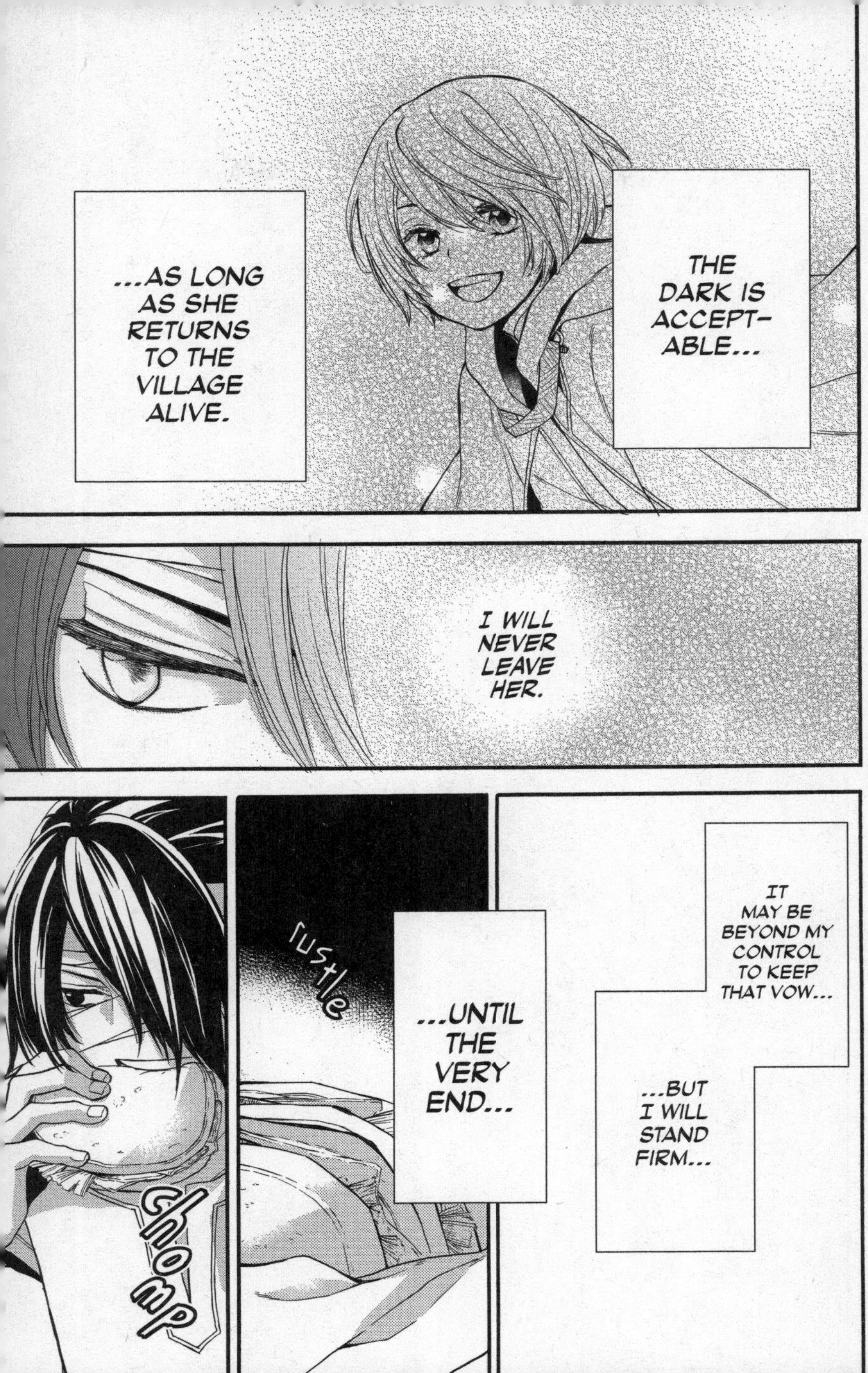
THE DARK IS ACCEPT-ABLE...
...AS LONG AS SHE RETURNS TO THE VILLAGE ALIVE.
I WILL NEVER LEAVE HER.
IT MAY BE BEYOND MY CONTROL TO KEEP THAT VOW...
...BUT I WILL STAND FIRM...
rustle
...UNTIL THE VERY END...
chomp

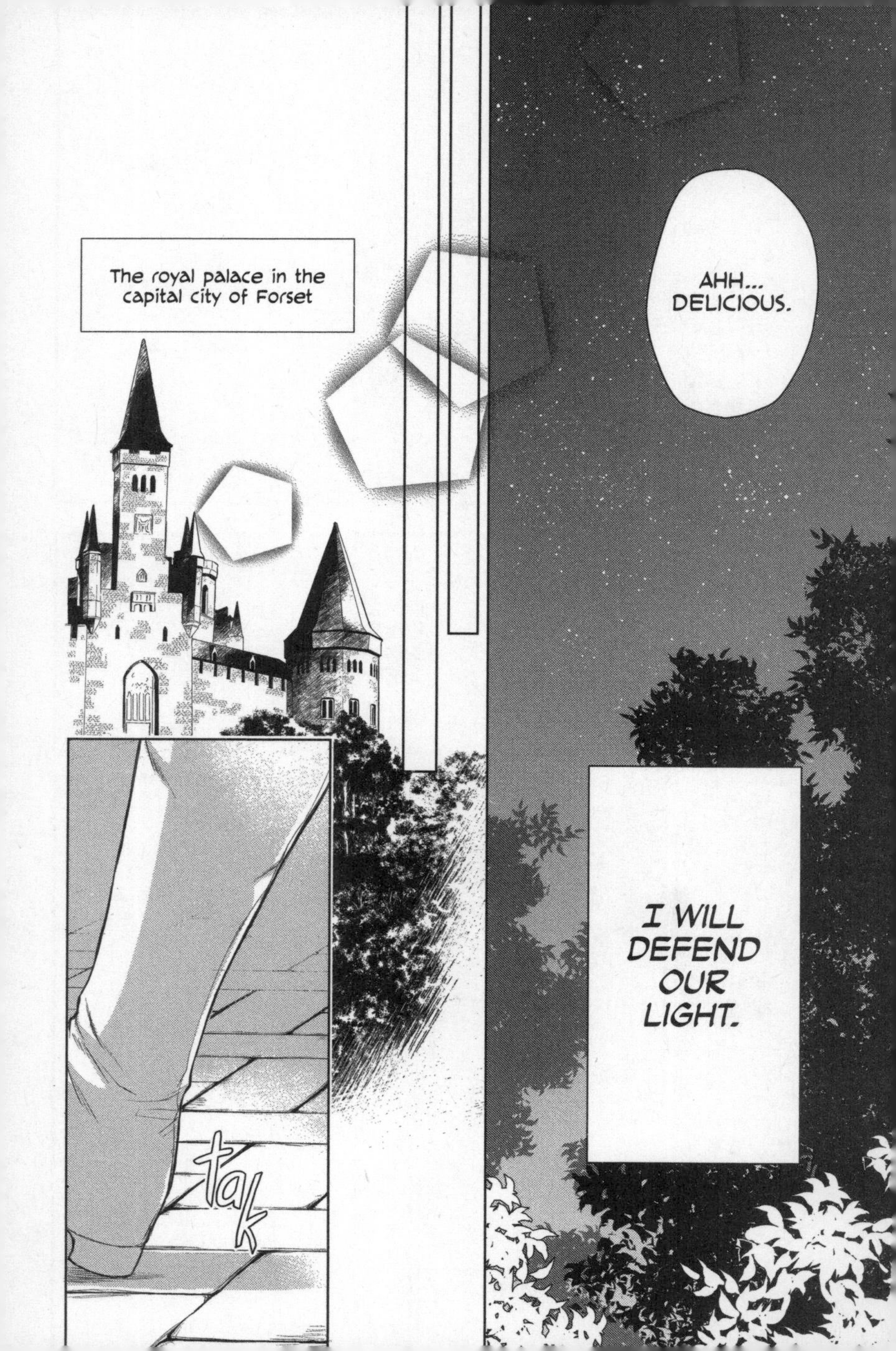
AHH... DELICIOUS.
I WILL DEFEND OUR LIGHT.
The royal palace in the capital city of Forset
tak

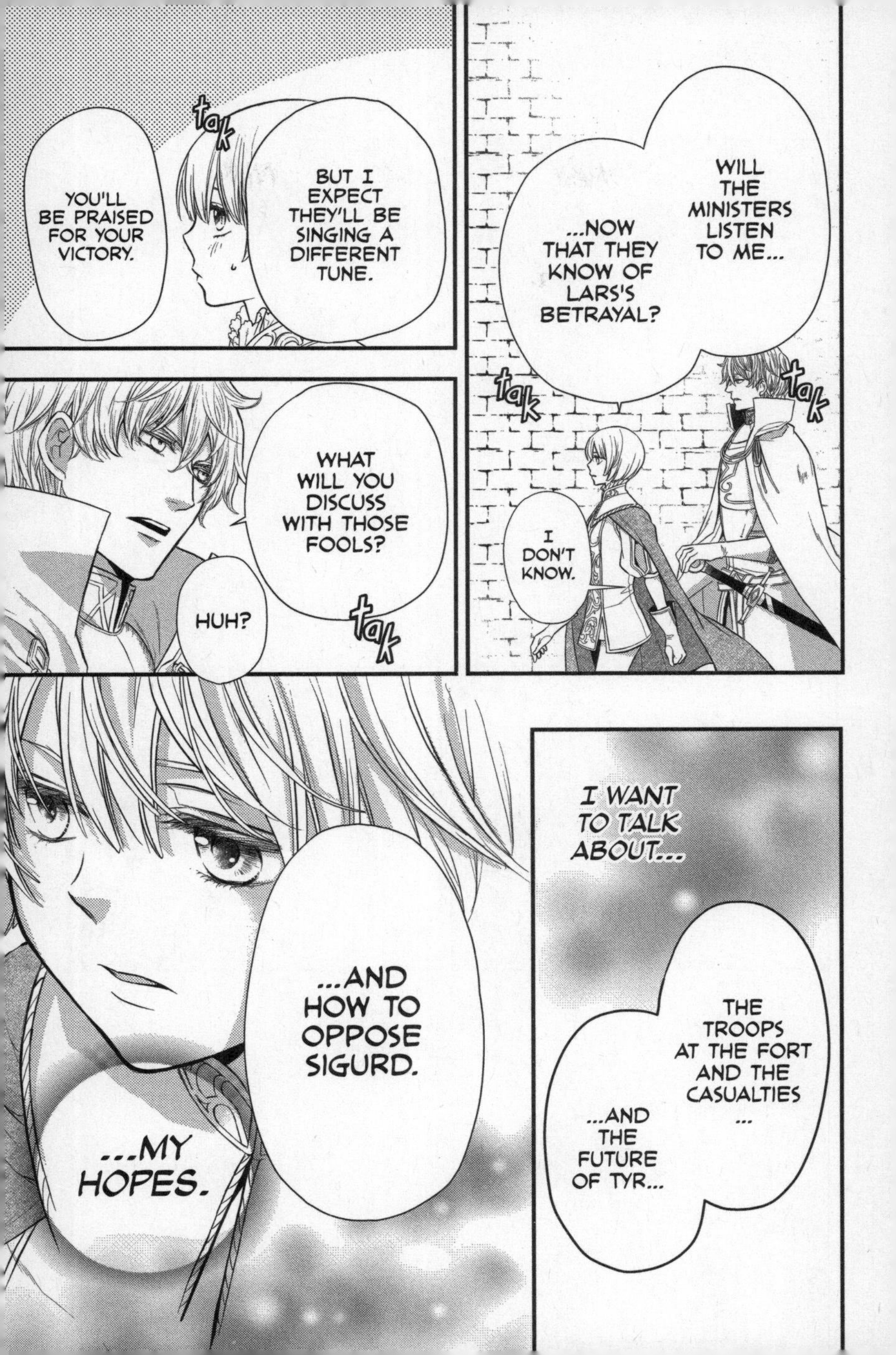
WILL THE MINISTERS LISTEN TO ME...
...NOW THAT THEY KNOW OF LARS'S BETRAYAL?
tak
tak
I DON'T KNOW.
tak
BUT I EXPECT THEY'LL BE SINGING A DIFFERENT TUNE.
YOU'LL BE PRAISED FOR YOUR VICTORY.
WHAT WILL YOU DISCUSS WITH THOSE FOOLS?
tak
HUH?
I WANT TO TALK ABOUT...
THE TROOPS AT THE FORT AND THE CASUALTIES...
...AND THE FUTURE OF TYR...
...AND HOW TO OPPOSE SIGURD.
...MY HOPES.

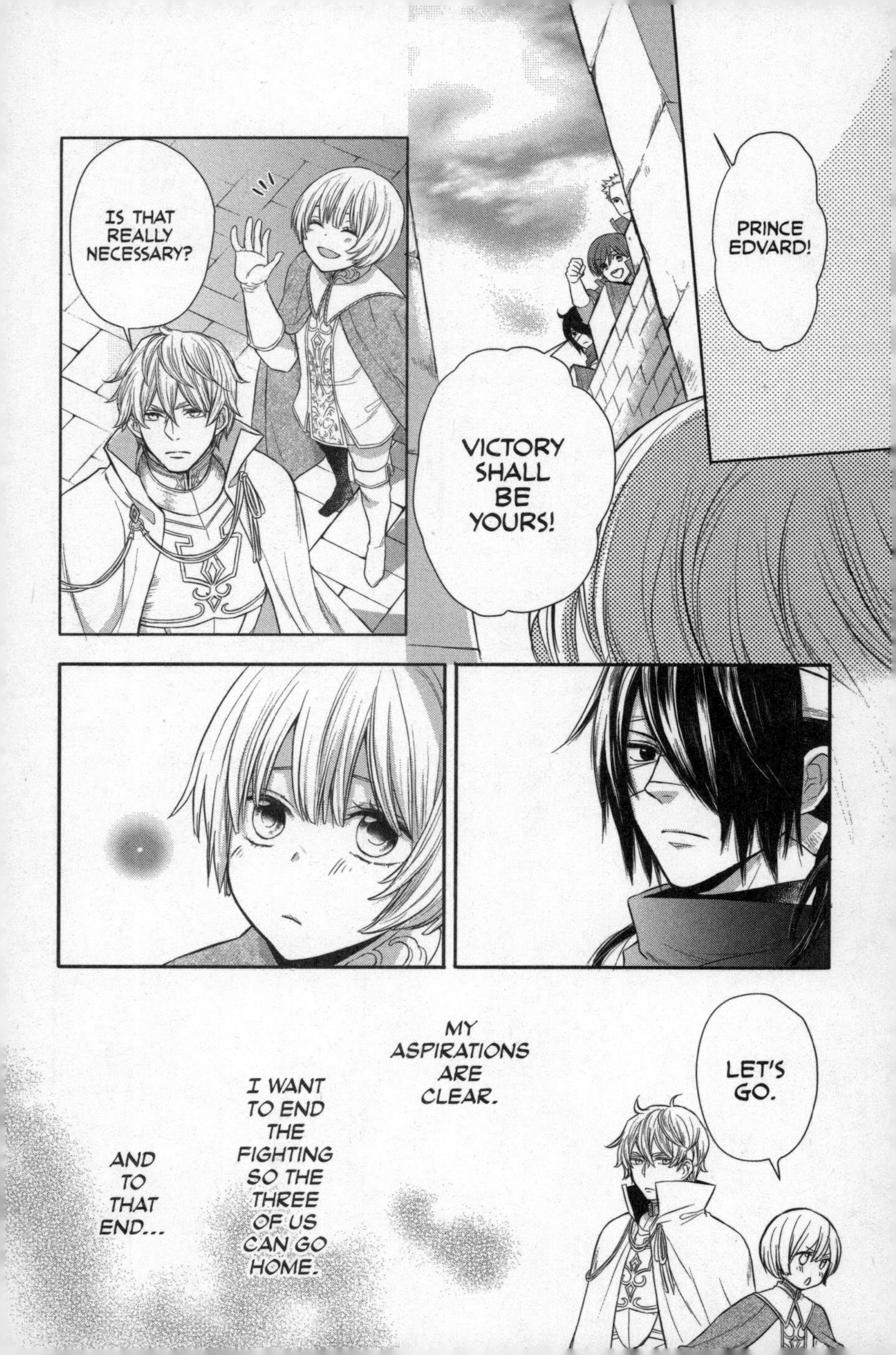
PRINCE EDVARD!
VICTORY SHALL BE YOURS!
IS THAT REALLY NECESSARY?
LET'S GO.
MY ASPIRATIONS ARE CLEAR.
I WANT TO END THE FIGHTING SO THE THREE OF US CAN GO HOME.
AND TO THAT END...

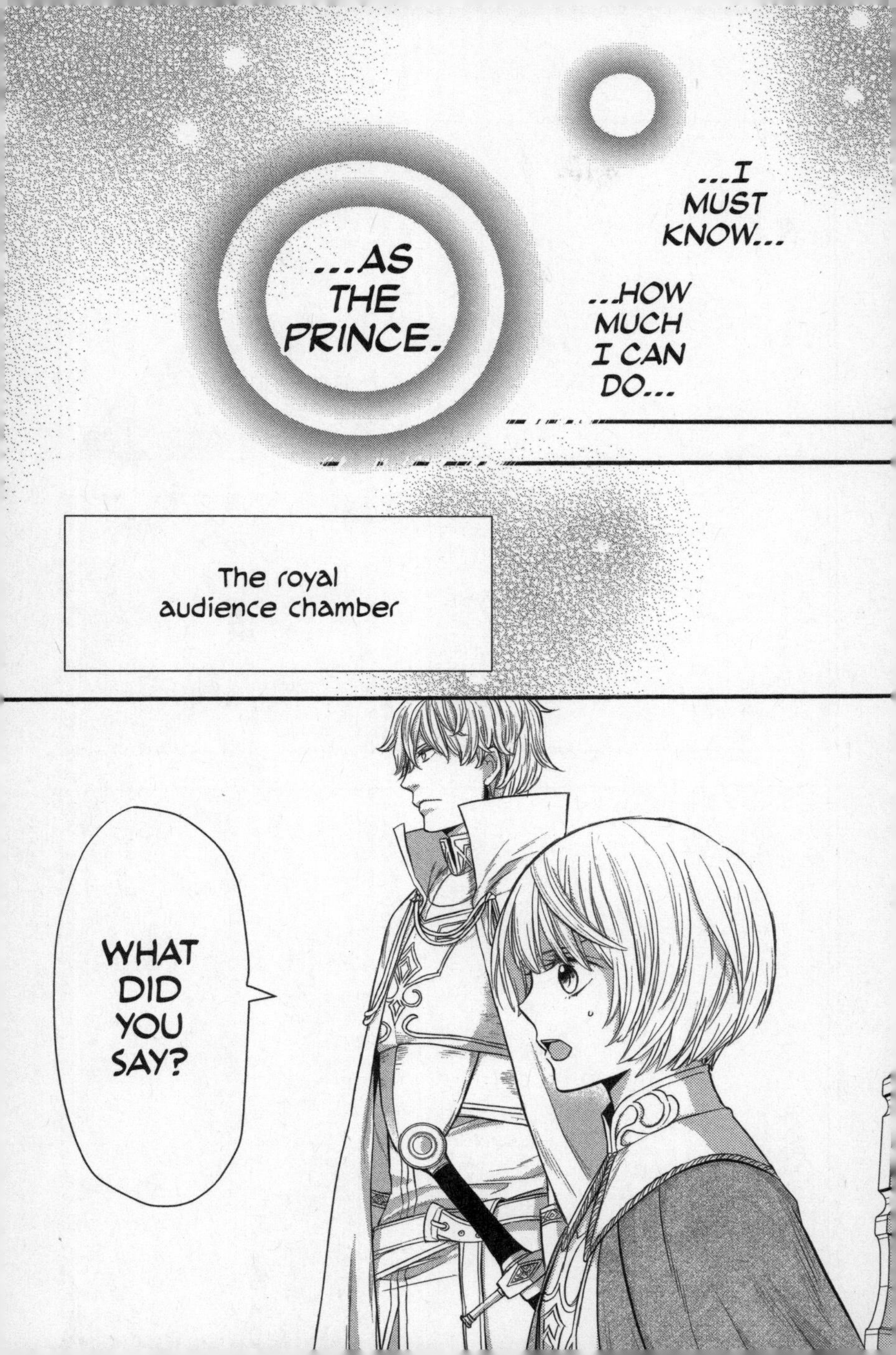
...I MUST KNOW...
...HOW MUCH I CAN DO...
...AS THE PRINCE.
The royal audience chamber
WHAT DID YOU SAY?

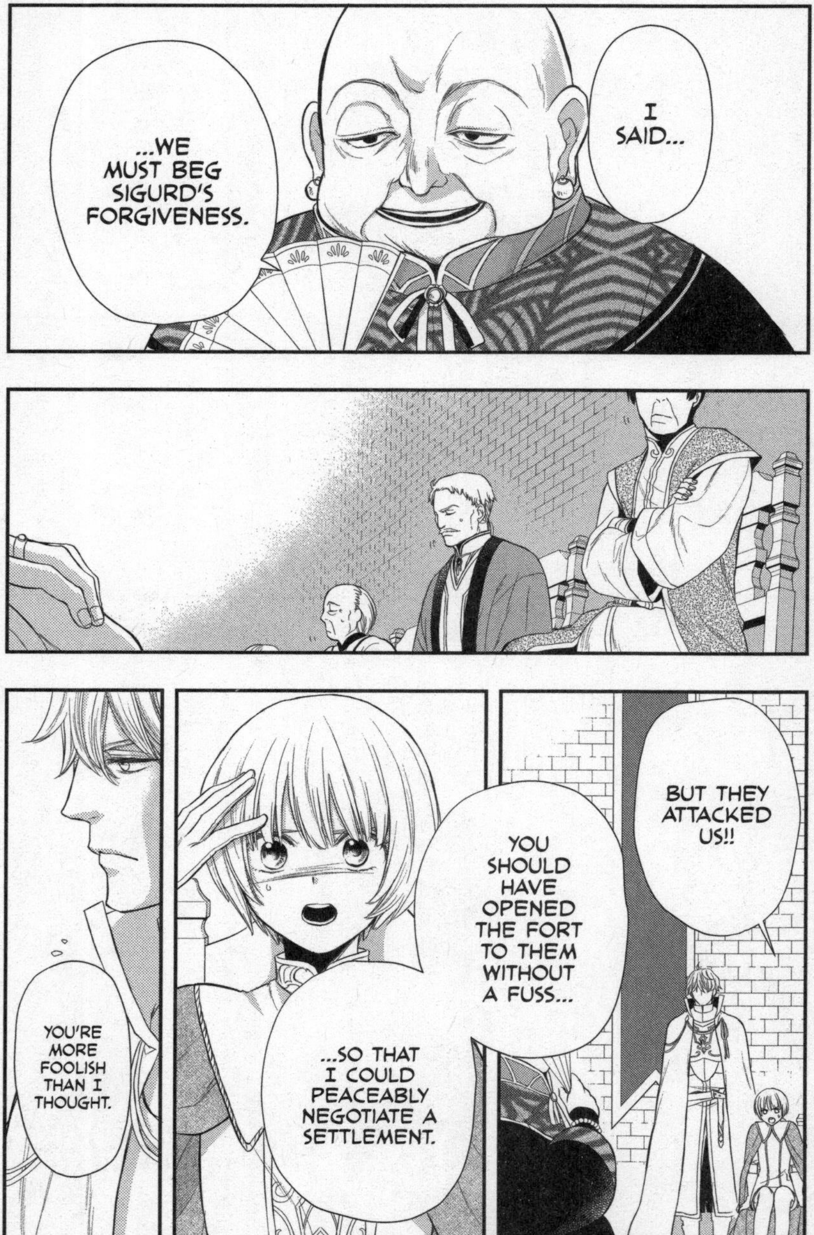
I SAID...
...WE MUST BEG SIGURD'S FORGIVENESS.
BUT THEY ATTACKED US!!
YOU SHOULD HAVE OPENED THE FORT TO THEM WITHOUT A FUSS...
...SO THAT I COULD PEACEABLY NEGOTIATE A SETTLEMENT.
YOU'RE MORE FOOLISH THAN I THOUGHT.

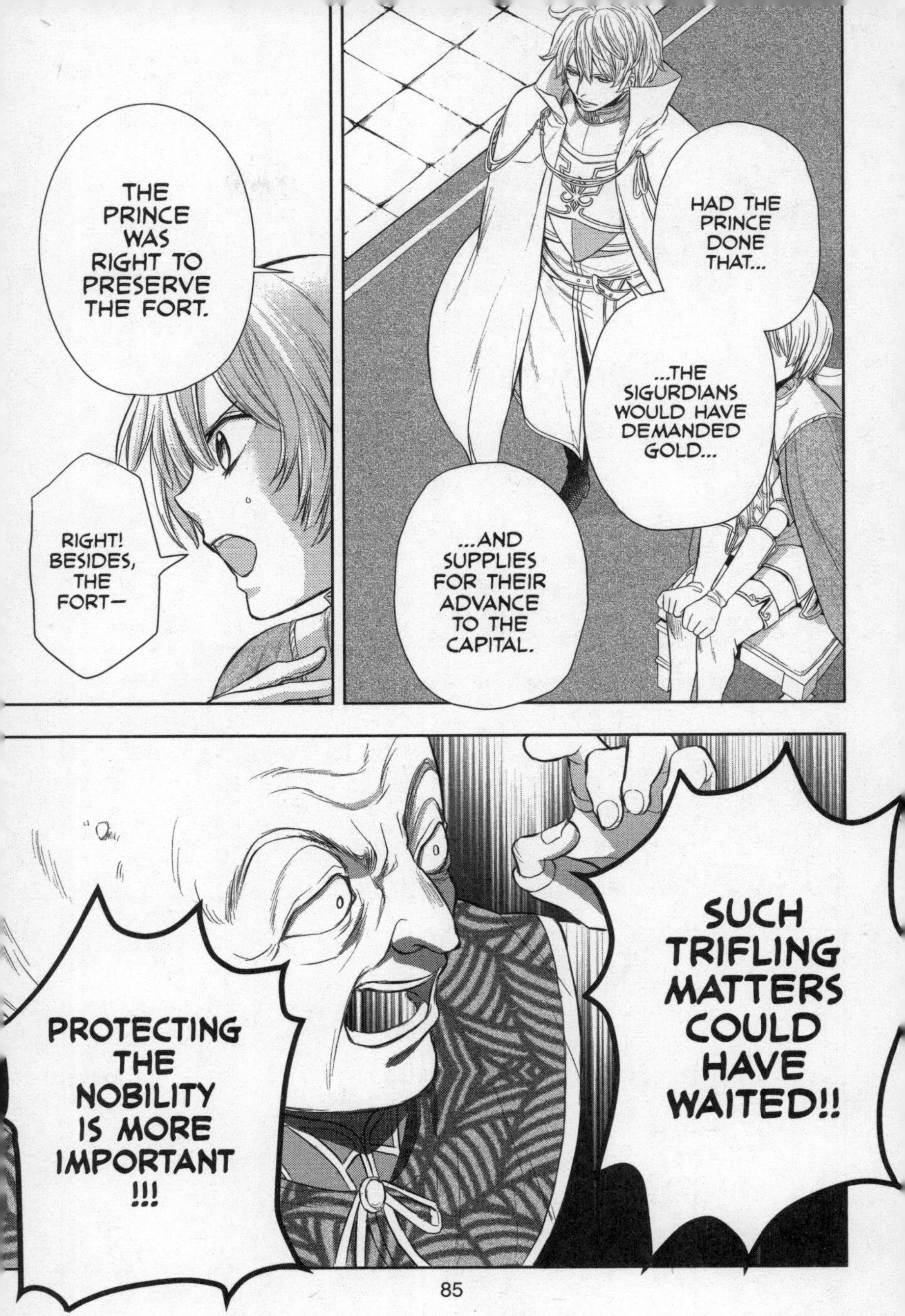
HAD THE PRINCE DONE THAT...
...THE SIGURDIANS WOULD HAVE DEMANDED GOLD...
...AND SUPPLIES FOR THEIR ADVANCE TO THE CAPITAL.
THE PRINCE WAS RIGHT TO PRESERVE THE FORT.
RIGHT! BESIDES, THE FORT—
SUCH TRIFLING MATTERS COULD HAVE WAITED!!
PROTECTING THE NOBILITY IS MORE IMPORTANT !!!

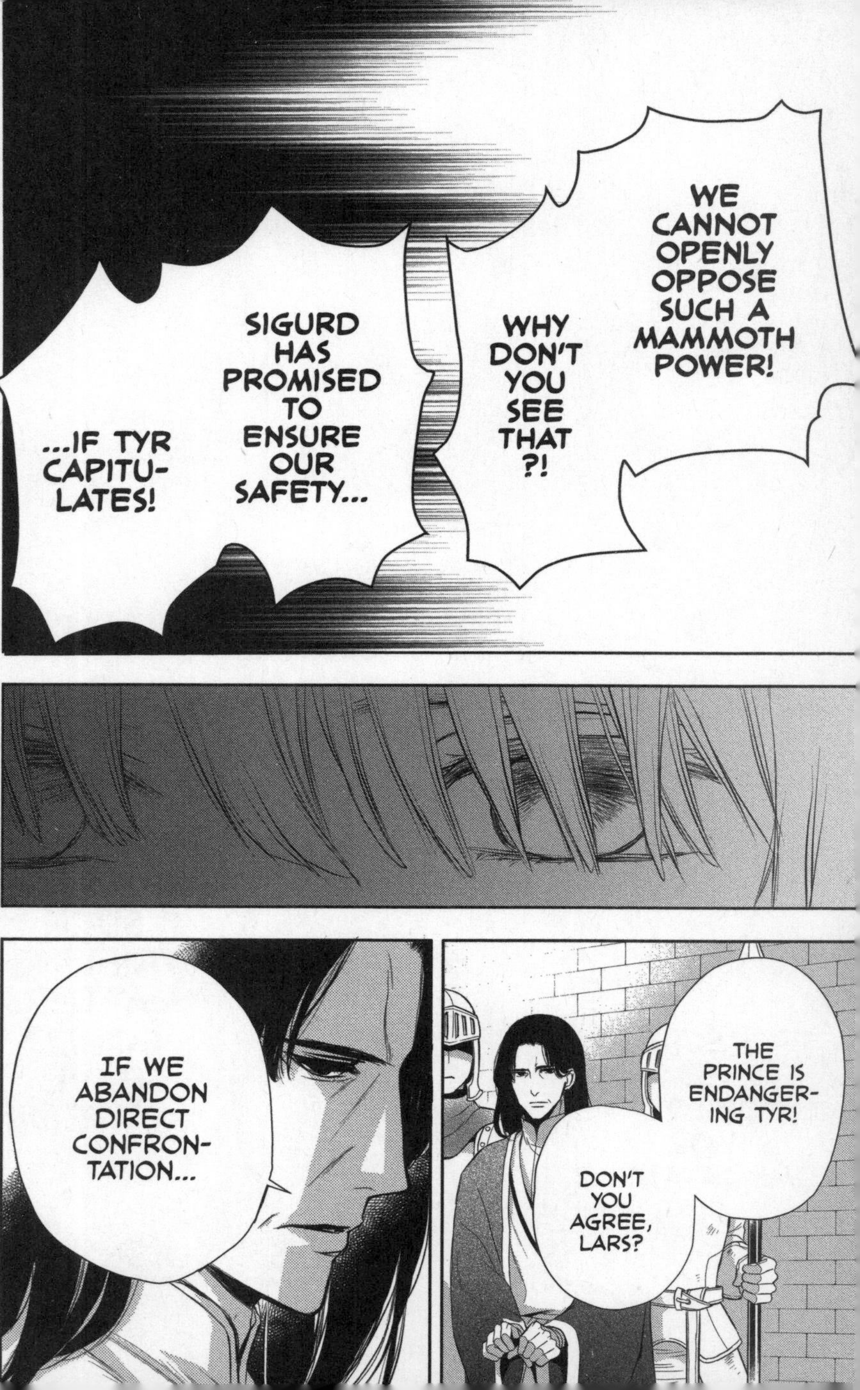
WE CANNOT OPENLY OPPOSE SUCH A MAMMOTH POWER!
WHY DON'T YOU SEE THAT?!
SIGURD HAS PROMISED TO ENSURE OUR SAFETY...
...IF TYR CAPITULATES!
THE PRINCE IS ENDANGERING TYR!
DON'T YOU AGREE, LARS?
IF WE ABANDON DIRECT CONFRONTATION...

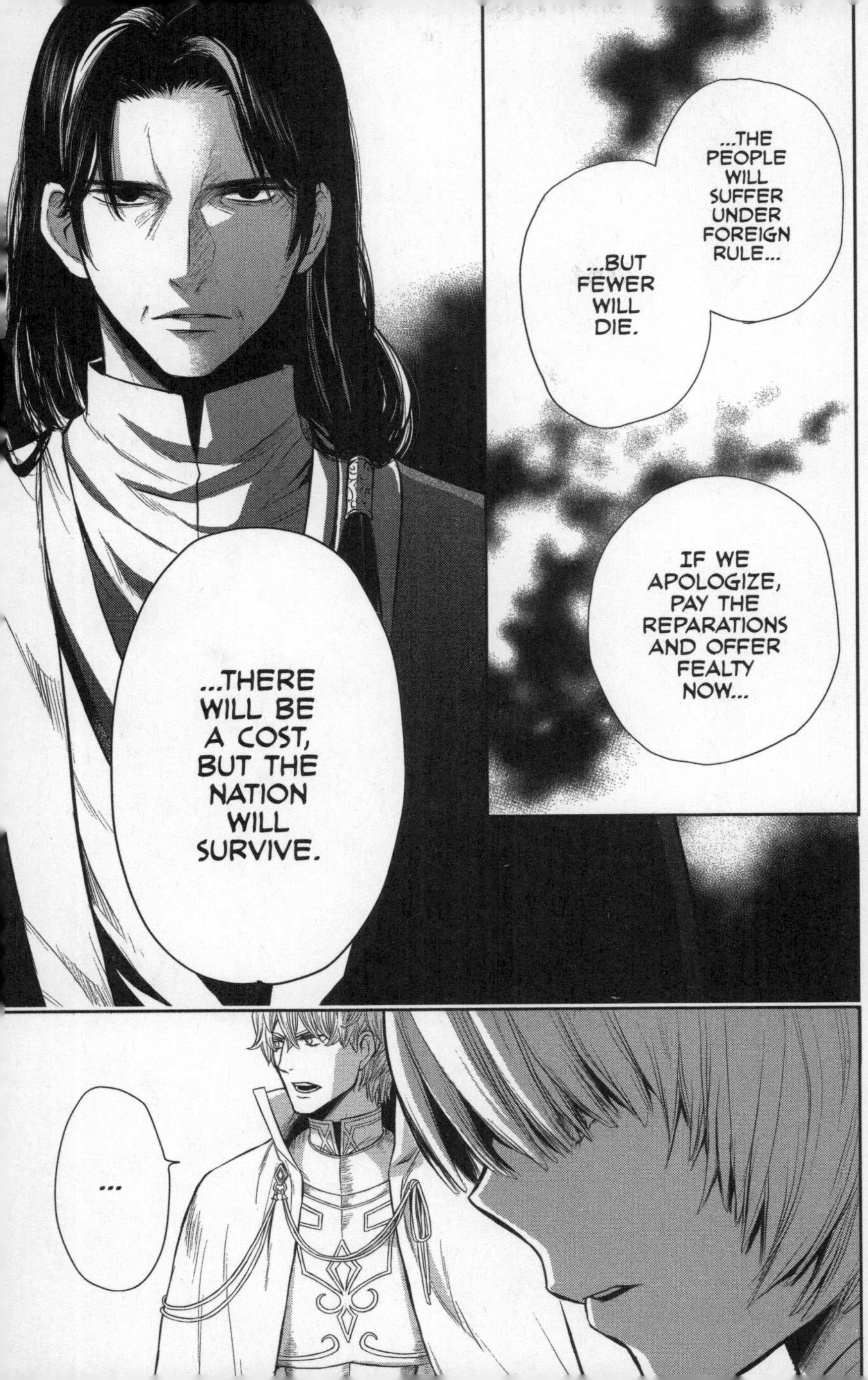
...THE PEOPLE WILL SUFFER UNDER FOREIGN RULE...
...BUT FEWER WILL DIE.
IF WE APOLOGIZE, PAY THE REPARATIONS AND OFFER FEALTY NOW...
...THERE WILL BE A COST, BUT THE NATION WILL SURVIVE.
...

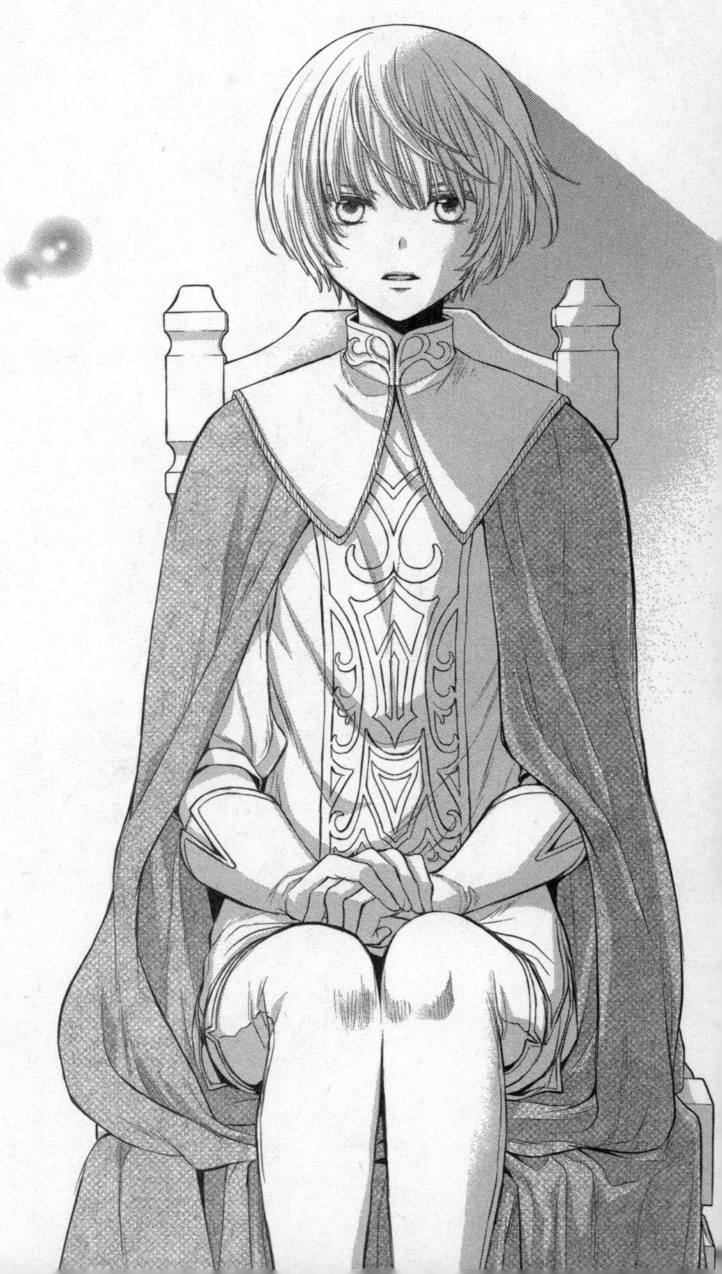

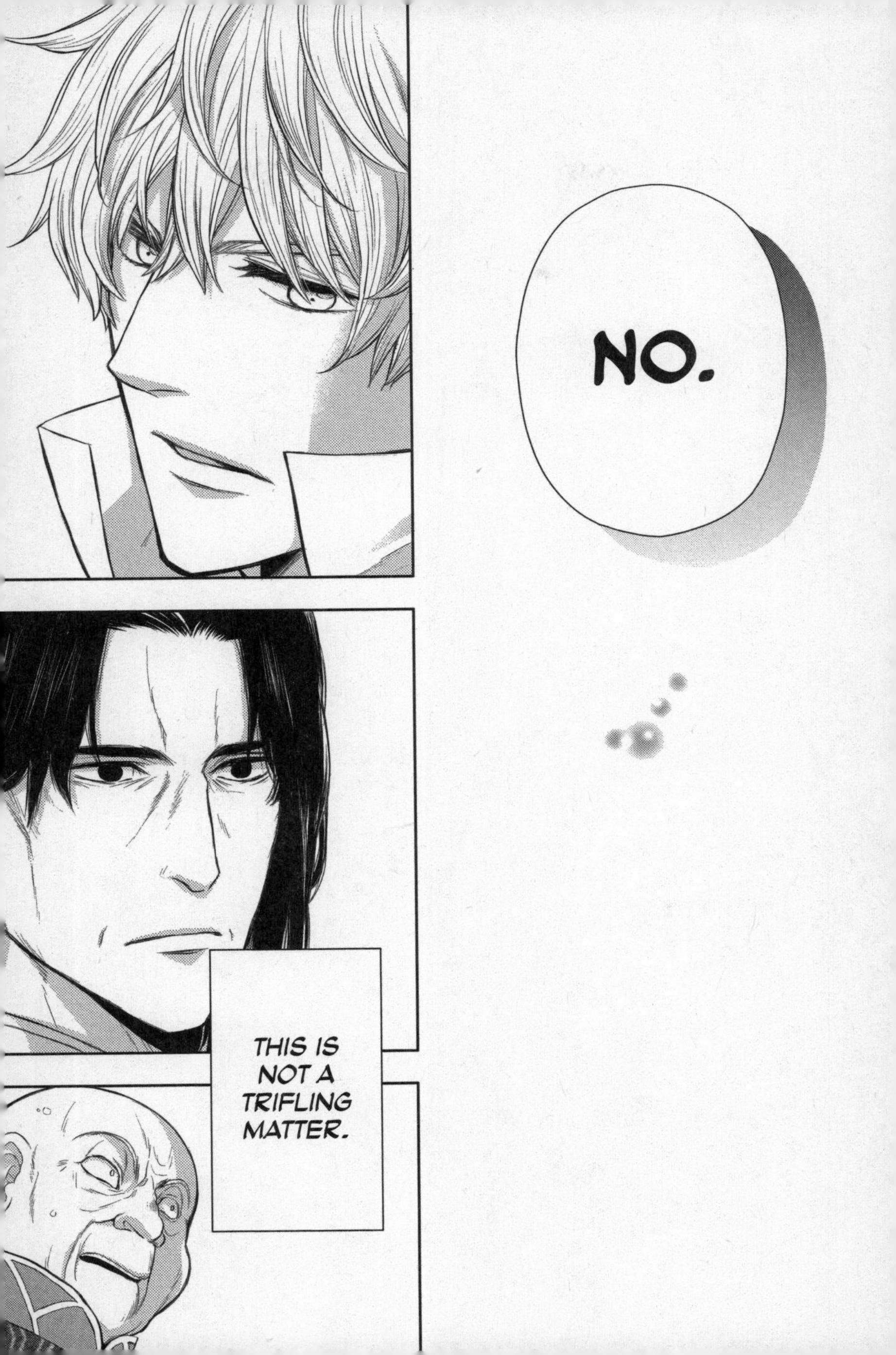
NO.
THIS IS NOT A TRIFLING MATTER.

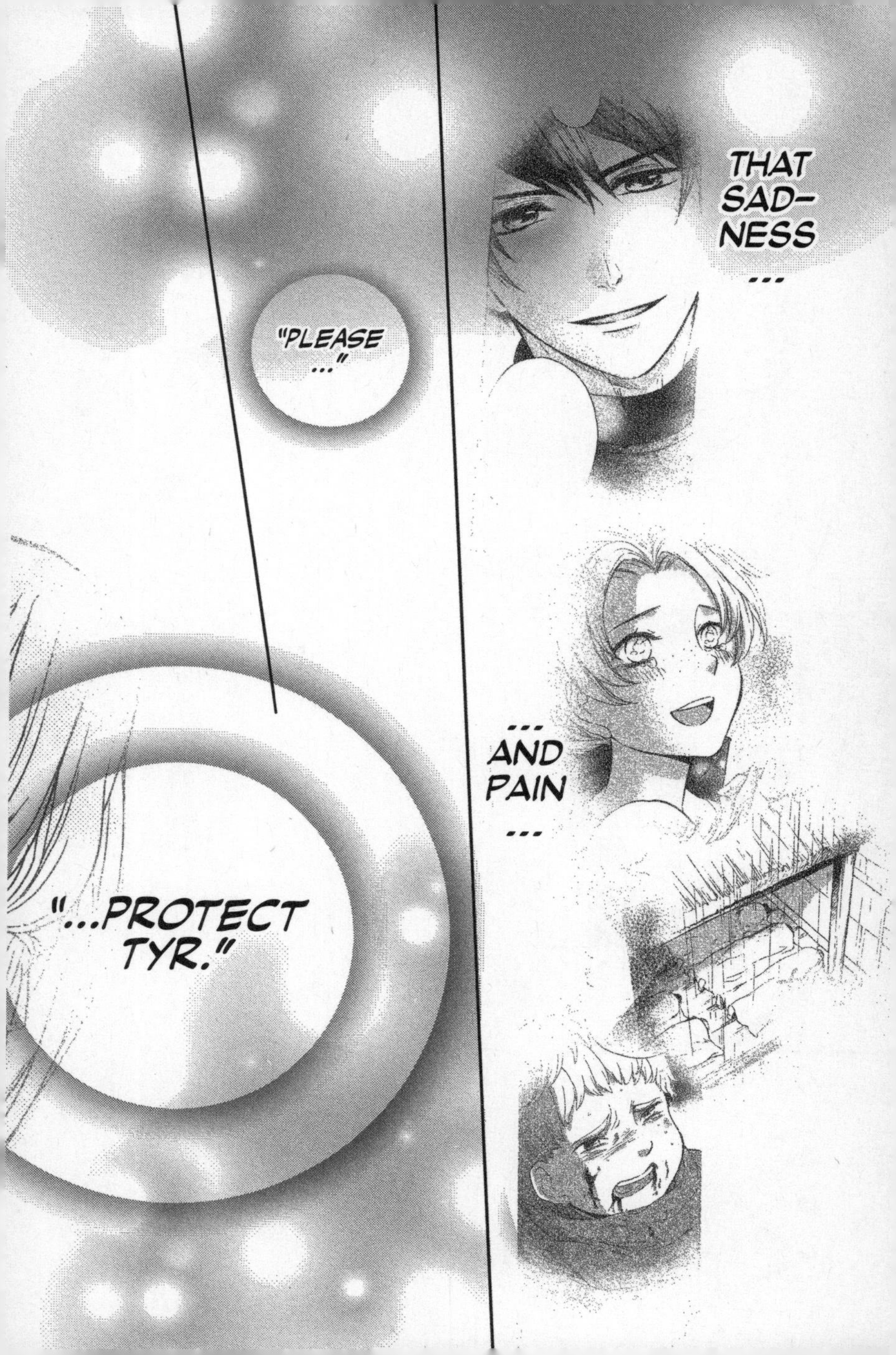
THAT SAD-NESS ...
... AND PAIN ...
"PLEASE ..."
"...PROTECT TYR."

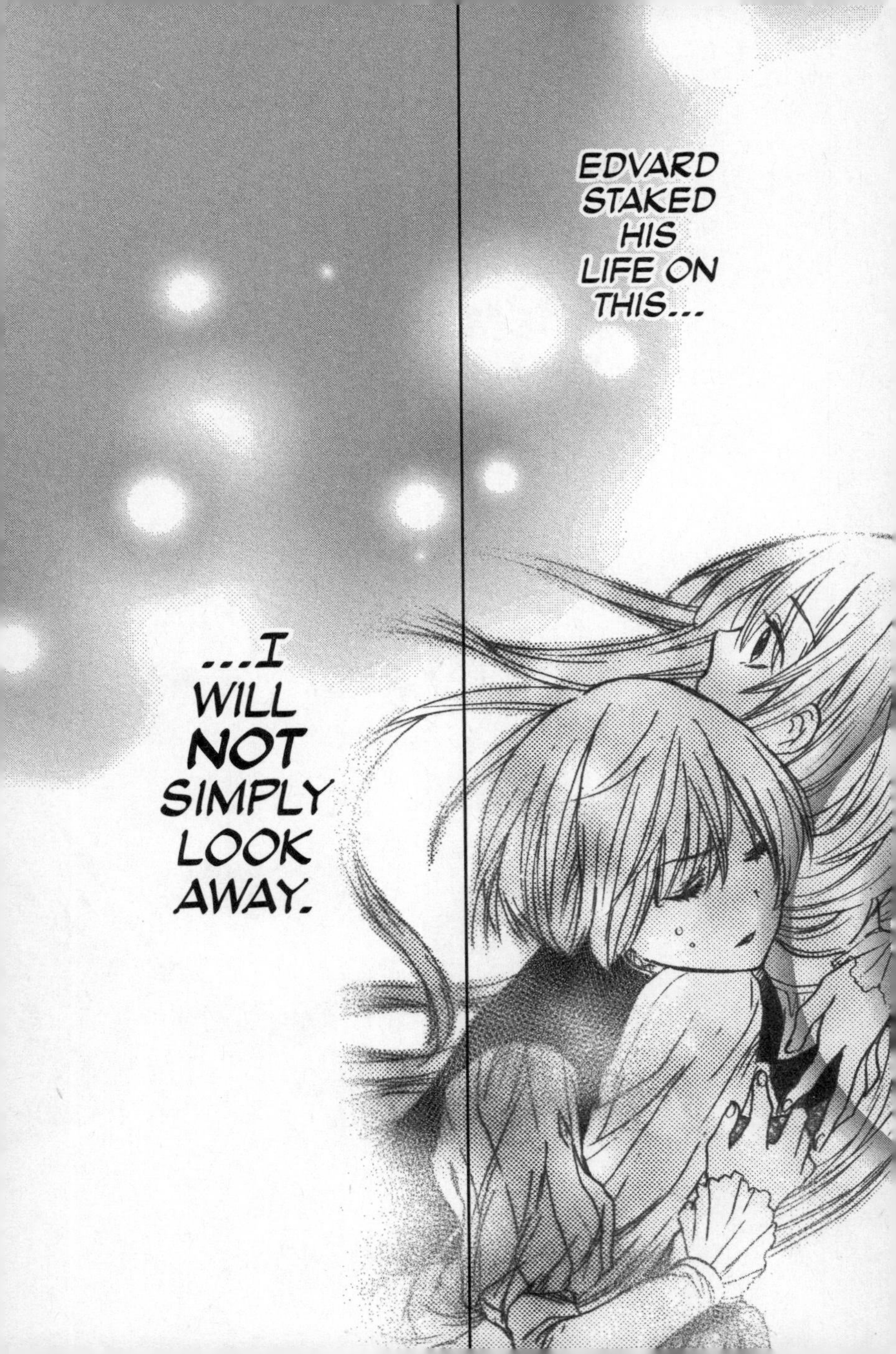
EDVARD STAKED HIS LIFE ON THIS...
...I WILL NOT SIMPLY LOOK AWAY.

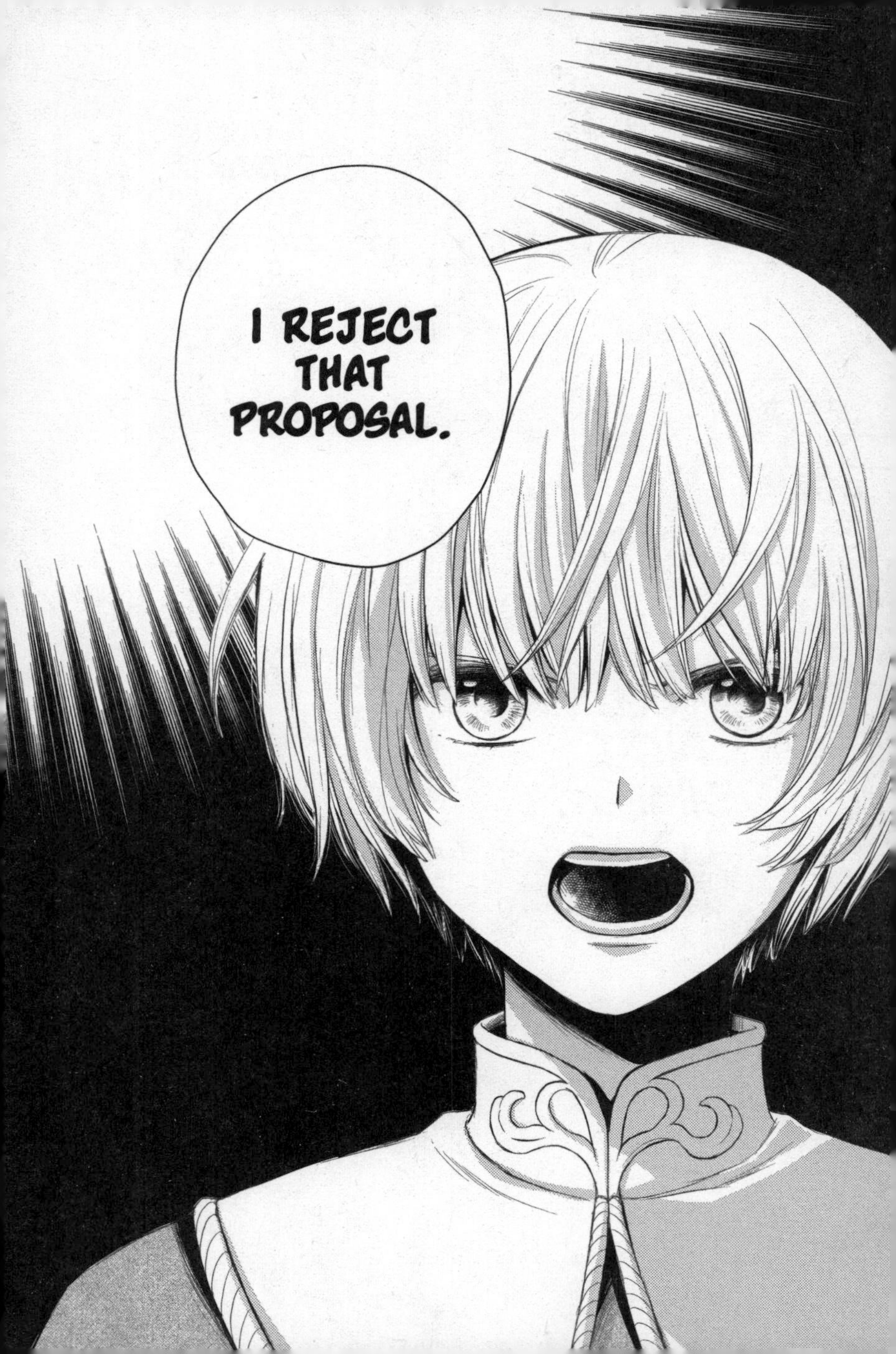
I REJECT THAT PROPOSAL.

Chapter 12: The Oath

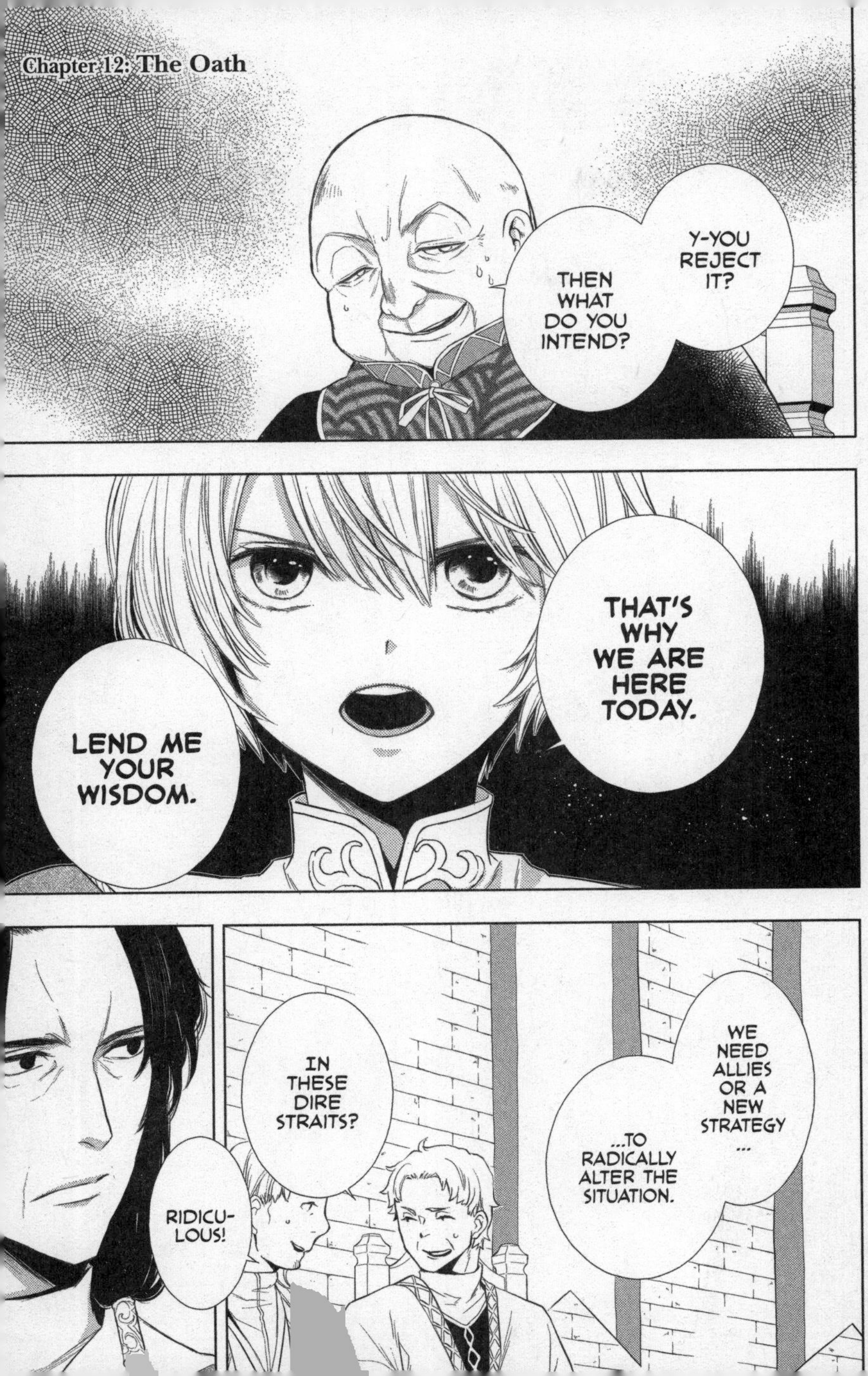
Y-YOU REJECT IT?
THEN WHAT DO YOU INTEND?
THAT'S WHY WE ARE HERE TODAY.
LEND ME YOUR WISDOM.
WE NEED ALLIES OR A NEW STRATEGY ...
...TO RADICALLY ALTER THE SITUATION.
IN THESE DIRE STRAITS?
RIDICU-LOUS!

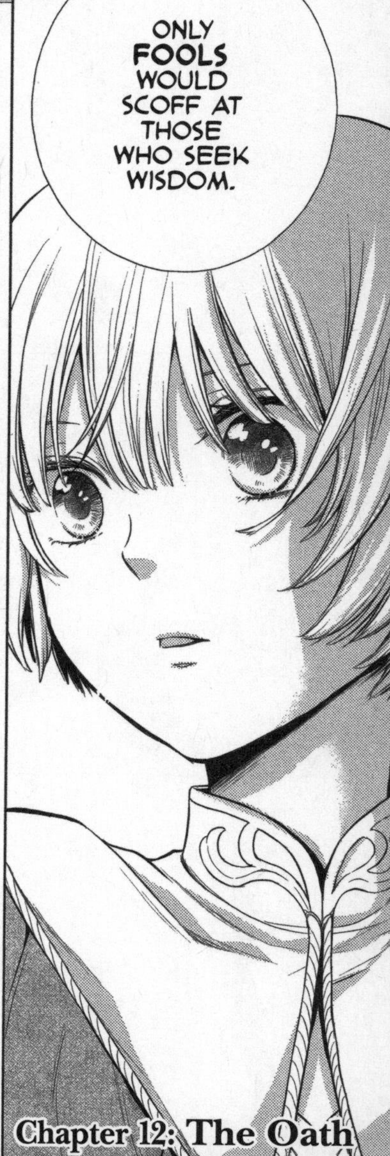
ONLY FOOLS WOULD SCOFF AT THOSE WHO SEEK WISDOM.

Chapter 12: The Oath

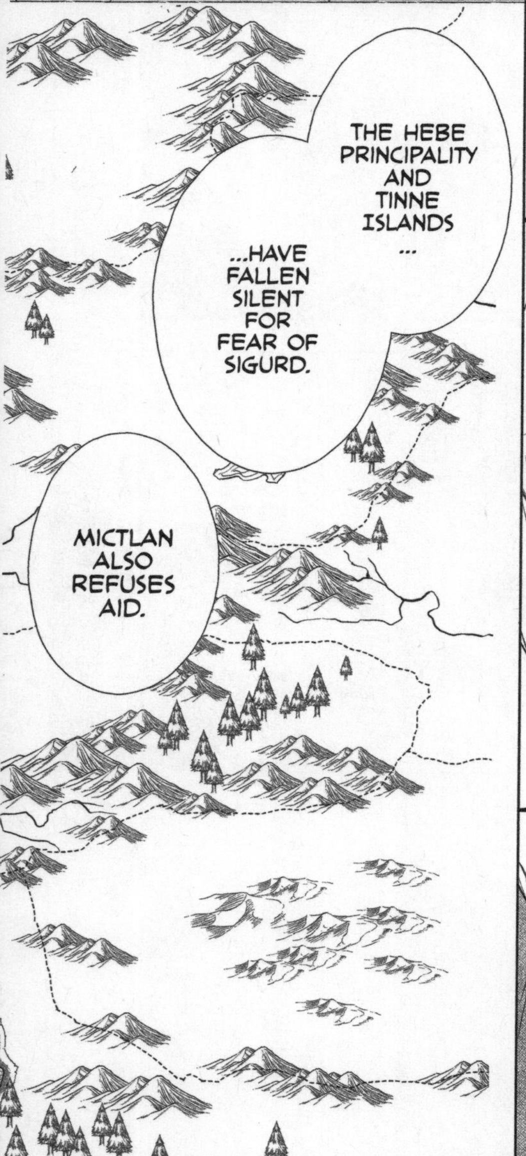
THE HEBE PRINCIPALITY AND TINNE ISLANDS ...
...HAVE FALLEN SILENT FOR FEAR OF SIGURD.
MICTLAN ALSO REFUSES AID.

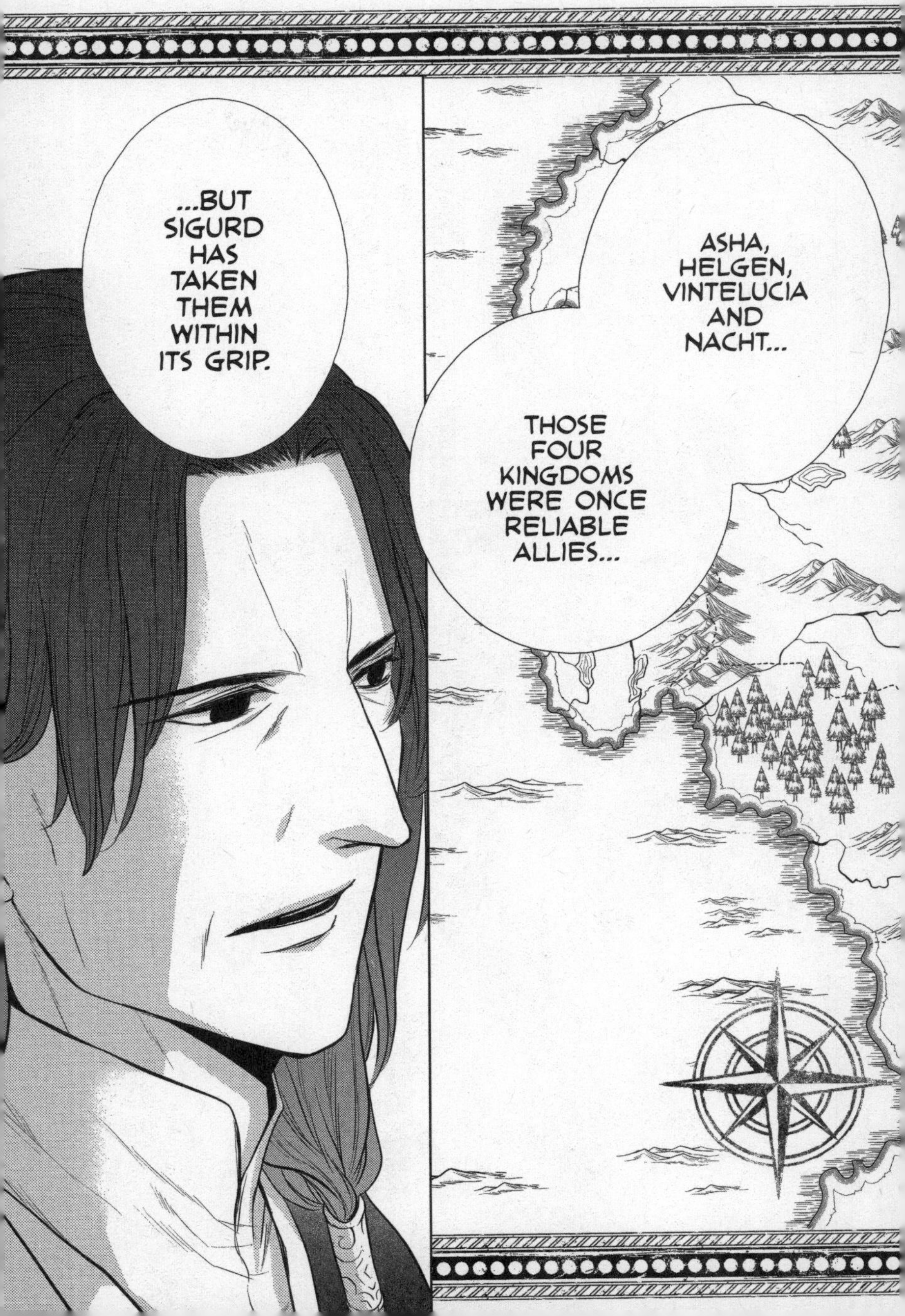
ASHA, HELGEN, VINTELUCIA AND NACHT...
THOSE FOUR KINGDOMS WERE ONCE RELIABLE ALLIES...
...BUT SIGURD HAS TAKEN THEM WITHIN ITS GRIP.

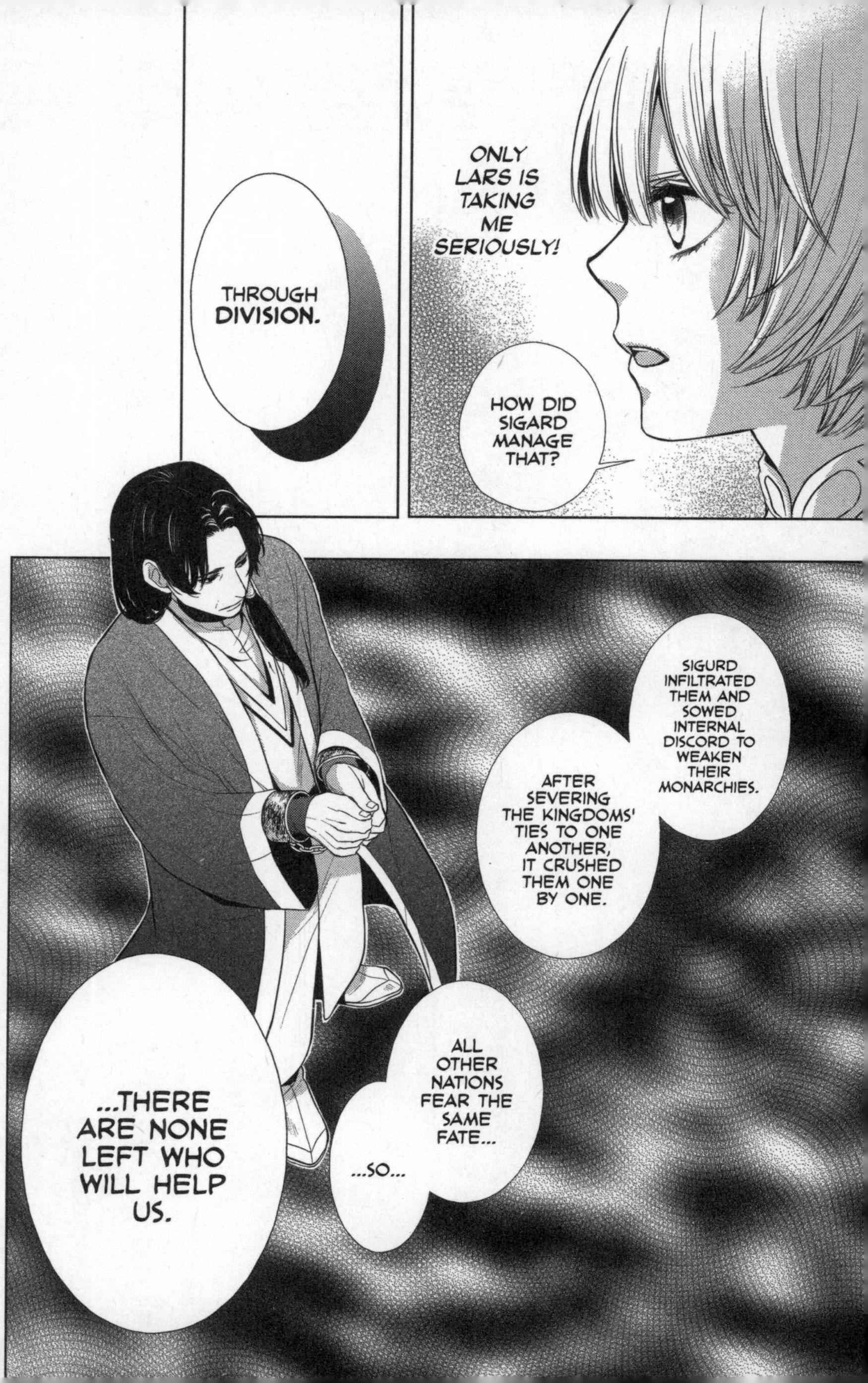
ONLY LARS IS TAKING ME SERIOUSLY!
HOW DID SIGARD MANAGE THAT?
THROUGH DIVISION.
SIGURD INFILTRATED THEM AND SOWED INTERNAL DISCORD TO WEAKEN THEIR MONARCHIES.
AFTER SEVERING THE KINGDOMS' TIES TO ONE ANOTHER, IT CRUSHED THEM ONE BY ONE.
ALL OTHER NATIONS FEAR THE SAME FATE...
...SO...
...THERE ARE NONE LEFT WHO WILL HELP US.

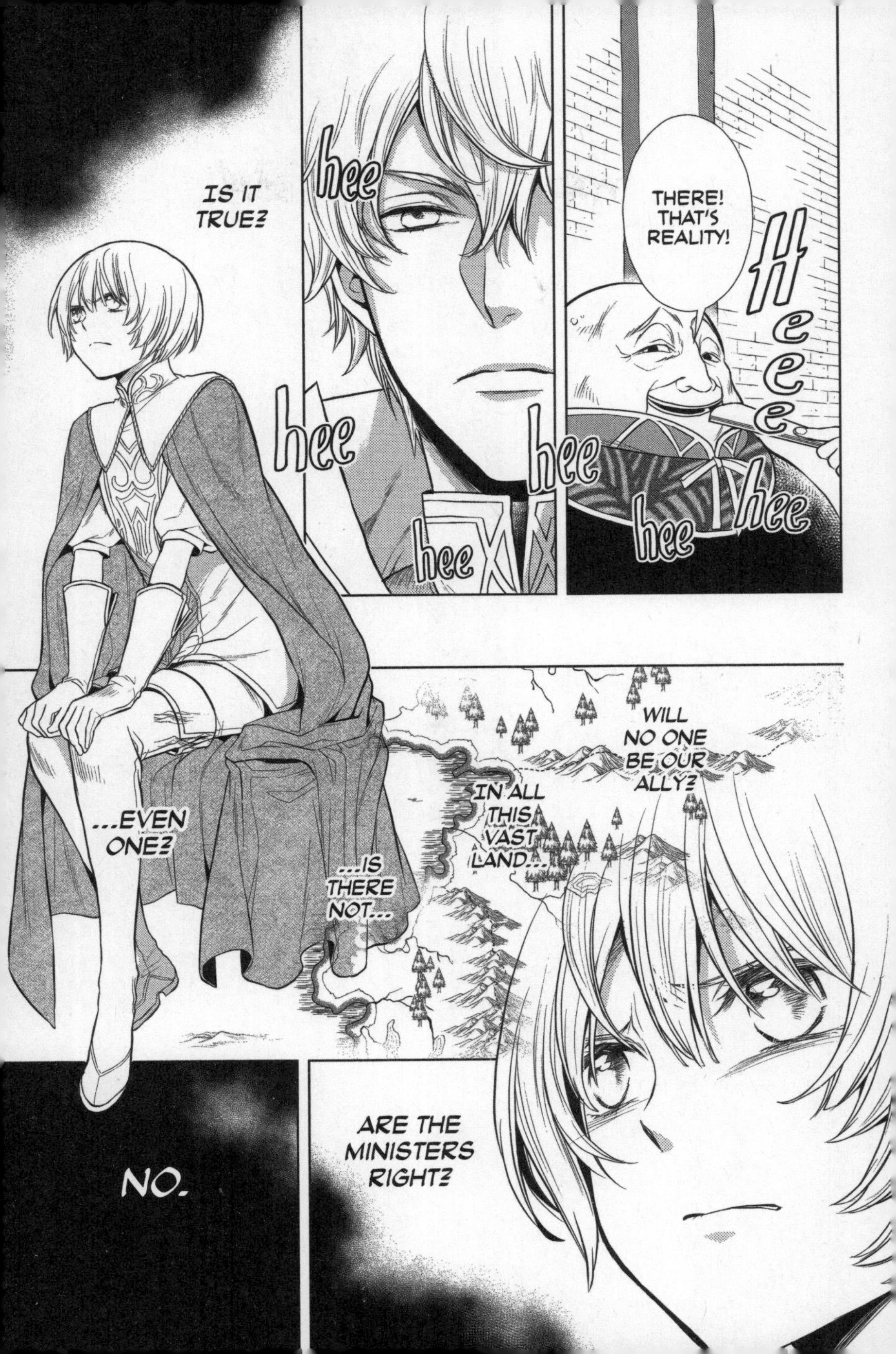
THERE! THAT'S REALITY!
Heeee...
hee
hee
hee
hee
hee
hee
IS IT TRUE?
WILL NO ONE BE OUR ALLY?
IN ALL THIS VAST LAND...
...IS THERE NOT...
...EVEN ONE?
ARE THE MINISTERS RIGHT?
NO.

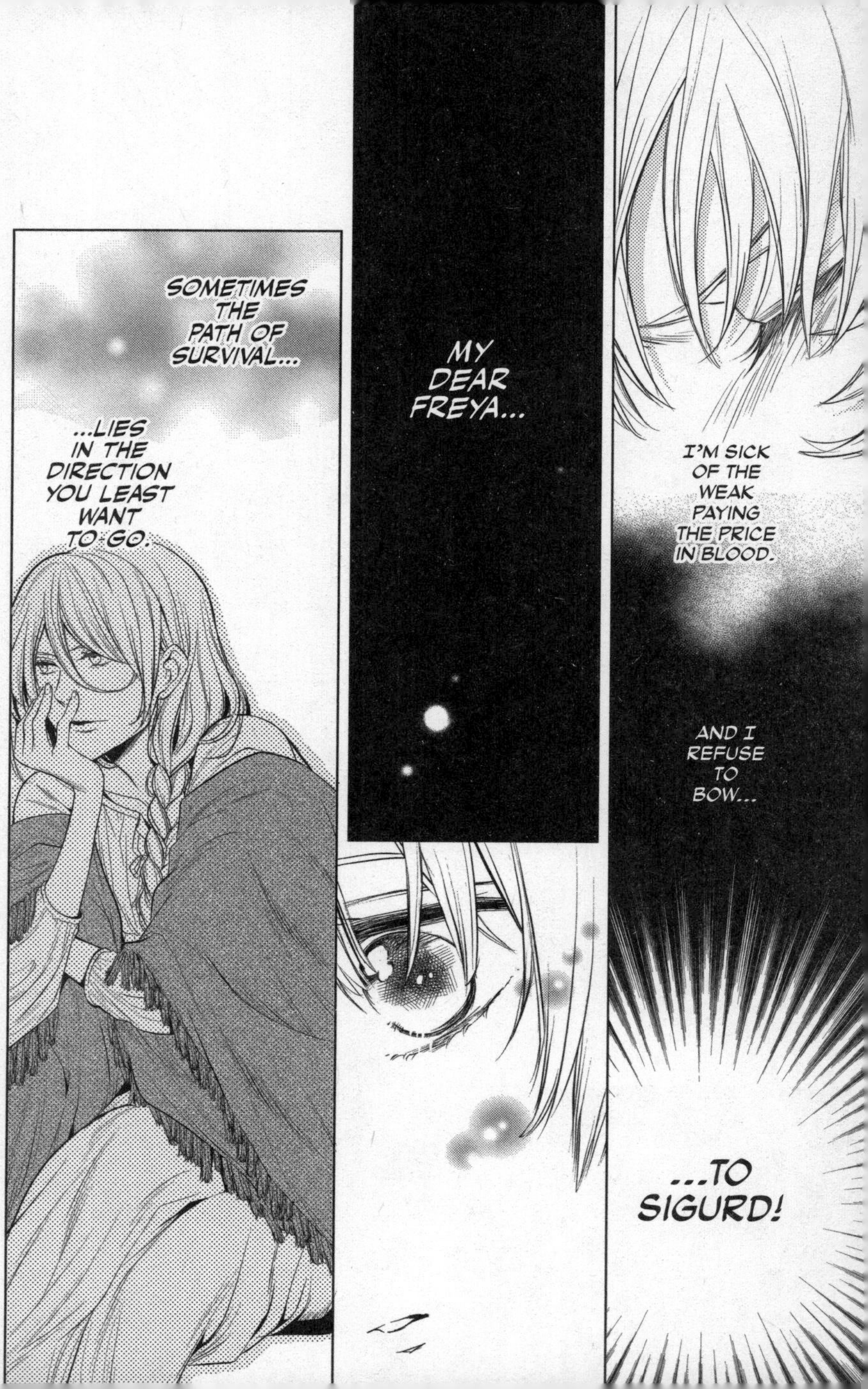
I'M SICK OF THE WEAK PAYING THE PRICE IN BLOOD.
AND I REFUSE TO BOW...
...TO SIGURD!
MY DEAR FREYA...
SOMETIMES THE PATH OF SURVIVAL...
...LIES IN THE DIRECTION YOU LEAST WANT TO GO.

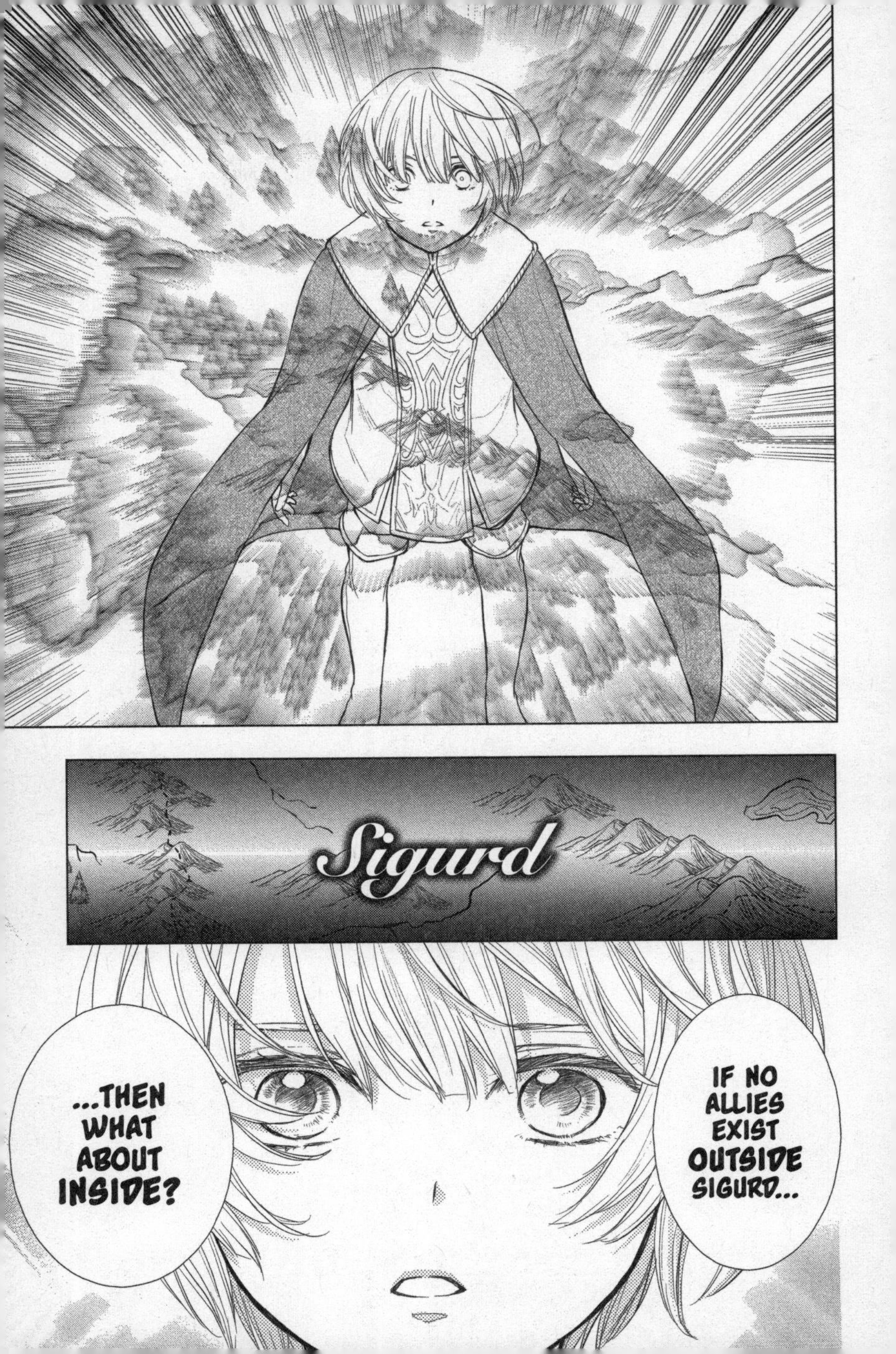
Sigurd
IF NO ALLIES EXIST OUTSIDE SIGURD...
...THEN WHAT ABOUT INSIDE?

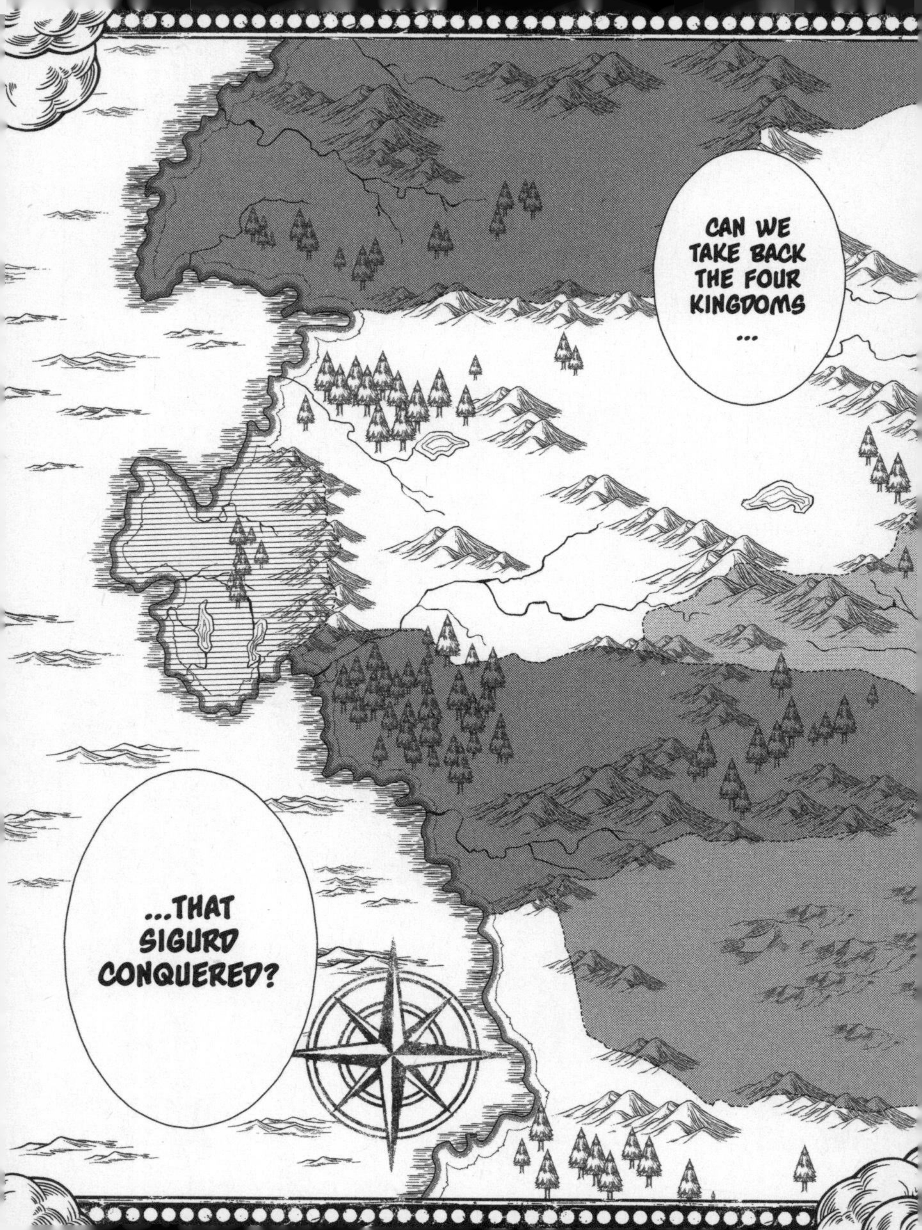
CAN WE TAKE BACK THE FOUR KINGDOMS ...
...THAT SIGURD CONQUERED?

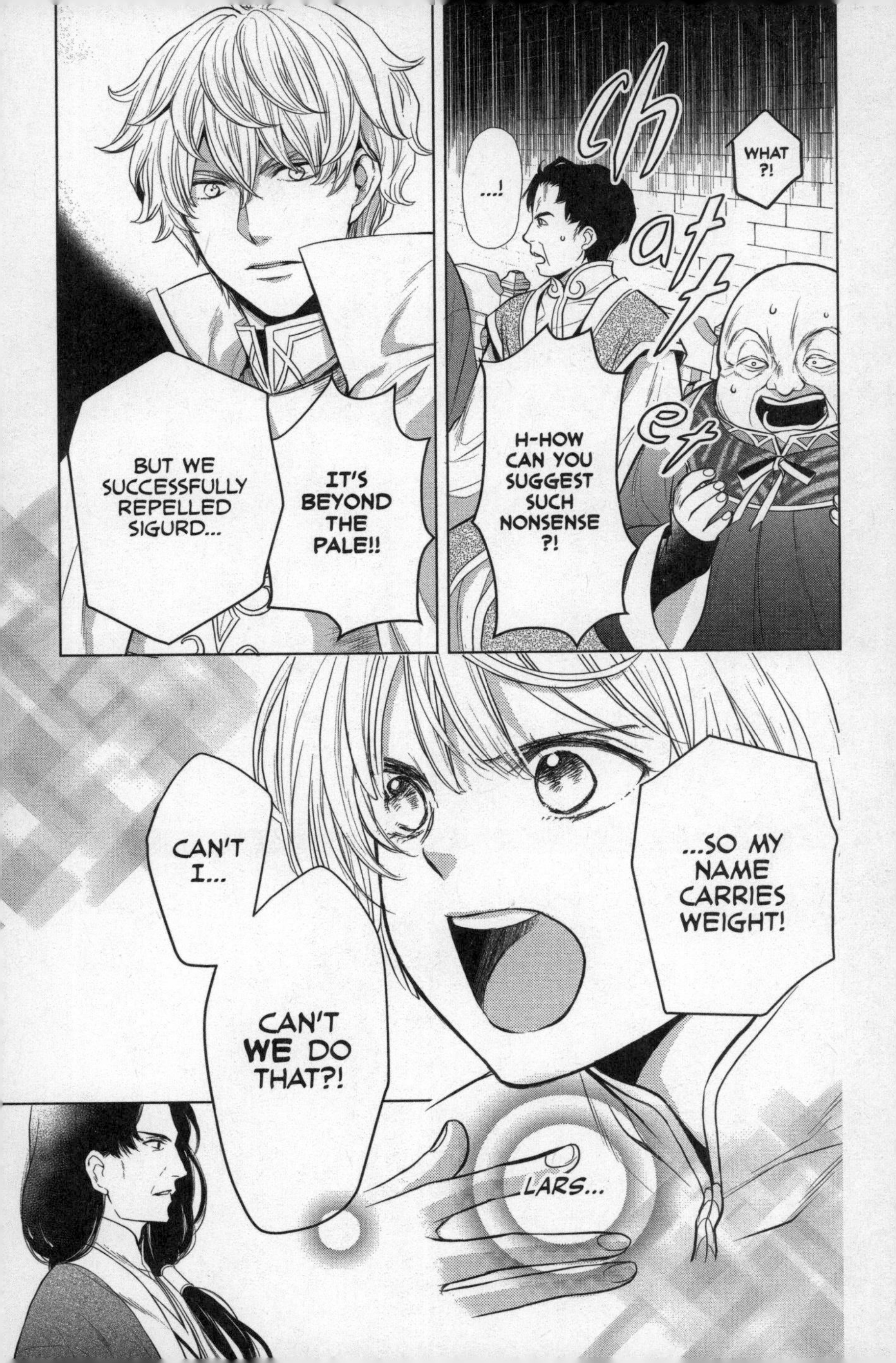
WHAT ?!
...!
chatter
H-HOW CAN YOU SUGGEST SUCH NONSENSE ?!
IT'S BEYOND THE PALE!!
BUT WE SUCCESSFULLY REPELLED SIGURD...
...SO MY NAME CARRIES WEIGHT!
CAN'T I...
CAN'T **WE** DO THAT?!
LARS...

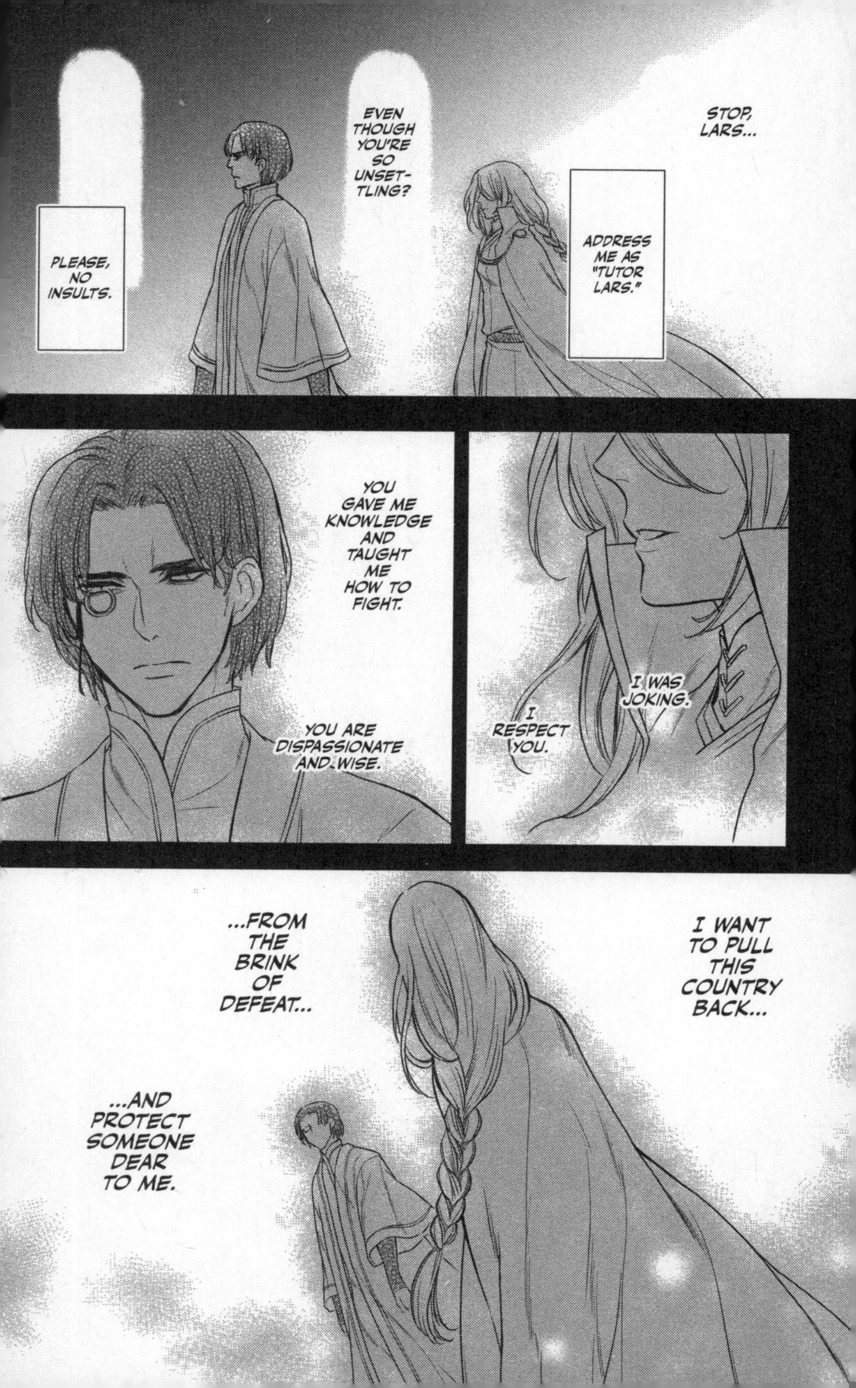
STOP, LARS...
ADDRESS ME AS "TUTOR LARS."
EVEN THOUGH YOU'RE SO UNSET-TLING?
PLEASE, NO INSULTS.
I WAS JOKING.
I RESPECT YOU.
YOU GAVE ME KNOWLEDGE AND TAUGHT ME HOW TO FIGHT.
YOU ARE DISPASSIONATE AND WISE.
I WANT TO PULL THIS COUNTRY BACK...
...FROM THE BRINK OF DEFEAT...
...AND PROTECT SOMEONE DEAR TO ME.

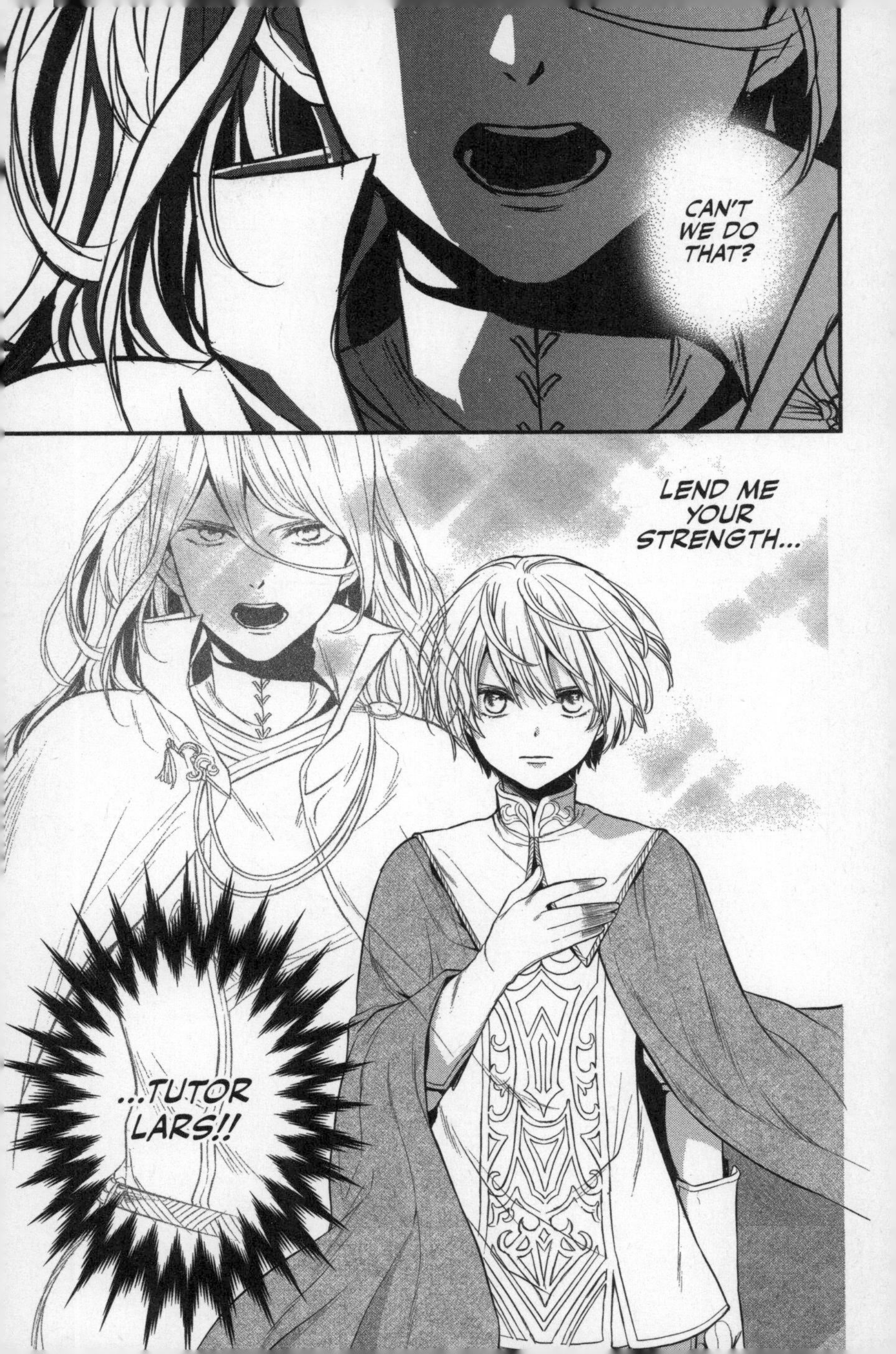
CAN'T WE DO THAT?
LEND ME YOUR STRENGTH...
...TUTOR LARS!!

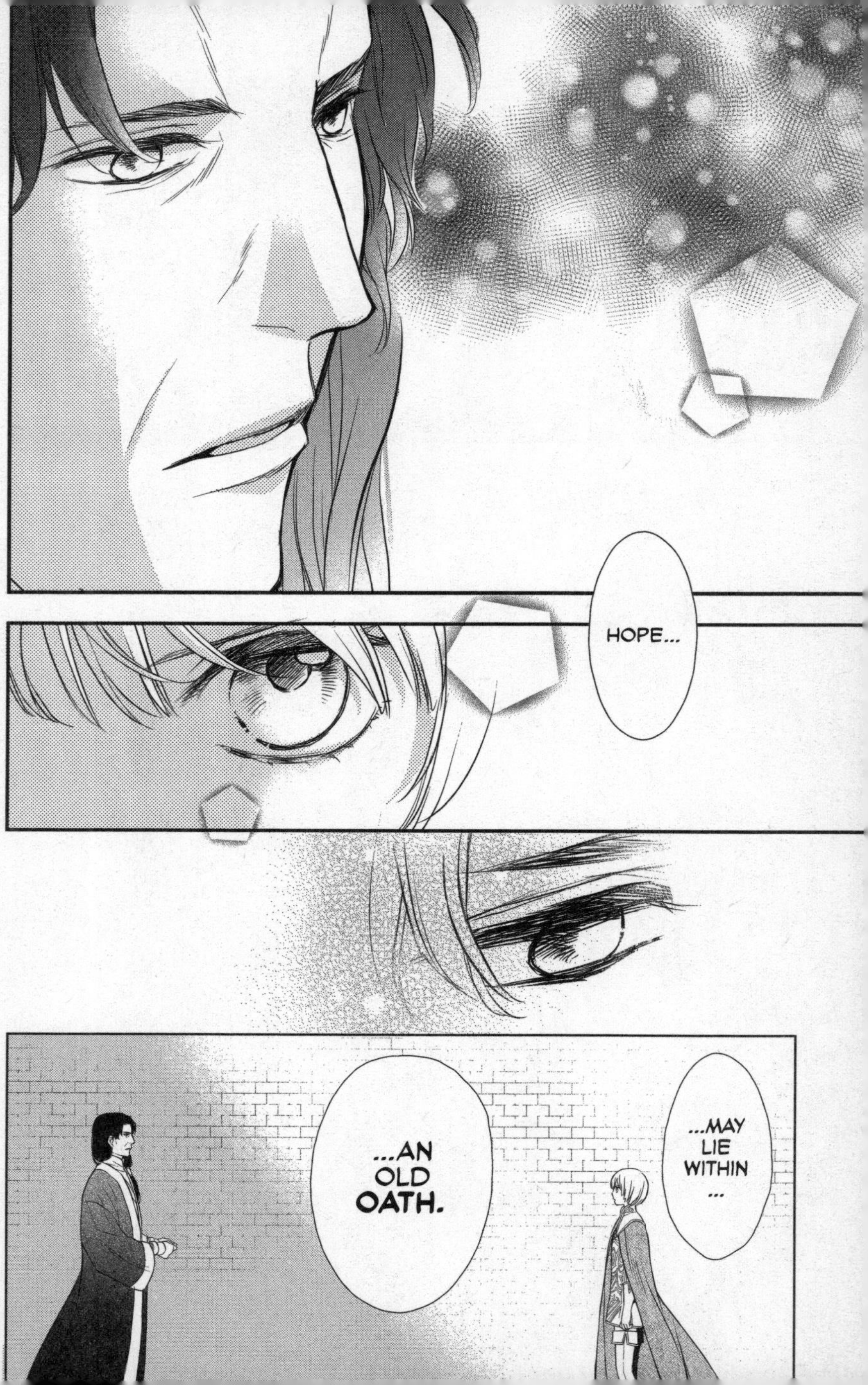
HOPE...
...MAY LIE WITHIN ...
...AN OLD OATH.

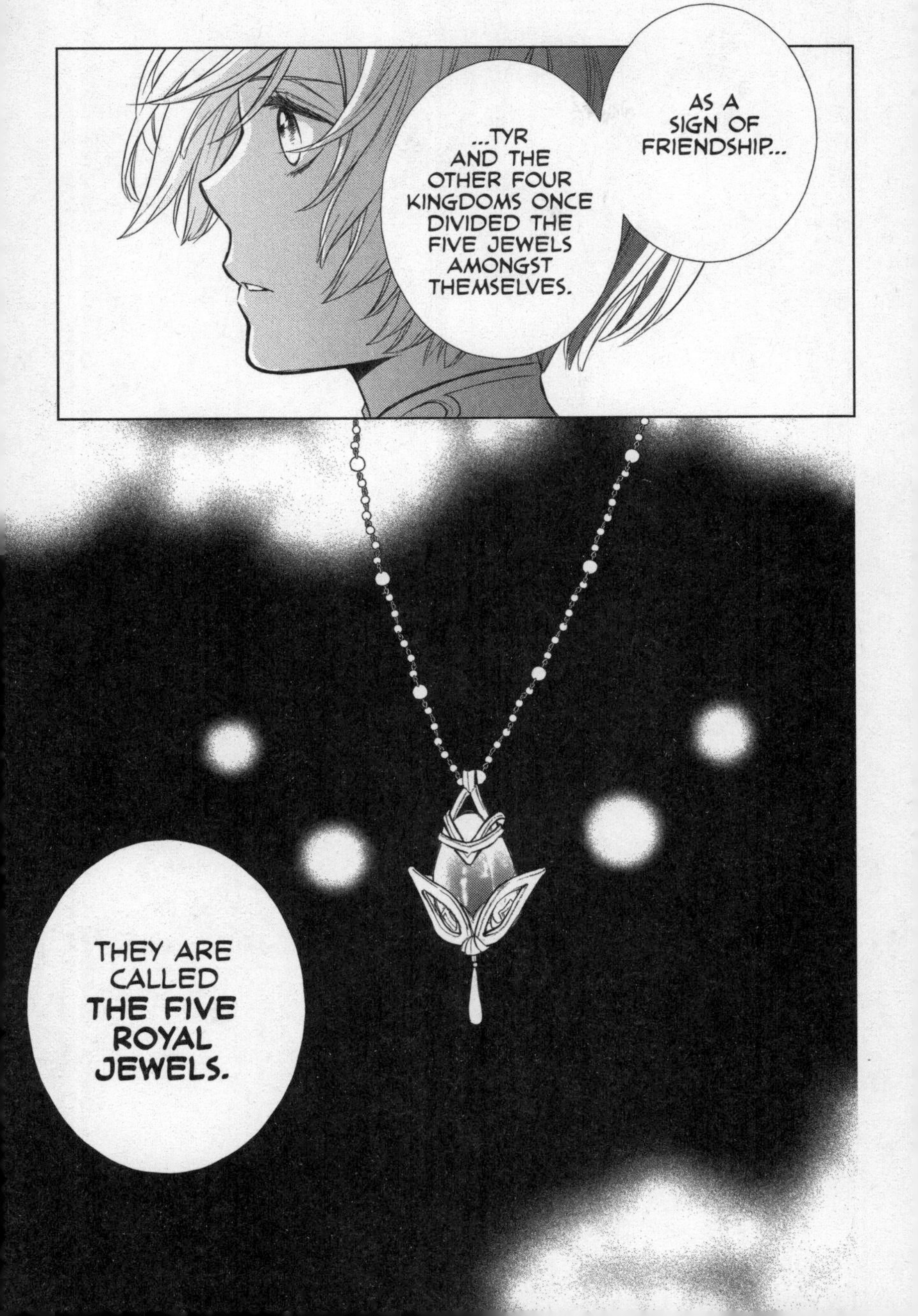
AS A SIGN OF FRIENDSHIP...
...TYR AND THE OTHER FOUR KINGDOMS ONCE DIVIDED THE FIVE JEWELS AMONGST THEMSELVES.
THEY ARE CALLED THE FIVE ROYAL JEWELS.

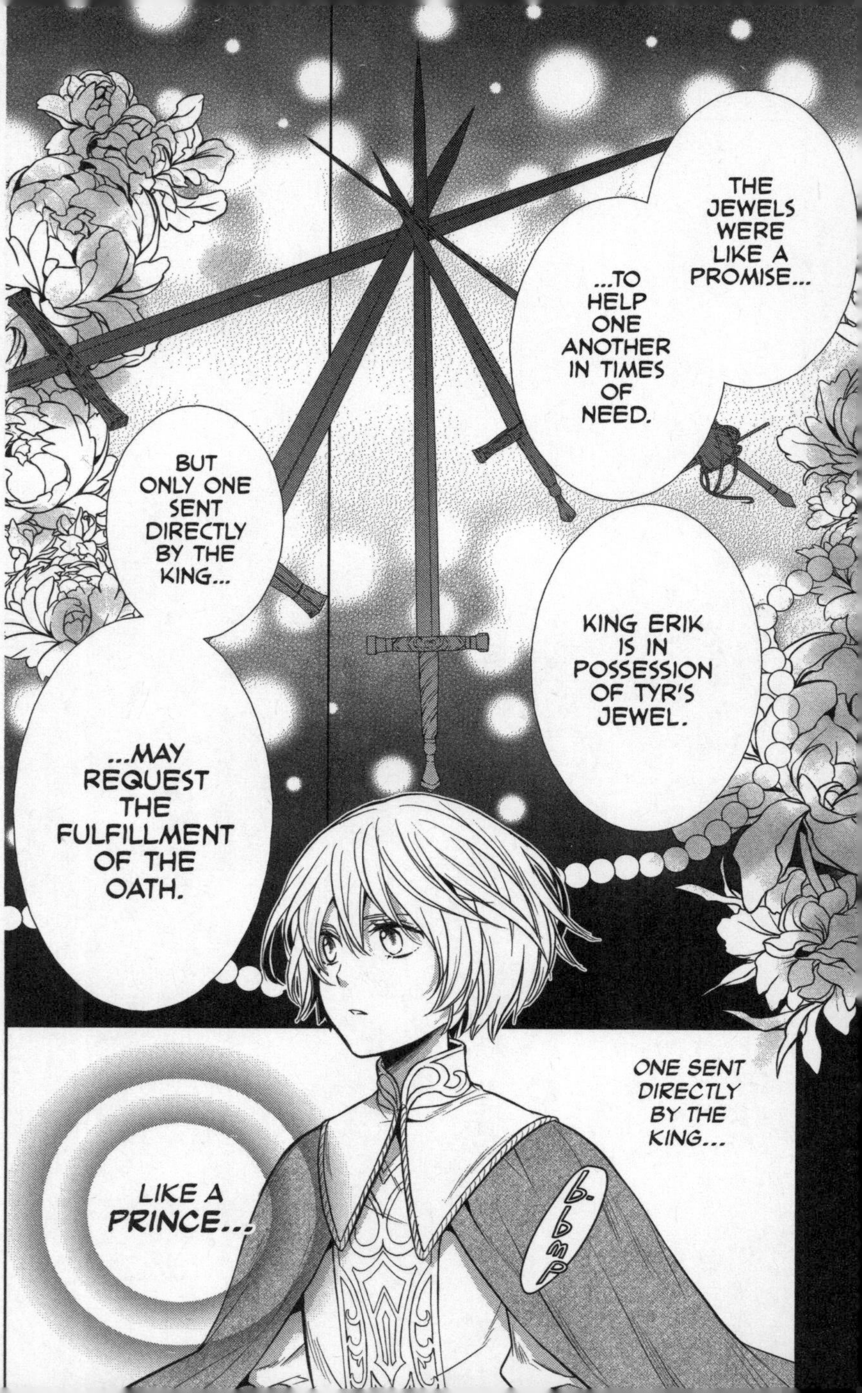
THE JEWELS WERE LIKE A PROMISE...
...TO HELP ONE ANOTHER IN TIMES OF NEED.
BUT ONLY ONE SENT DIRECTLY BY THE KING...
...MAY REQUEST THE FULFILLMENT OF THE OATH.
KING ERIK IS IN POSSESSION OF TYR'S JEWEL.
ONE SENT DIRECTLY BY THE KING...
b-bmp
LIKE A PRINCE...

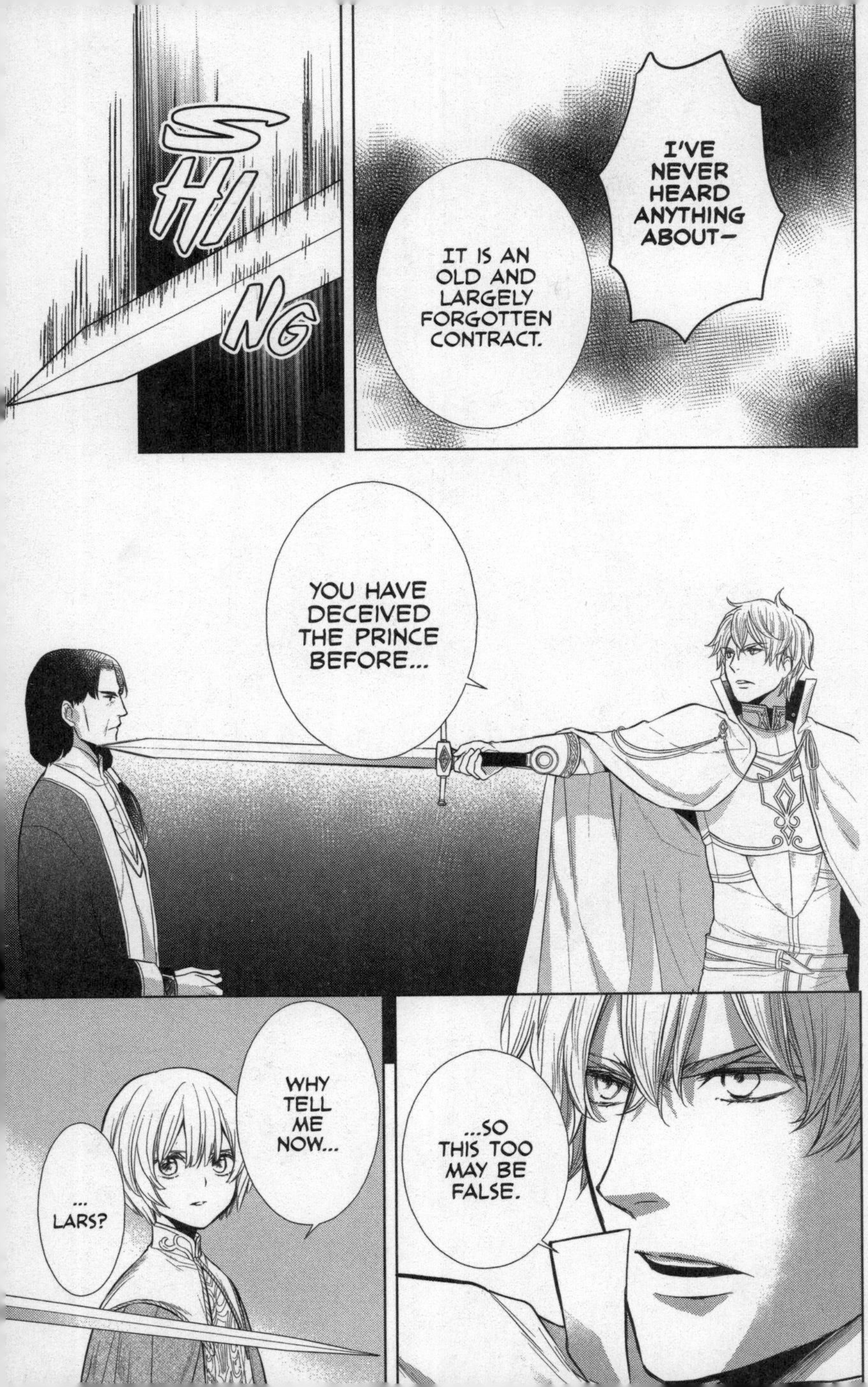
I'VE NEVER HEARD ANYTHING ABOUT—
IT IS AN OLD AND LARGELY FORGOTTEN CONTRACT.
SHING
YOU HAVE DECEIVED THE PRINCE BEFORE...
...SO THIS TOO MAY BE FALSE.
WHY TELL ME NOW...
... LARS?

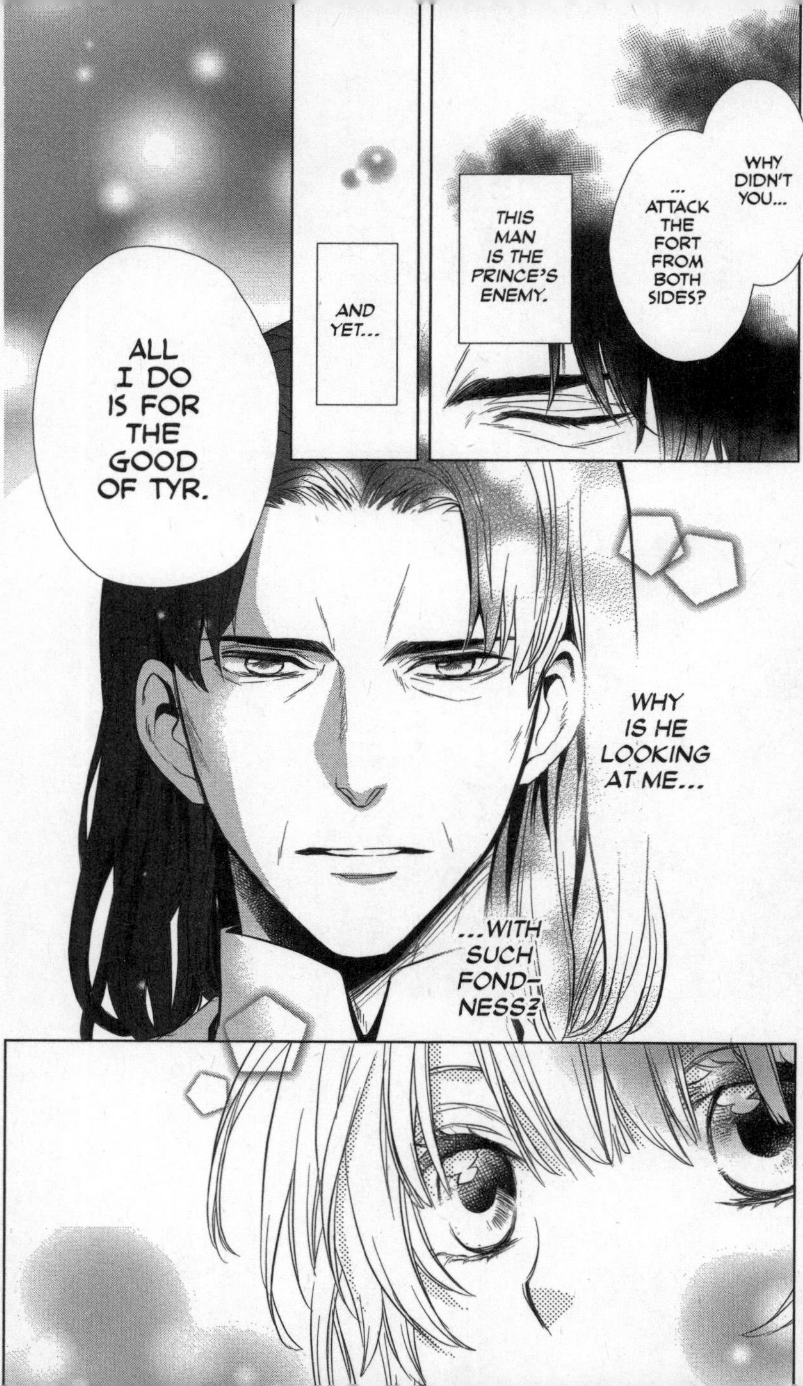
WHY DIDN'T YOU...
...ATTACK THE FORT FROM BOTH SIDES?
THIS MAN IS THE PRINCE'S ENEMY.
AND YET...
ALL I DO IS FOR THE GOOD OF TYR.
WHY IS HE LOOKING AT ME...
...WITH SUCH FONDNESS?

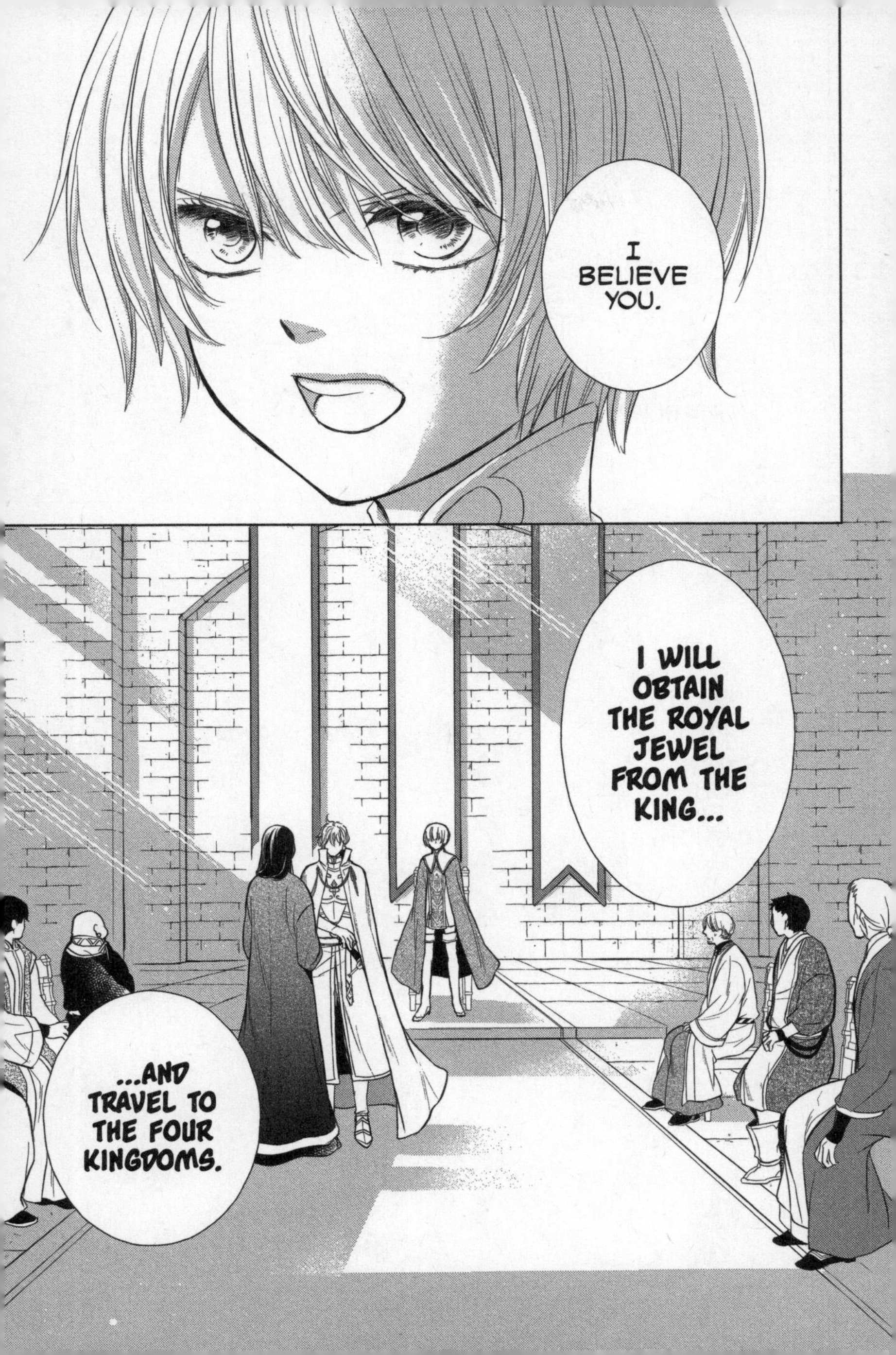
I BELIEVE YOU.
I WILL OBTAIN THE ROYAL JEWEL FROM THE KING...
...AND TRAVEL TO THE FOUR KINGDOMS.

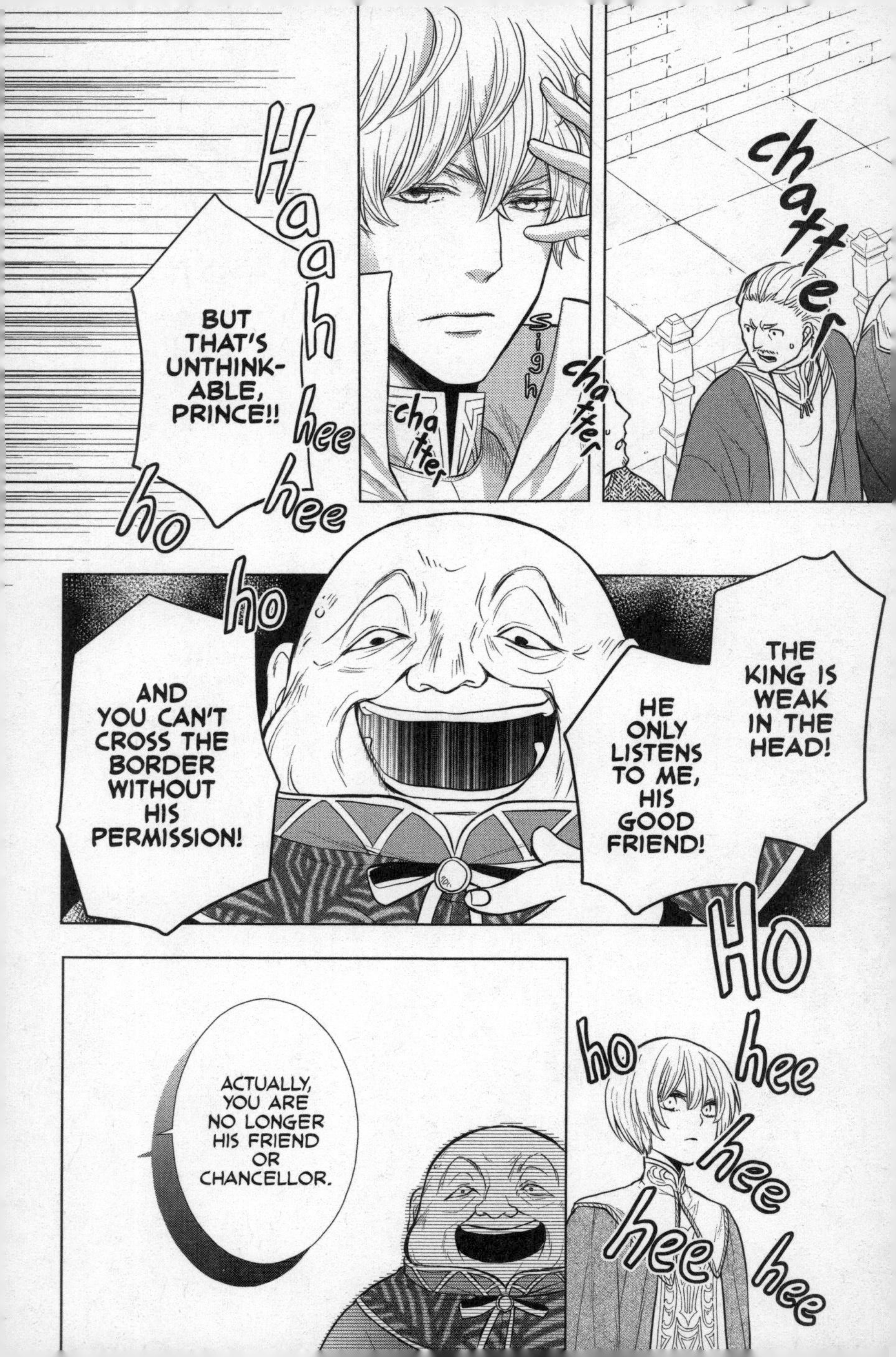
chatter!
sigh
chatter
chatter
BUT THAT'S UNTHINKABLE, PRINCE!!
Haaah hee hee ho
ho
THE KING IS WEAK IN THE HEAD!
HE ONLY LISTENS TO ME, HIS GOOD FRIEND!
AND YOU CAN'T CROSS THE BORDER WITHOUT HIS PERMISSION!
HO ho hee hee hee hee
ACTUALLY, YOU ARE NO LONGER HIS FRIEND OR CHANCELLOR.

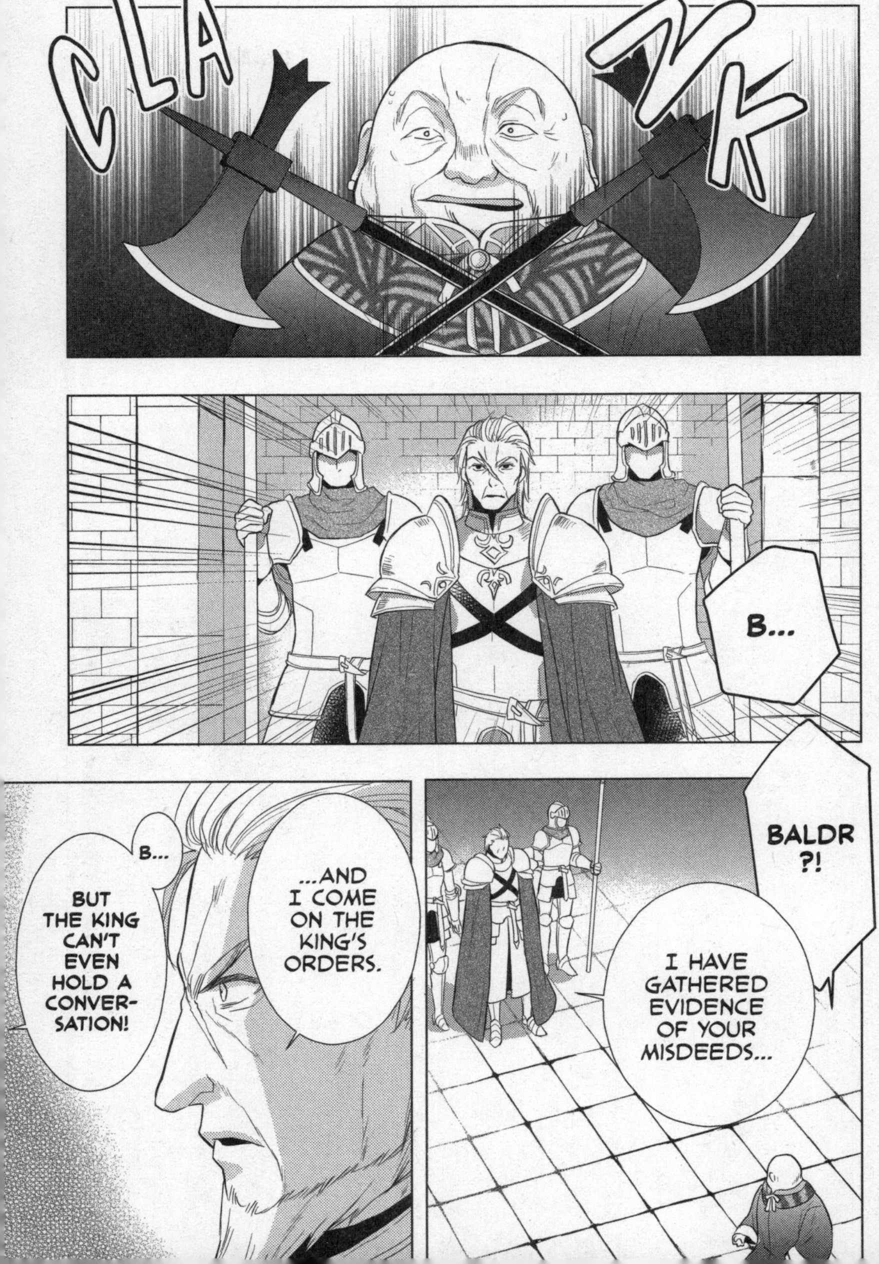
CLANK
B...
BALDR?!
I HAVE GATHERED EVIDENCE OF YOUR MISDEEDS...
...AND I COME ON THE KING'S ORDERS.
B...
BUT THE KING CAN'T EVEN HOLD A CONVERSATION!

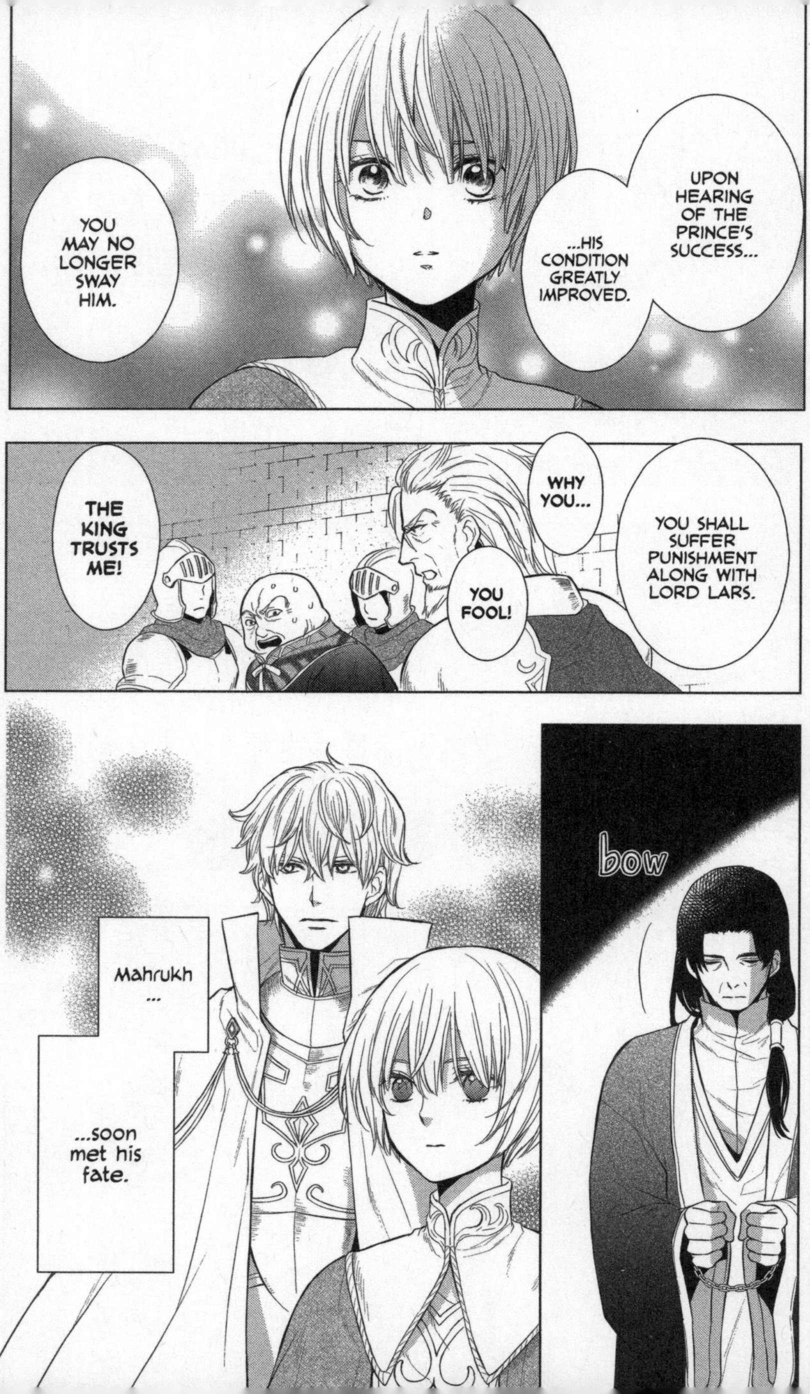
UPON HEARING OF THE PRINCE'S SUCCESS...
...HIS CONDITION GREATLY IMPROVED.
YOU MAY NO LONGER SWAY HIM.
YOU SHALL SUFFER PUNISHMENT ALONG WITH LORD LARS.
WHY YOU...
YOU FOOL!
THE KING TRUSTS ME!
bow
Mahrukh ...
...soon met his fate.

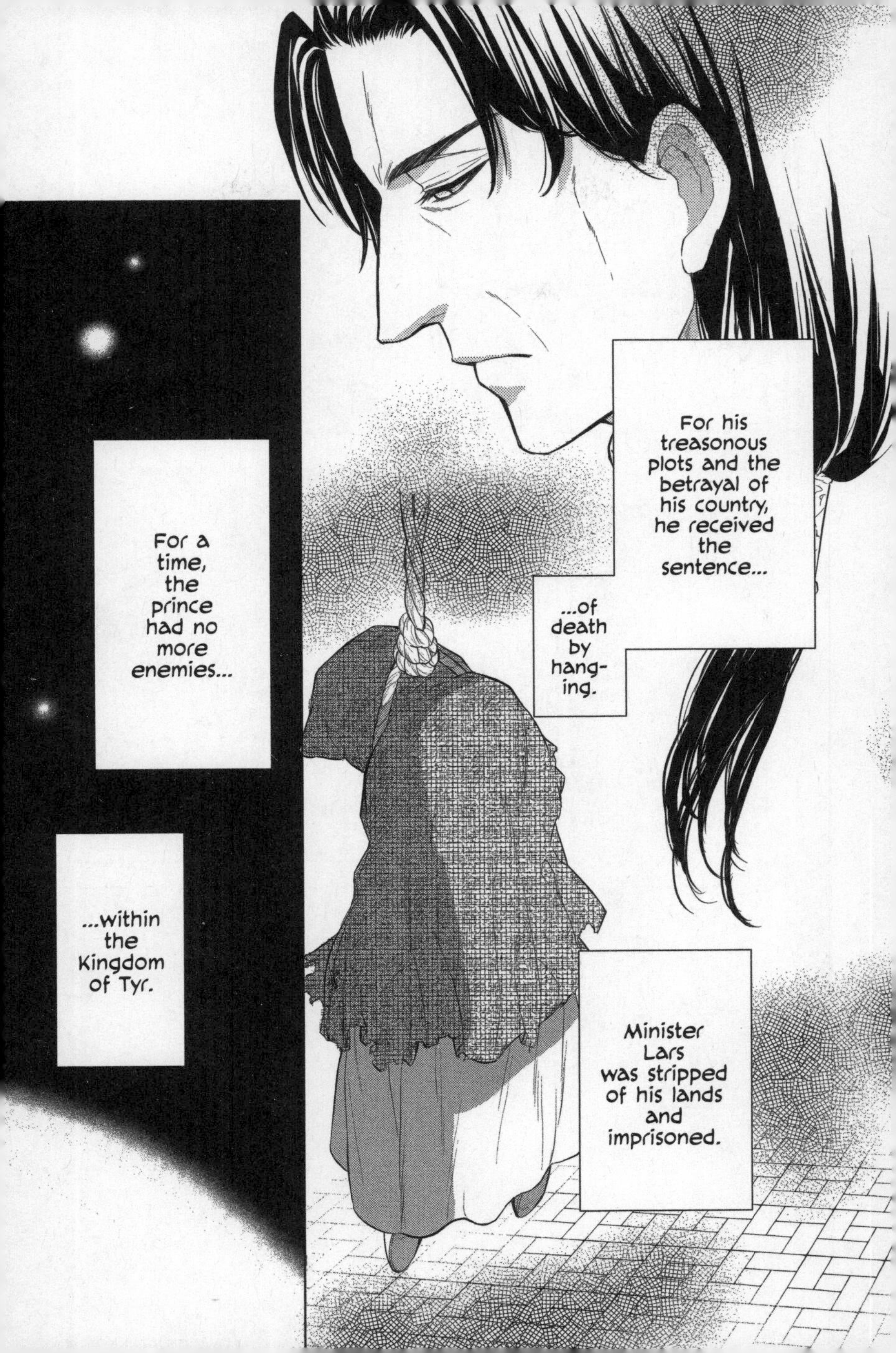
For his treasonous plots and the betrayal of his country, he received the sentence...
...of death by hang-ing.
Minister Lars was stripped of his lands and imprisoned.
For a time, the prince had no more enemies...
...within the Kingdom of Tyr.

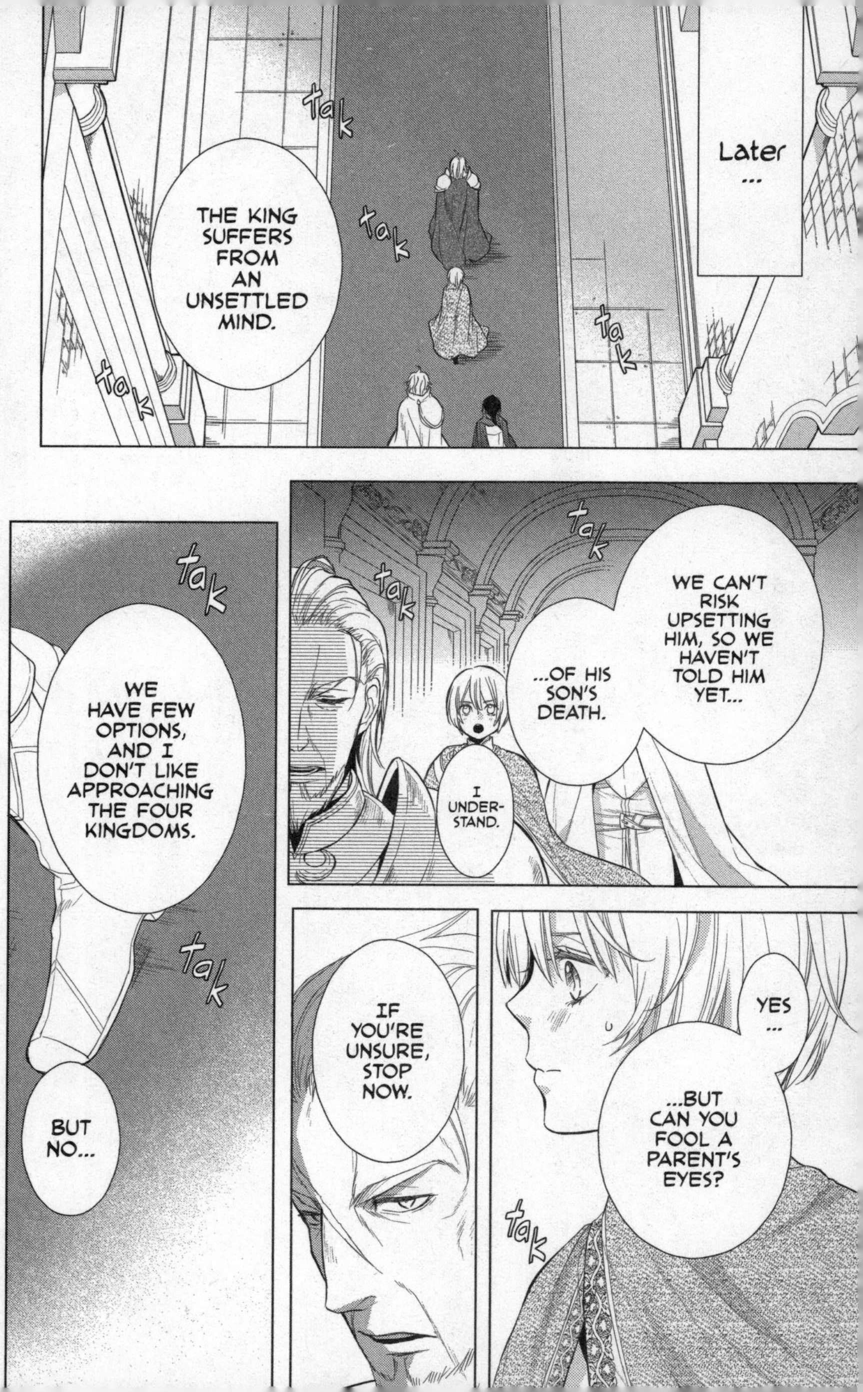
Later ...
tak
tak
tak
THE KING SUFFERS FROM AN UNSETTLED MIND.
tak
WE CAN'T RISK UPSETTING HIM, SO WE HAVEN'T TOLD HIM YET...
...OF HIS SON'S DEATH.
tak
tak
I UNDER-STAND.
YES ...
...BUT CAN YOU FOOL A PARENT'S EYES?
tak
IF YOU'RE UNSURE, STOP NOW.
tak
WE HAVE FEW OPTIONS, AND I DON'T LIKE APPROACHING THE FOUR KINGDOMS.
tak
BUT NO...

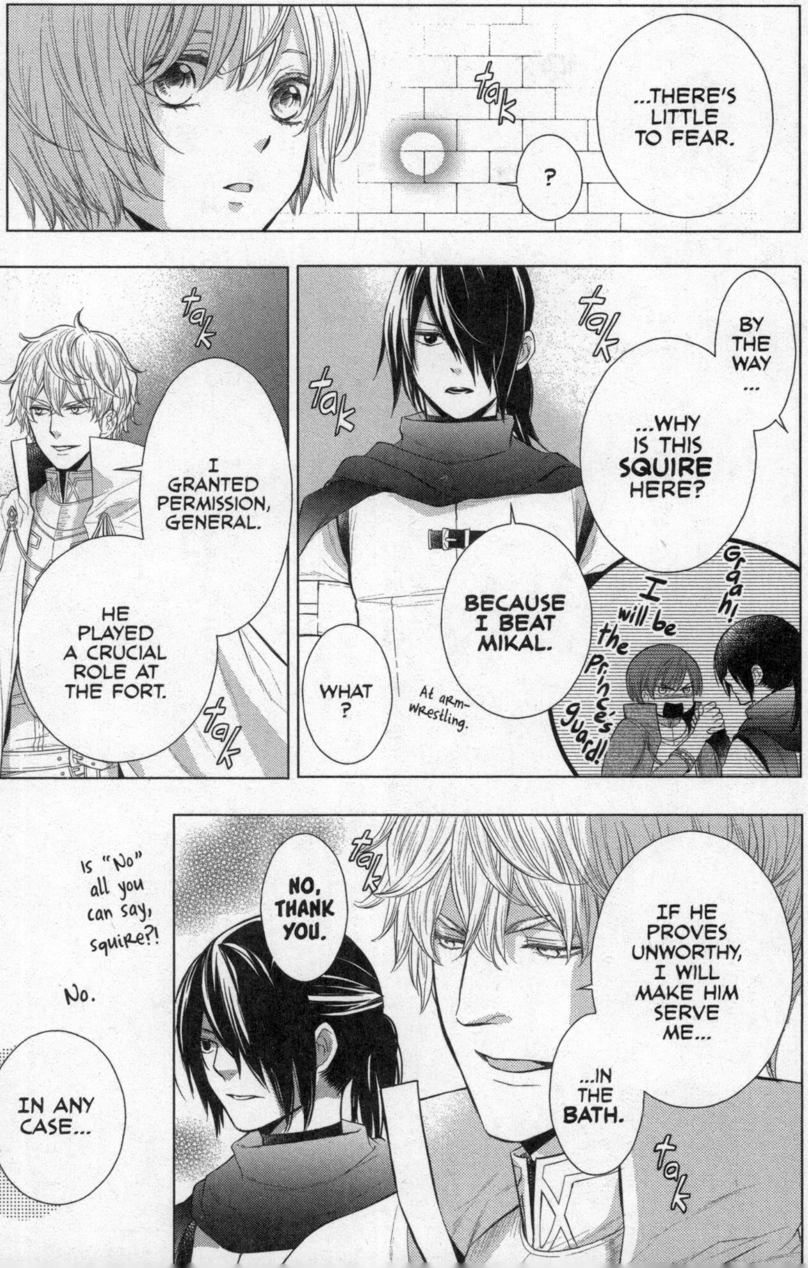
...THERE'S LITTLE TO FEAR.
?
tak
tak
tak
BY THE WAY ...
...WHY IS THIS SQUIRE HERE?
BECAUSE I BEAT MIKAL.
Graah! I will be the Prince's guard!
At arm-wrestling.
WHAT?
tak
I GRANTED PERMISSION, GENERAL.
HE PLAYED A CRUCIAL ROLE AT THE FORT.
tak
tak
IF HE PROVES UNWORTHY, I WILL MAKE HIM SERVE ME...
...IN THE BATH.
tak
NO, THANK YOU.
Is "No" all you can say, squire?!
No.
IN ANY CASE...

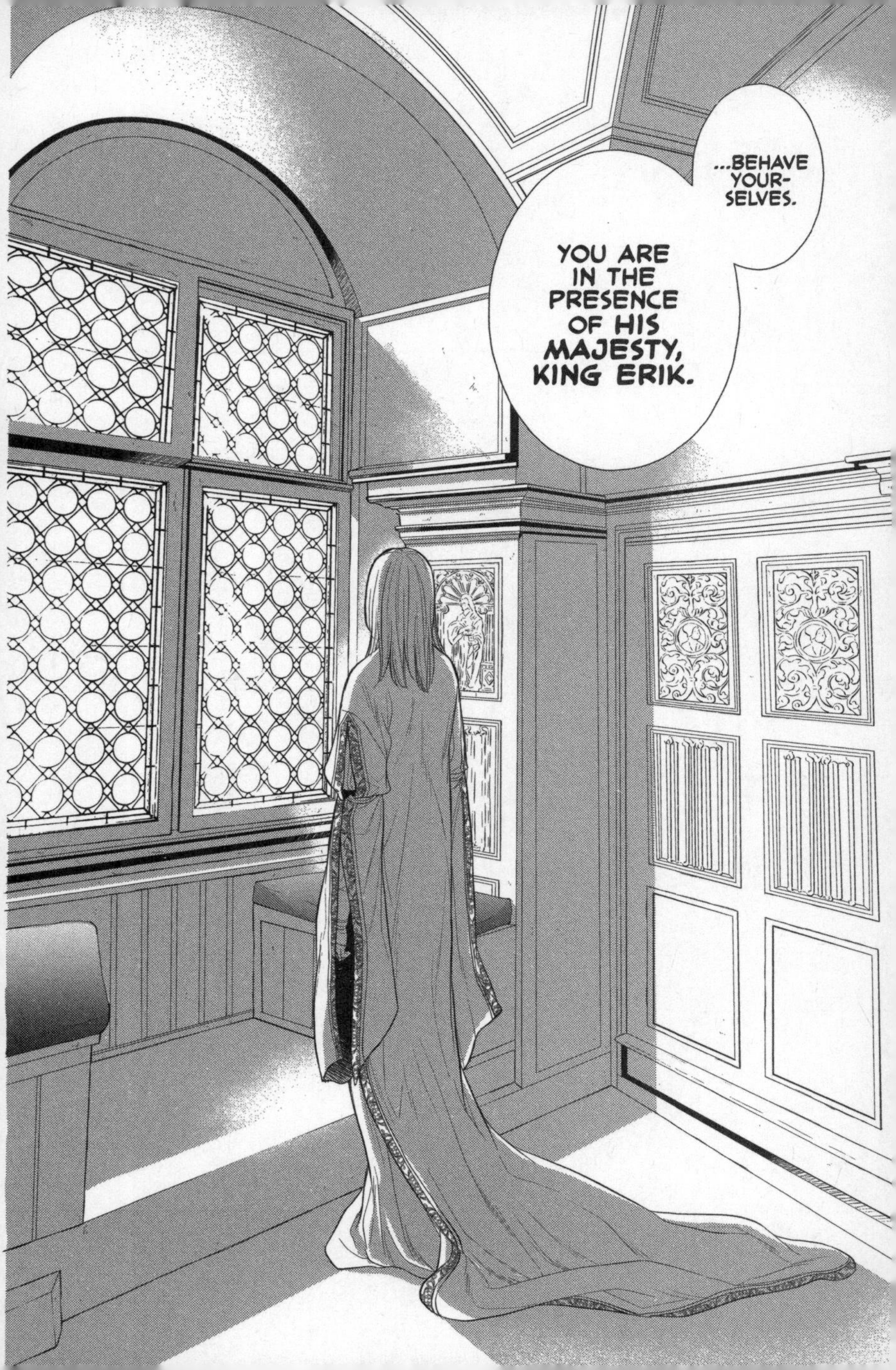
...BEHAVE YOUR-SELVES.
YOU ARE IN THE PRESENCE OF HIS MAJESTY, KING ERIK.

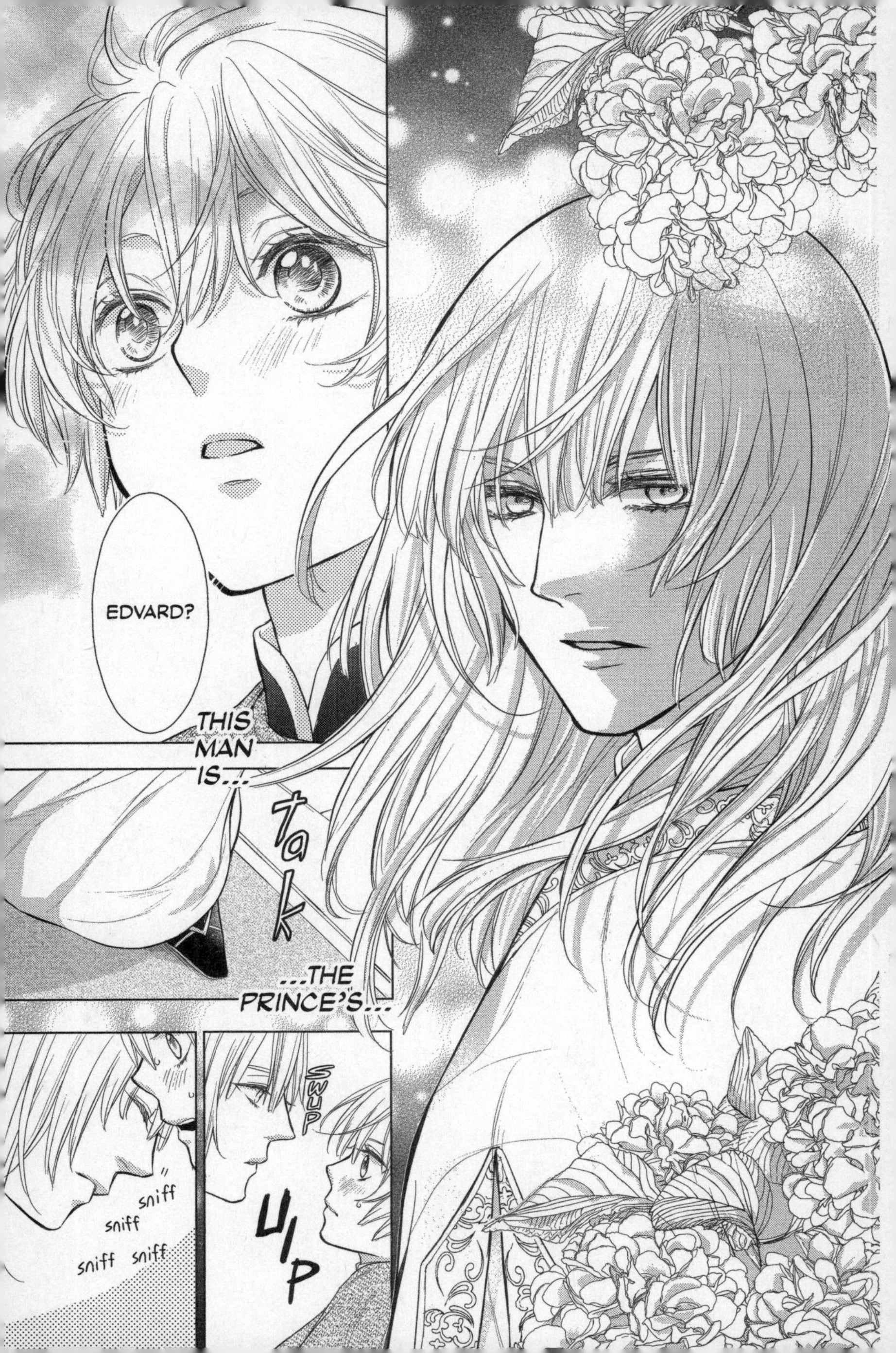

EDVARD?
THIS MAN IS...
tak
...THE PRINCE'S...
SWUP
UP
sniff sniff sniff sniff

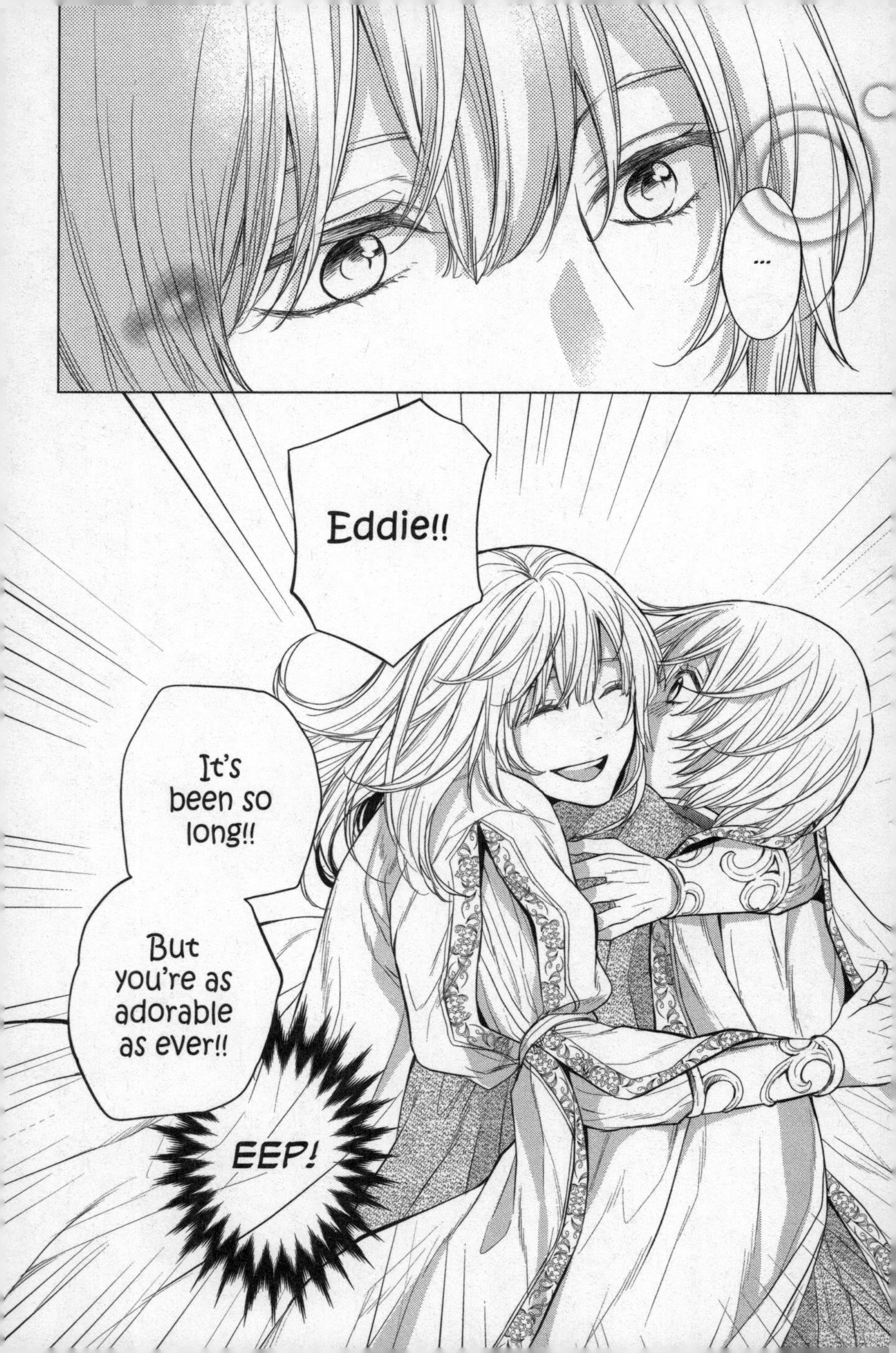
...
Eddie!!
It's been so long!!
But you're as adorable as ever!!
EEP!

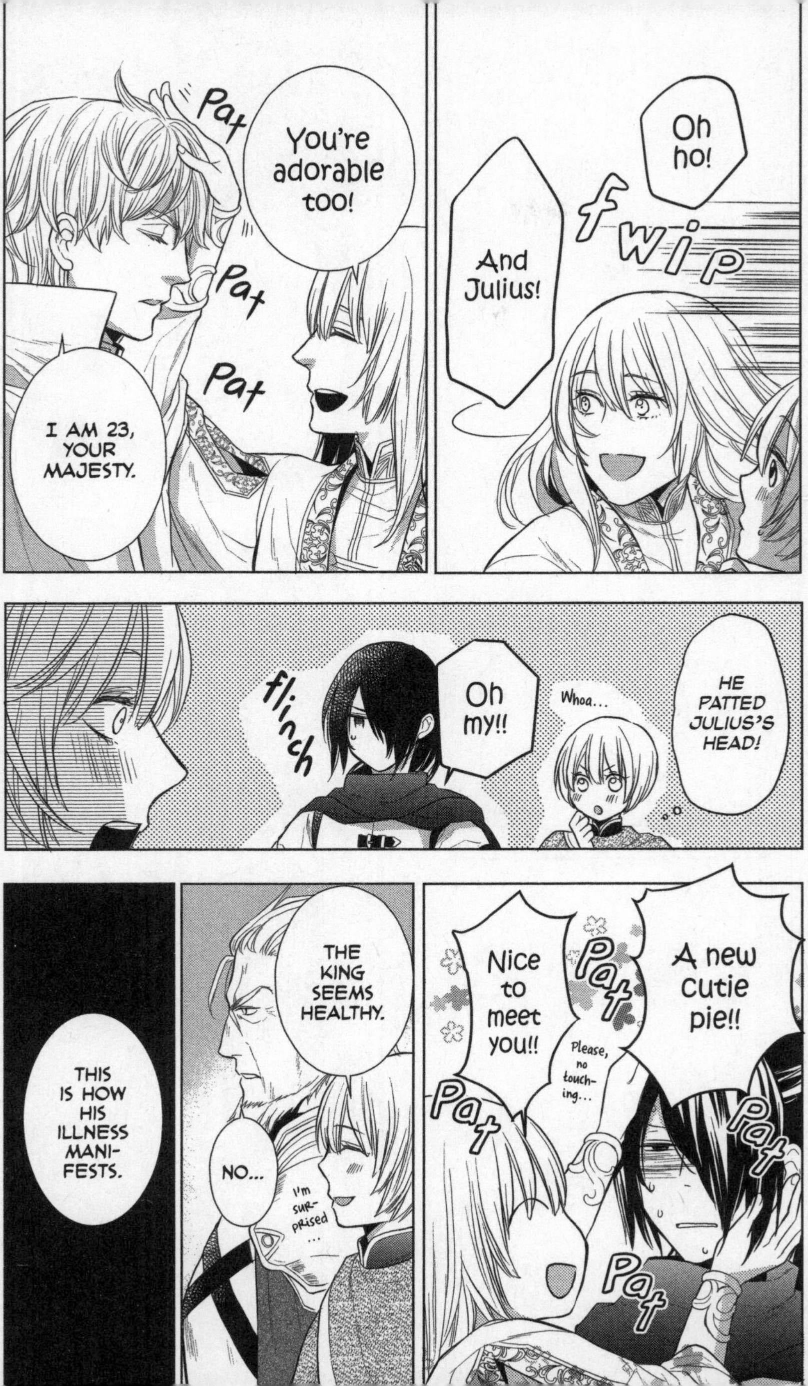
Oh ho!
fwip
And Julius!
Pat
You're adorable too!
Pat
Pat
I AM 23, YOUR MAJESTY.
HE PATTED JULIUS'S HEAD!
Whoa...
Oh my!!
flinch
A new cutie pie!!
Pat
Nice to meet you!!
Please, no touching...
Pat
Pat
Pat
THE KING SEEMS HEALTHY.
NO...
I'm surprised...
THIS IS HOW HIS ILLNESS MANIFESTS.

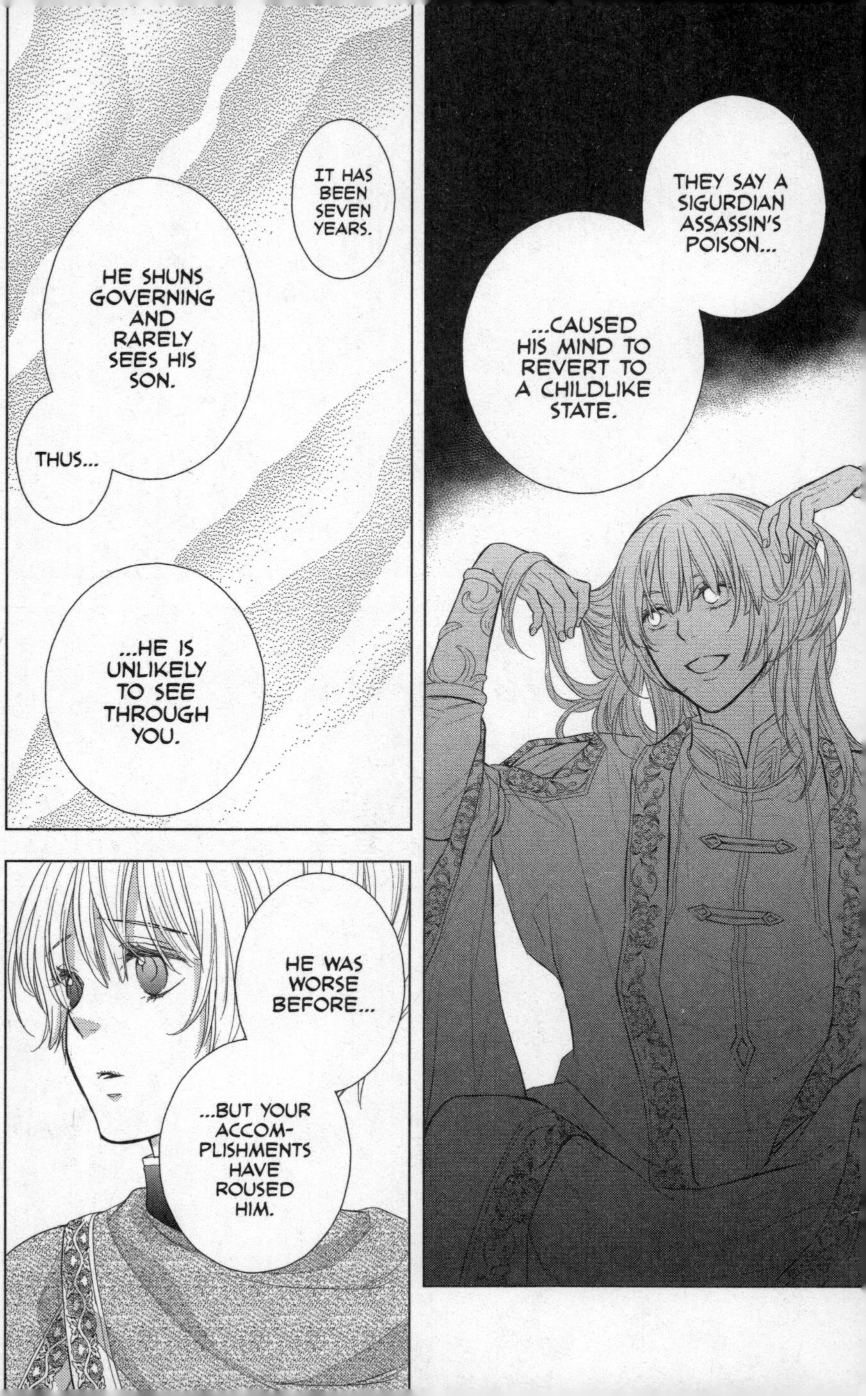
THEY SAY A SIGURDIAN ASSASSIN'S POISON...
...CAUSED HIS MIND TO REVERT TO A CHILDLIKE STATE.
IT HAS BEEN SEVEN YEARS.
HE SHUNS GOVERNING AND RARELY SEES HIS SON.
THUS...
...HE IS UNLIKELY TO SEE THROUGH YOU.
HE WAS WORSE BEFORE...
...BUT YOUR ACCOM-PLISHMENTS HAVE ROUSED HIM.

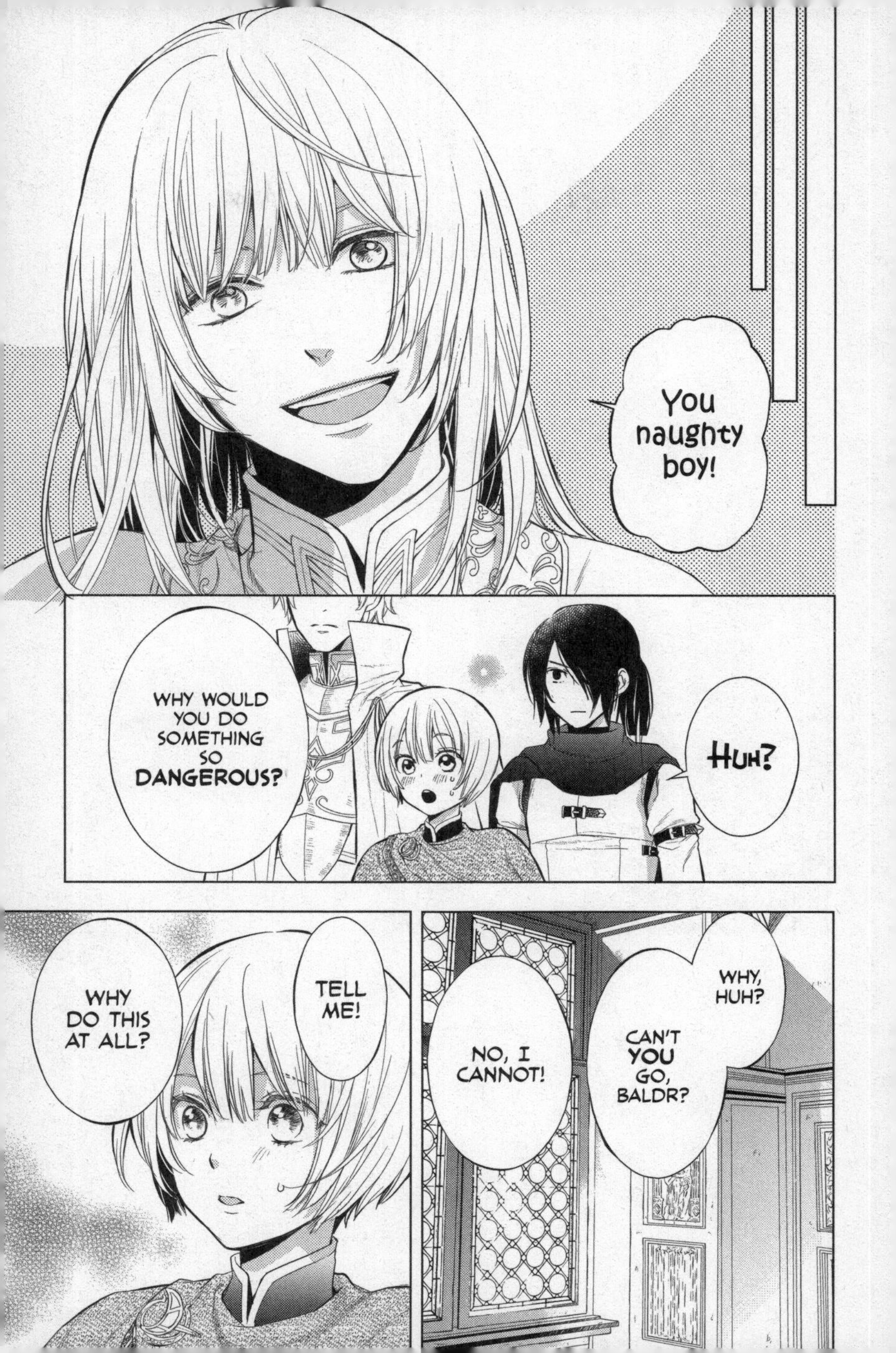
You naughty boy!
HUH?
WHY WOULD YOU DO SOMETHING SO DANGEROUS?
WHY, HUH? CAN'T YOU GO, BALDR?
NO, I CANNOT!
TELL ME!
WHY DO THIS AT ALL?

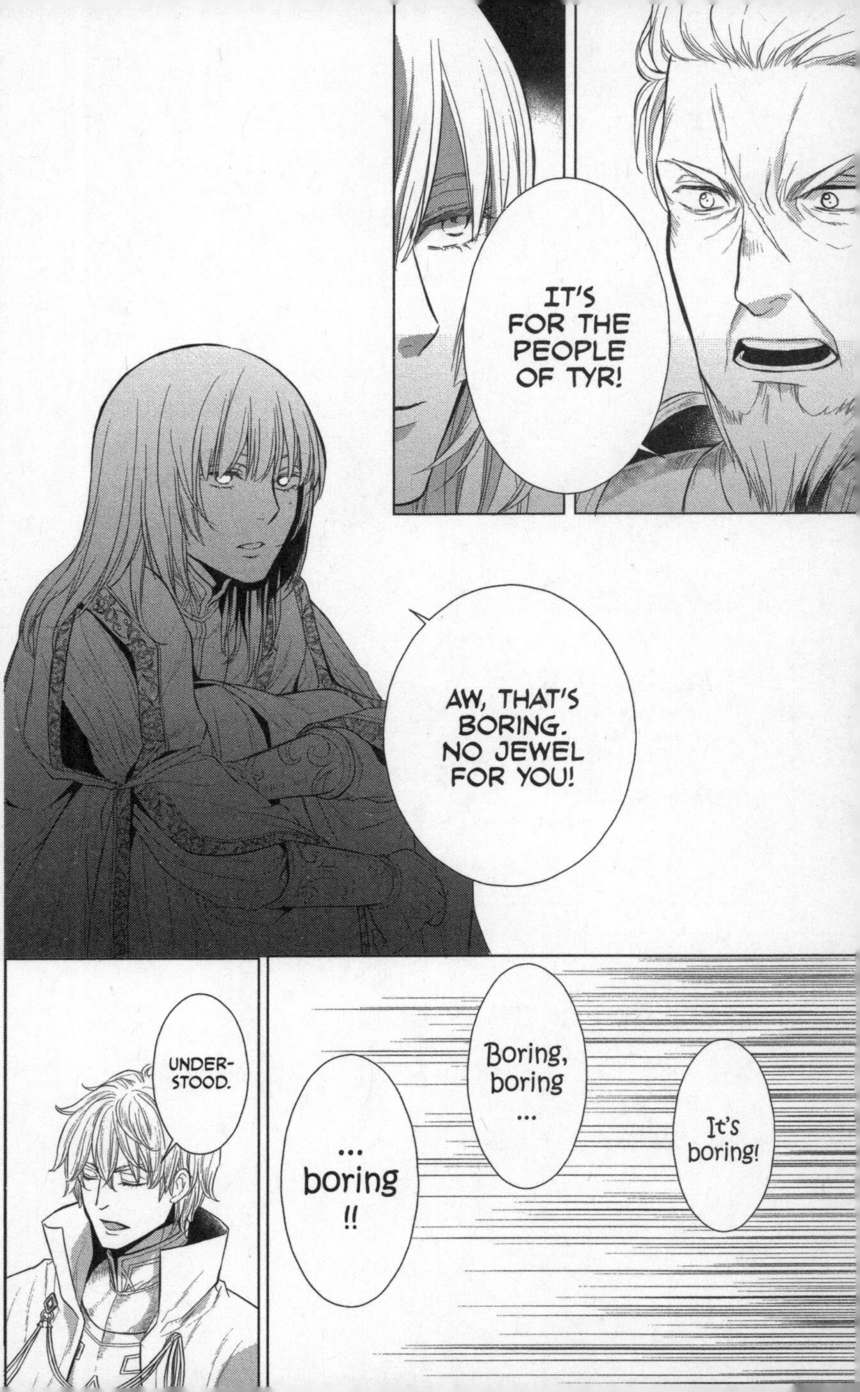
IT'S FOR THE PEOPLE OF TYR!
AW, THAT'S BORING. NO JEWEL FOR YOU!
It's boring!
Boring, boring ...
... boring !!
UNDER-STOOD.

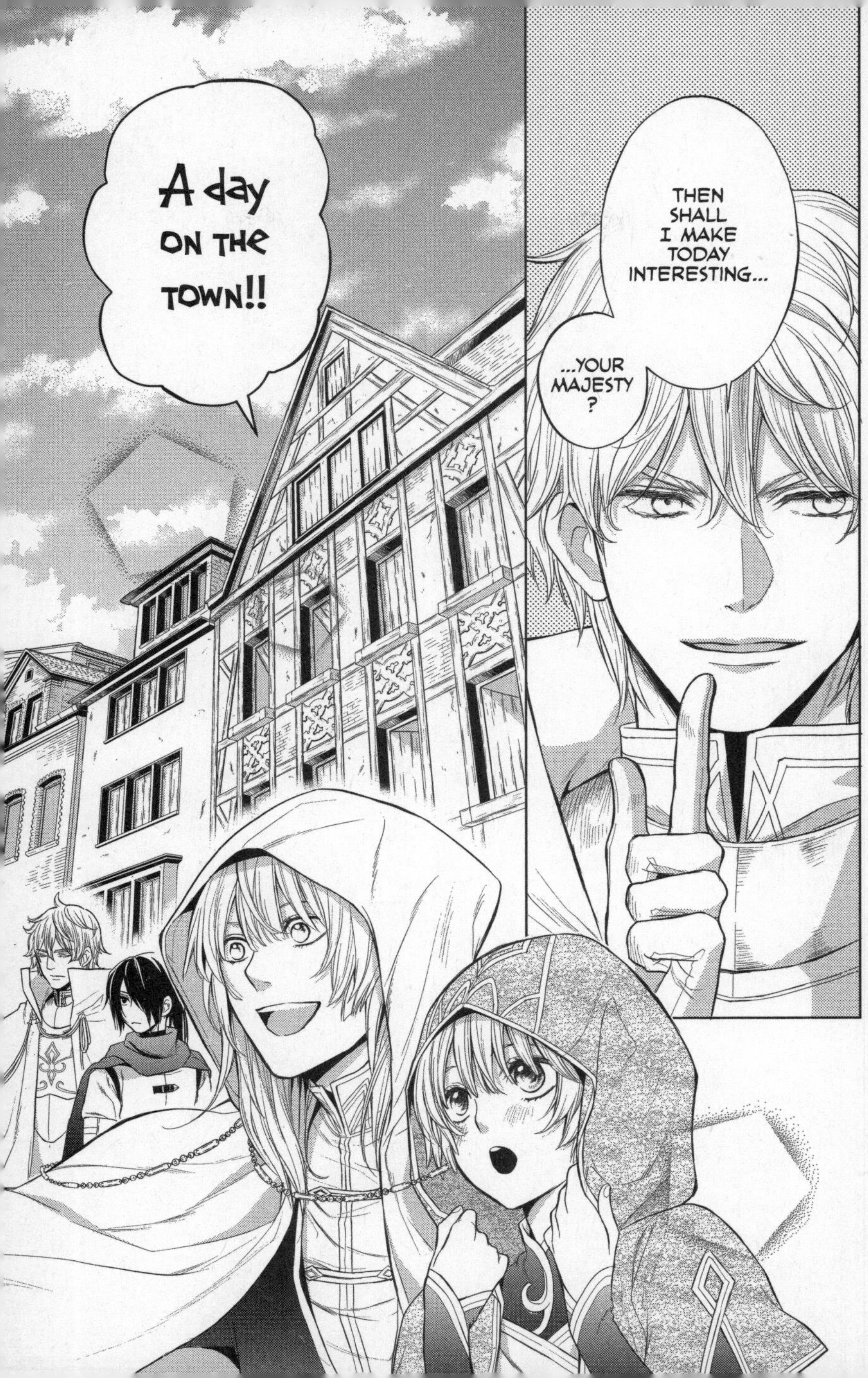
THEN SHALL I MAKE TODAY INTERESTING...
...YOUR MAJESTY?
A day ON THE TOWN!!

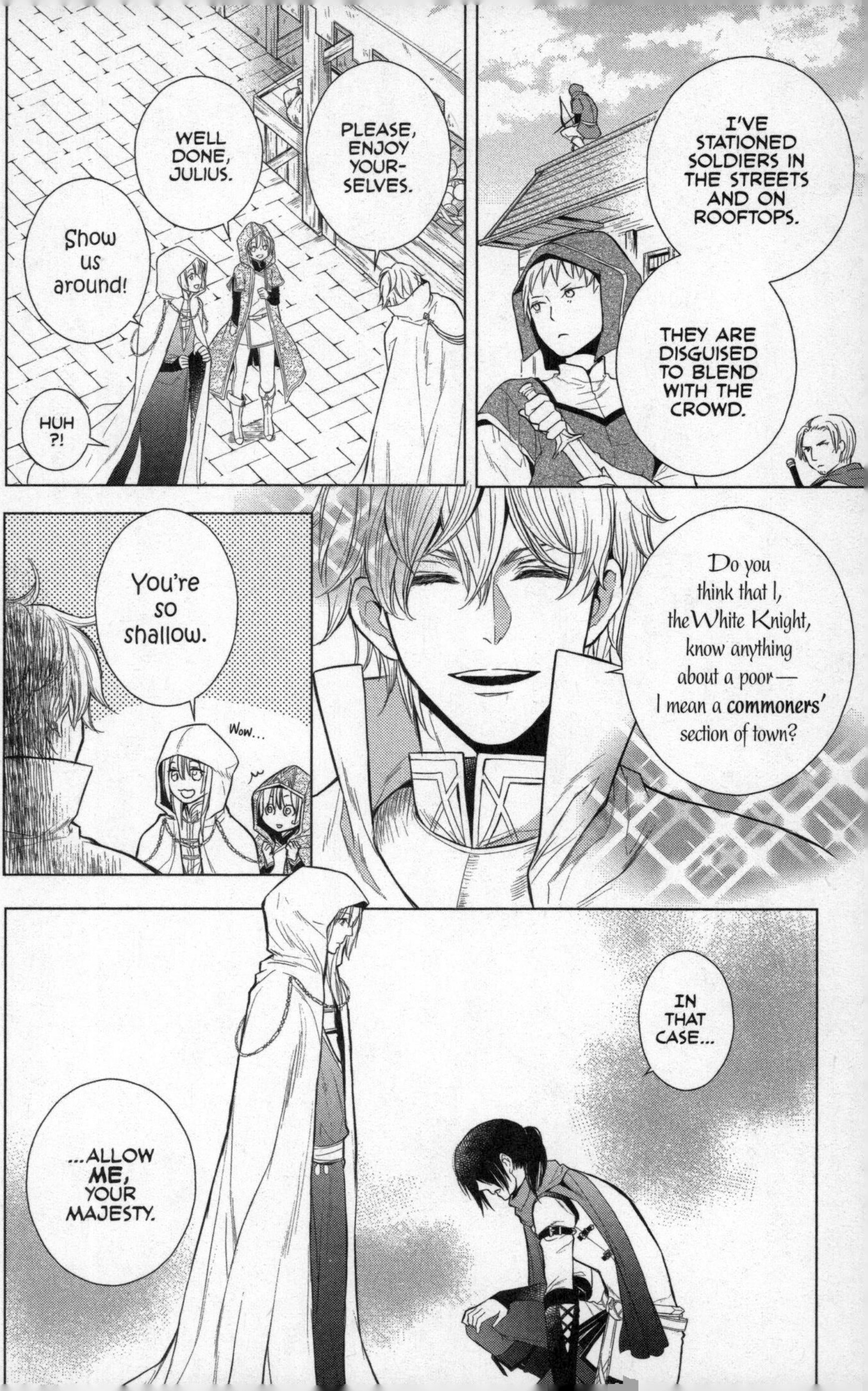
I'VE STATIONED SOLDIERS IN THE STREETS AND ON ROOFTOPS.
THEY ARE DISGUISED TO BLEND WITH THE CROWD.
PLEASE, ENJOY YOUR-SELVES.
WELL DONE, JULIUS.
Show us around!
HUH ?!
Do you think that I, the White Knight, know anything about a poor— I mean a **commoners'** section of town?
You're so shallow.
WOW...
IN THAT CASE...
...ALLOW **ME**, YOUR MAJESTY.

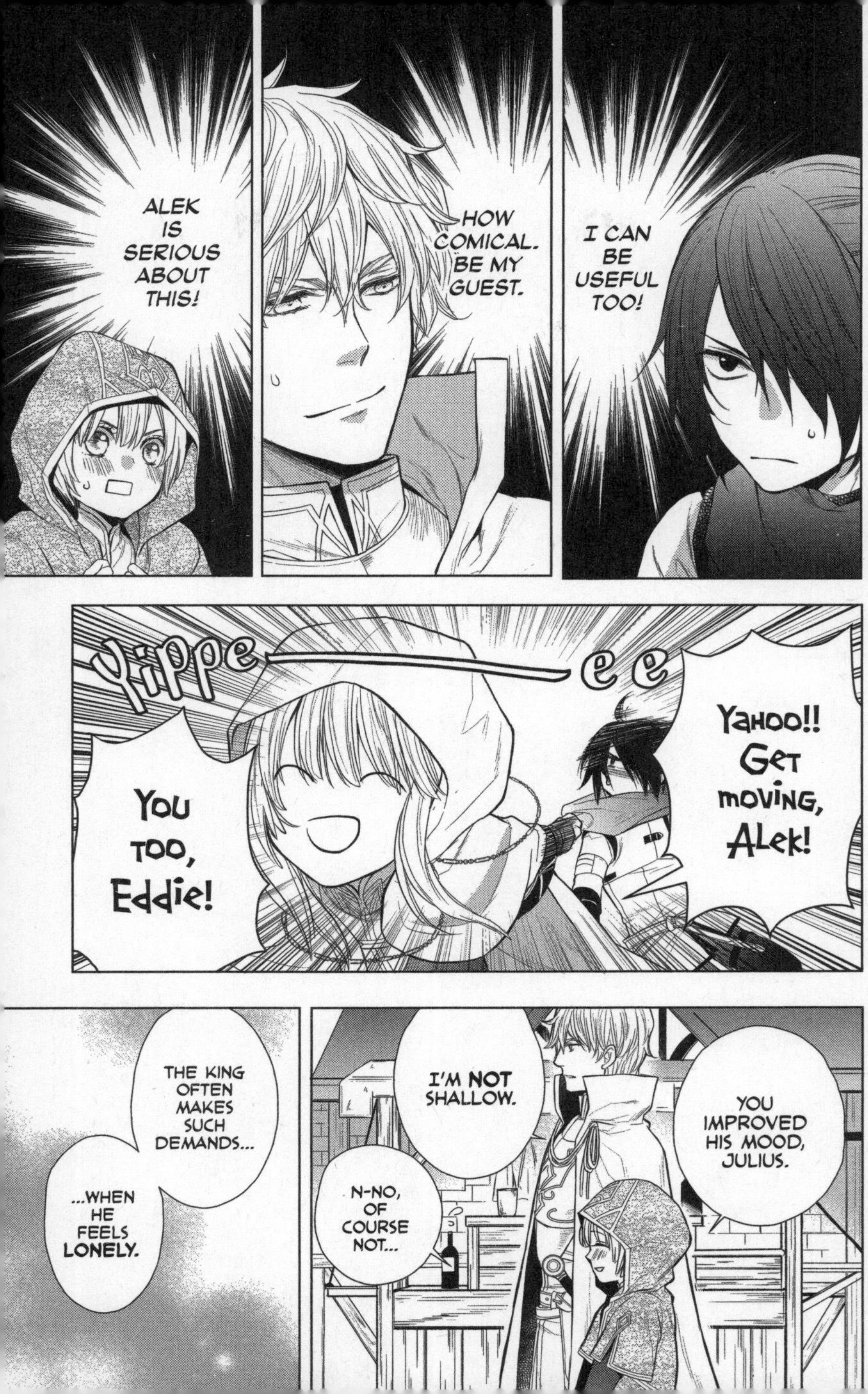
I CAN BE USEFUL TOO!
HOW COMICAL. BE MY GUEST.
ALEK IS SERIOUS ABOUT THIS!
YAHOO!! Get moving, Alek!
Yippe——ee
You too, Eddie!
YOU IMPROVED HIS MOOD, JULIUS.
I'M NOT SHALLOW.
N-NO, OF COURSE NOT...
THE KING OFTEN MAKES SUCH DEMANDS...
...WHEN HE FEELS LONELY.

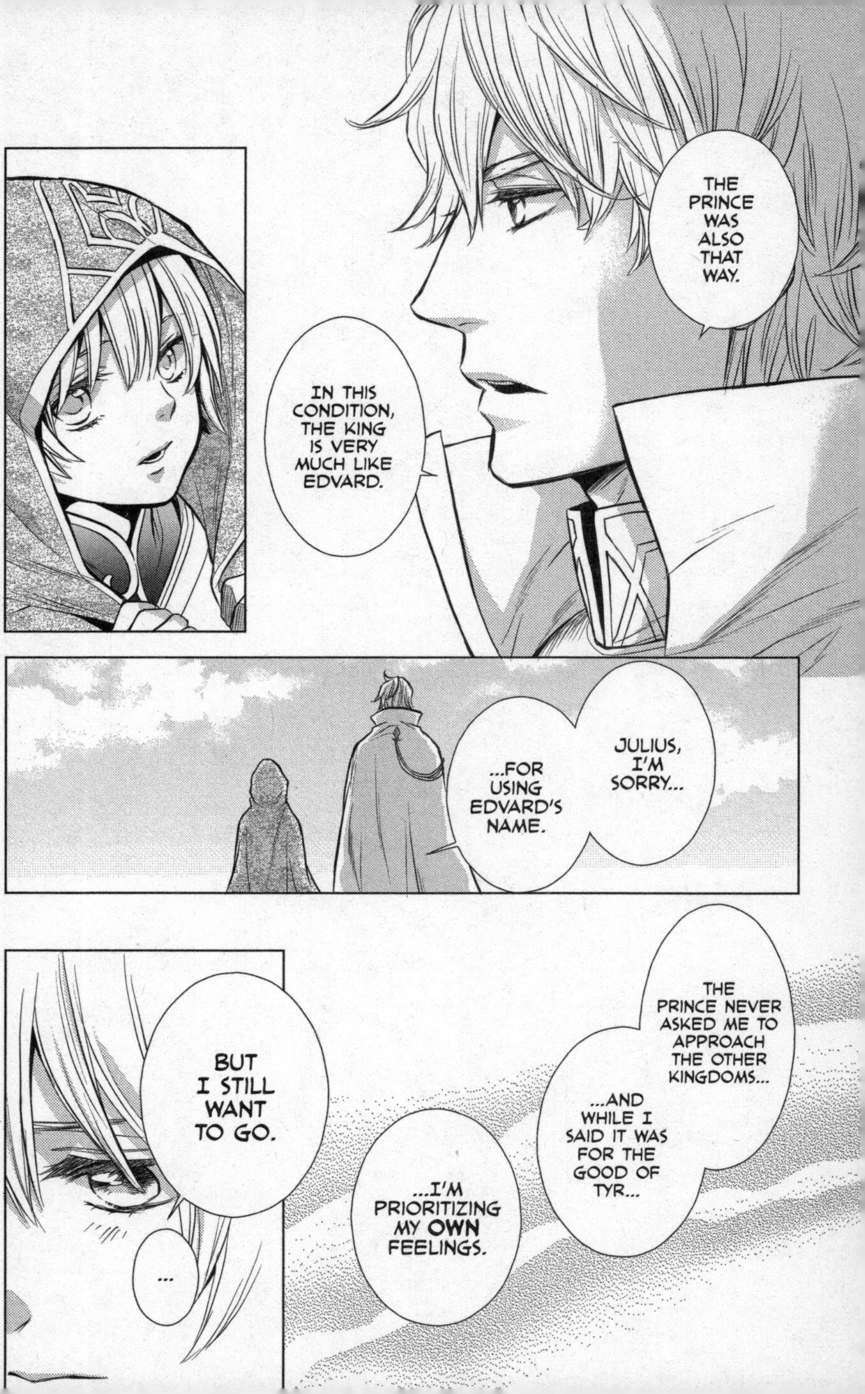
THE PRINCE WAS ALSO THAT WAY.
IN THIS CONDITION, THE KING IS VERY MUCH LIKE EDVARD.
JULIUS, I'M SORRY...
...FOR USING EDVARD'S NAME.
THE PRINCE NEVER ASKED ME TO APPROACH THE OTHER KINGDOMS...
...AND WHILE I SAID IT WAS FOR THE GOOD OF TYR...
...I'M PRIORITIZING MY **OWN** FEELINGS.
BUT I STILL WANT TO GO.
...

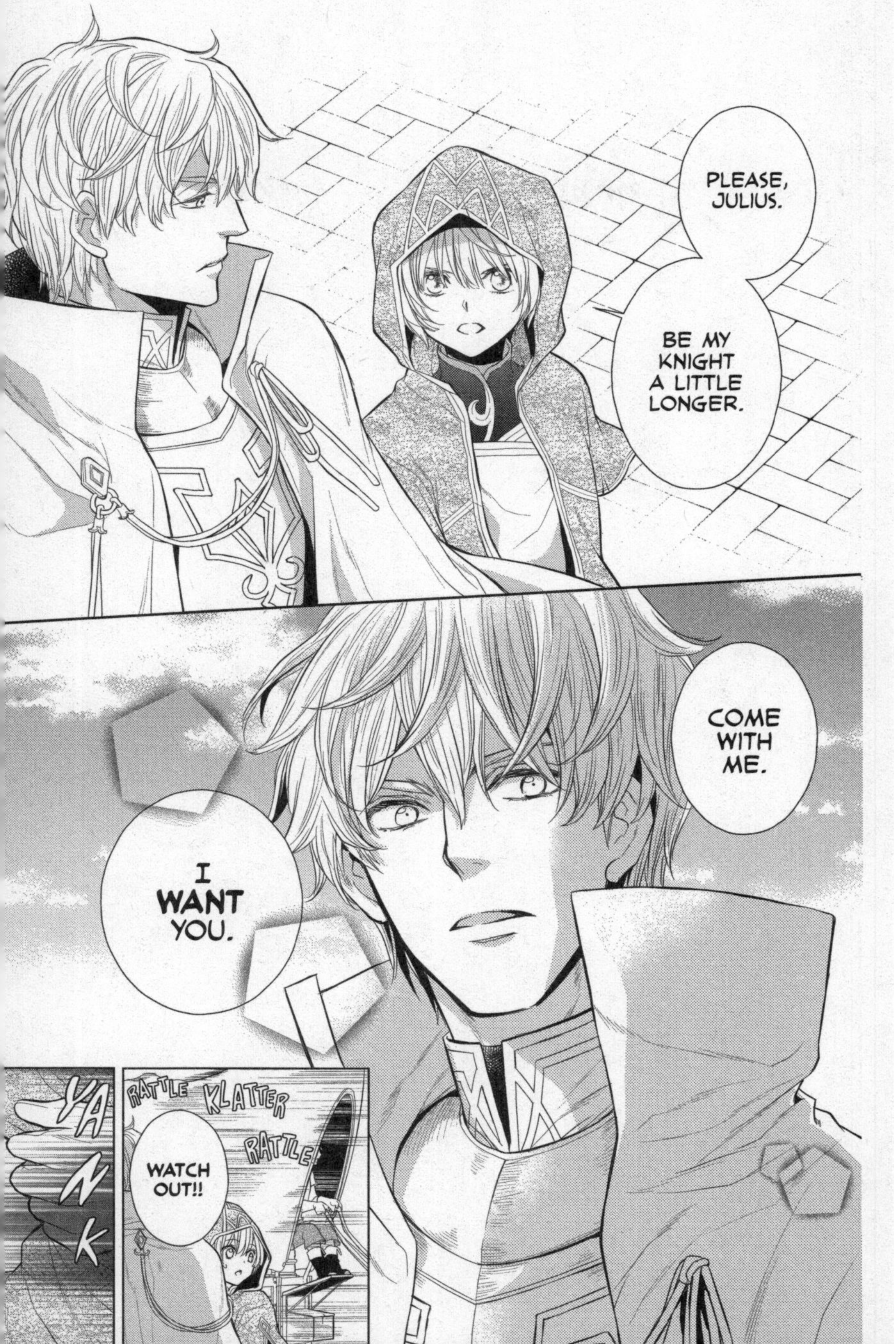
PLEASE, JULIUS.
BE MY KNIGHT A LITTLE LONGER.
COME WITH ME.
I WANT YOU.
RATTLE
KLATTER
RATTLE
WATCH OUT!!
YANK

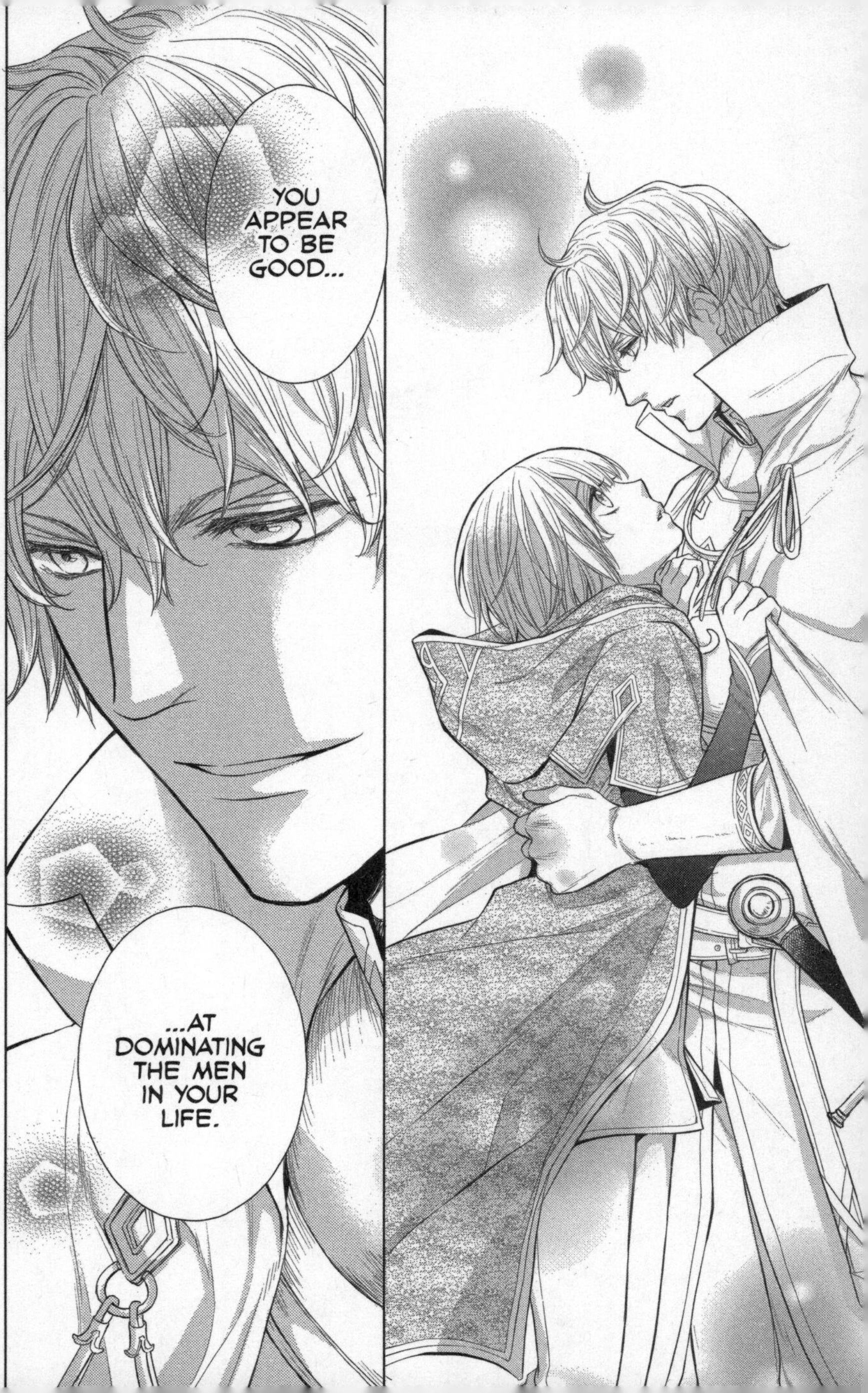
YOU APPEAR TO BE GOOD...
...AT DOMINATING THE MEN IN YOUR LIFE.

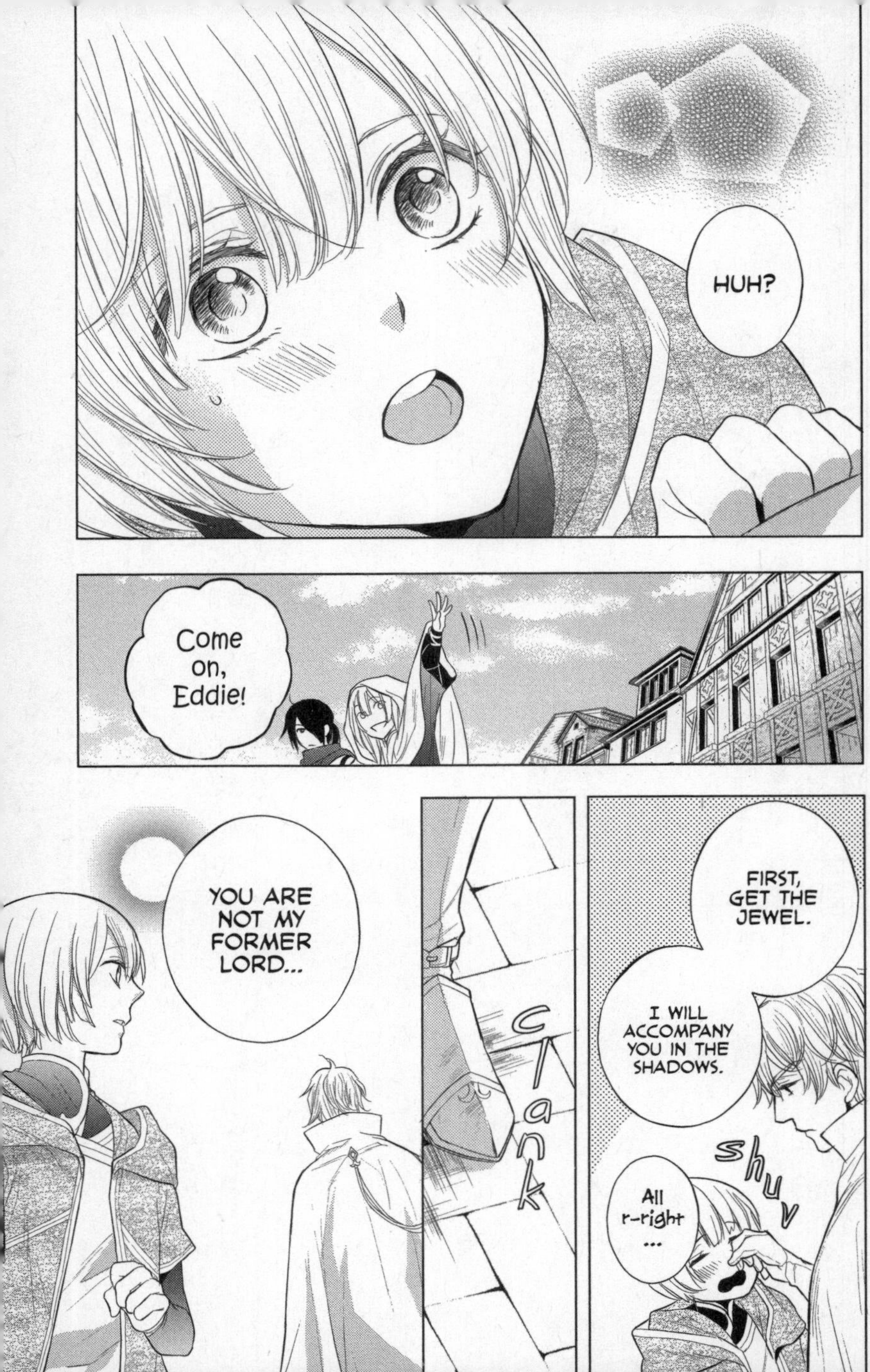
HUH?
Come on, Eddie!
FIRST, GET THE JEWEL.
I WILL ACCOMPANY YOU IN THE SHADOWS.
shuv
All r-right...
clank
YOU ARE NOT MY FORMER LORD...

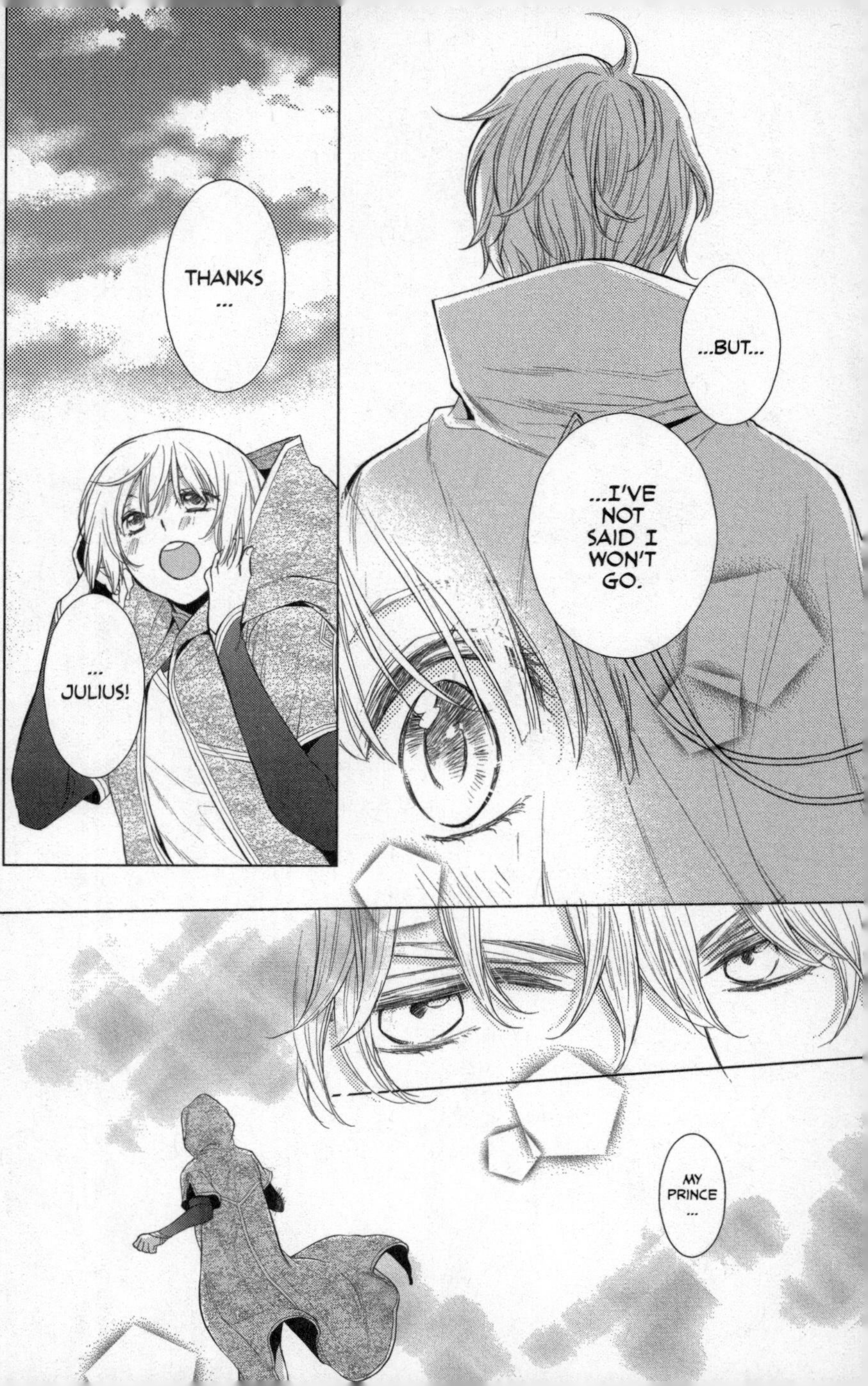
...BUT...
...I'VE NOT SAID I WON'T GO.
THANKS...
...JULIUS!
MY PRINCE...

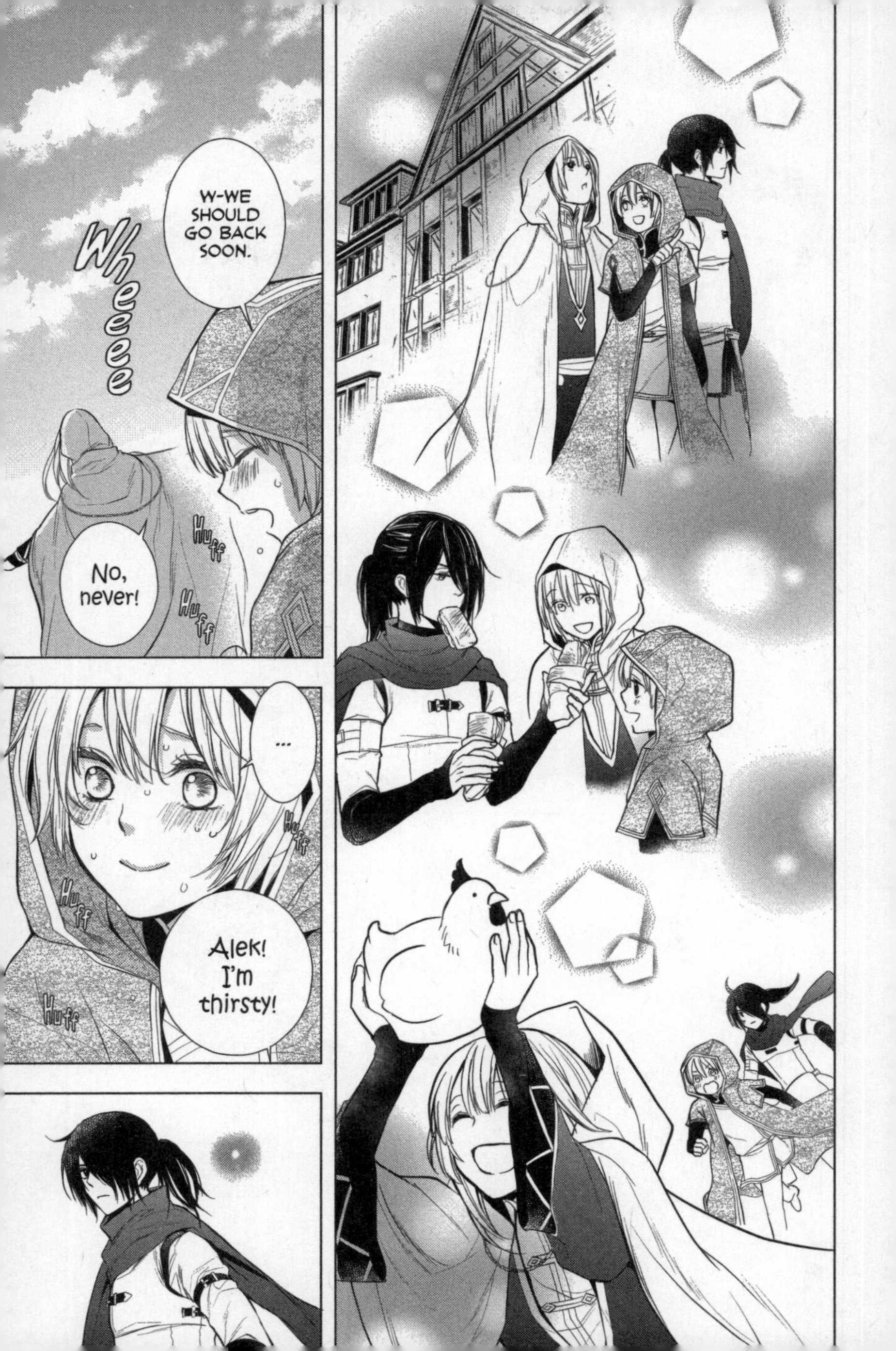
W-WE SHOULD GO BACK SOON.
Wheeeee
Huff
Huff
No, never!
...
Huff
Huff
Alek! I'm thirsty!
Huff

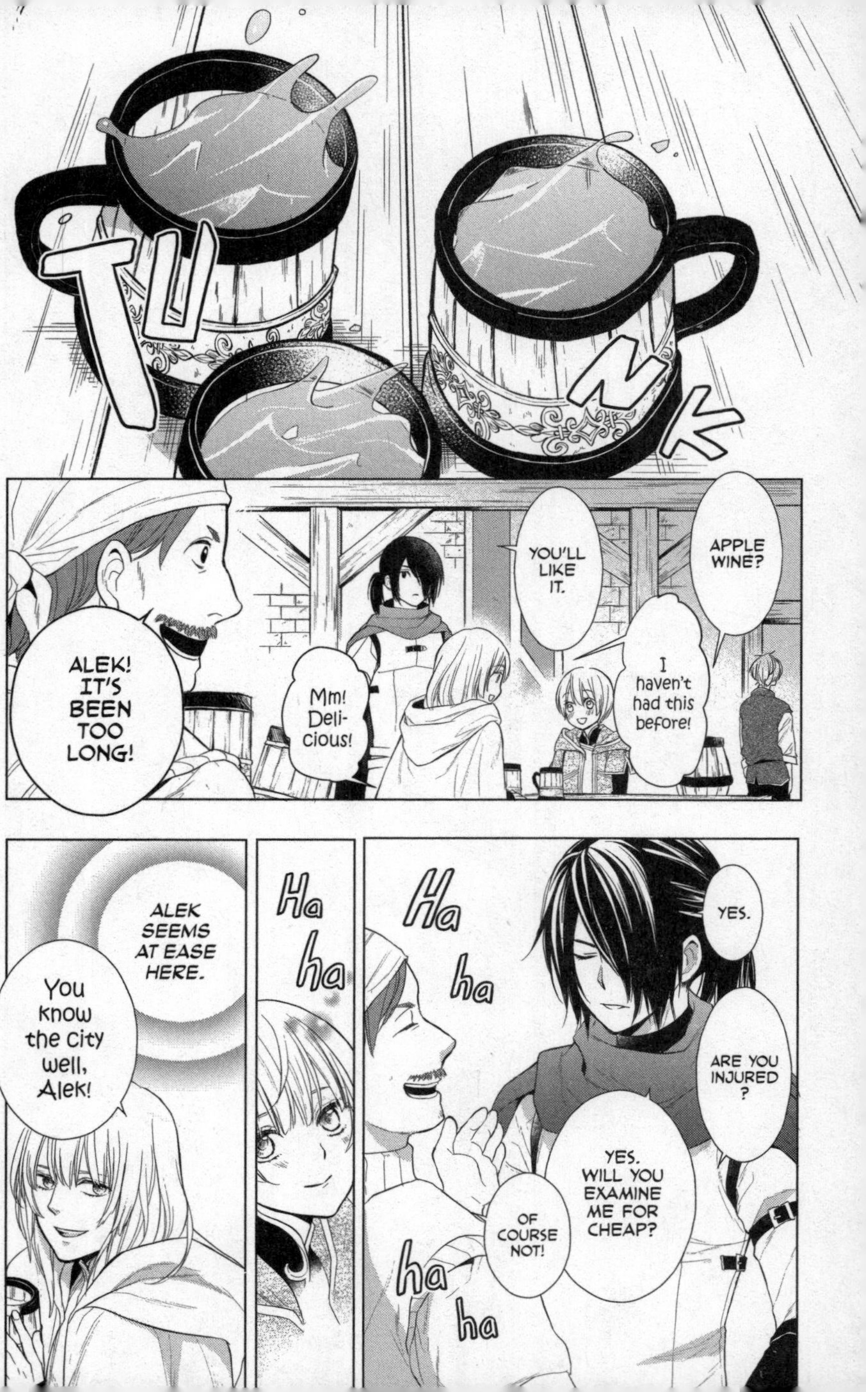
TUNK
APPLE WINE?
YOU'LL LIKE IT.
I haven't had this before!
Mm! Delicious!
ALEK! IT'S BEEN TOO LONG!
YES.
ARE YOU INJURED?
YES. WILL YOU EXAMINE ME FOR CHEAP?
OF COURSE NOT!
Ha ha
ha ha
Ha ha
ALEK SEEMS AT EASE HERE.
You know the city well, Alek!

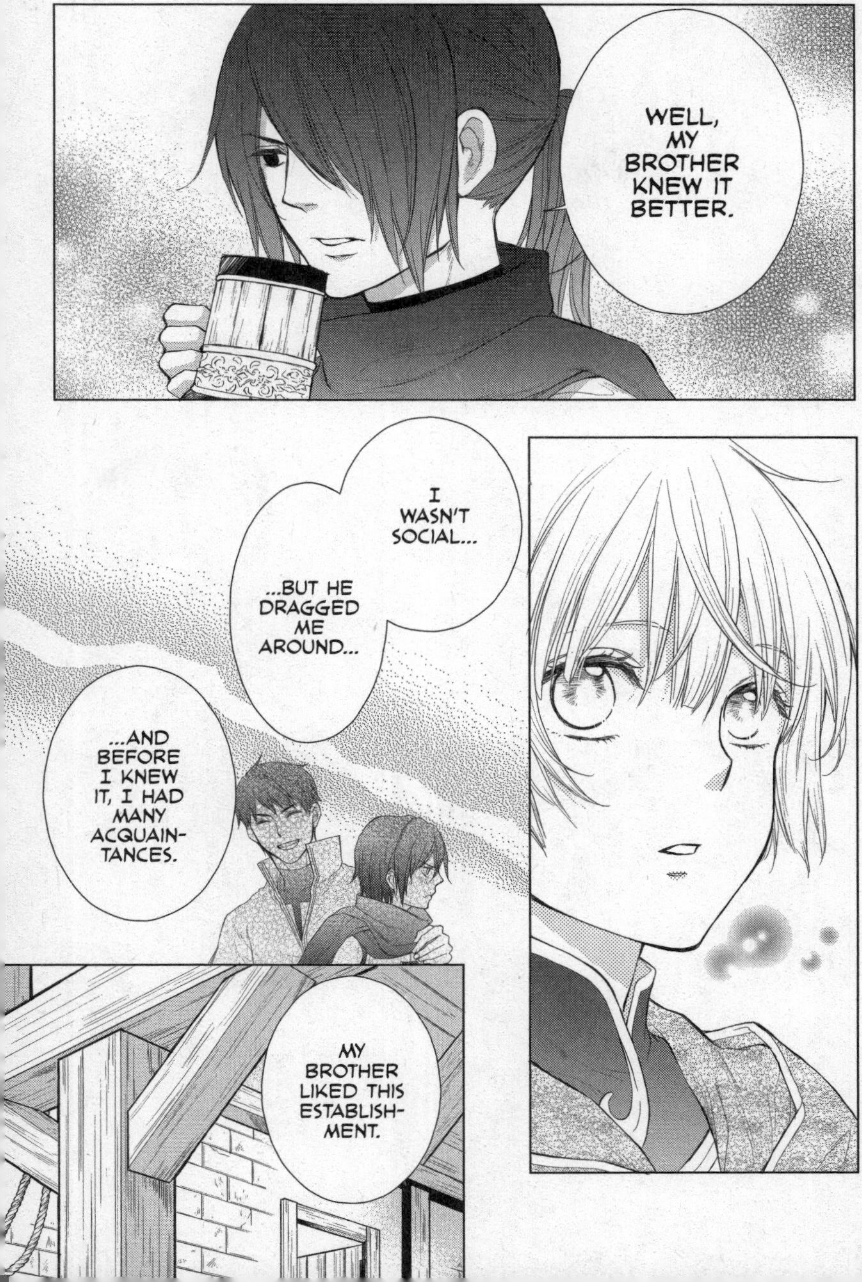
WELL, MY BROTHER KNEW IT BETTER.
I WASN'T SOCIAL...
...BUT HE DRAGGED ME AROUND...
...AND BEFORE I KNEW IT, I HAD MANY ACQUAIN-TANCES.
MY BROTHER LIKED THIS ESTABLISH-MENT.

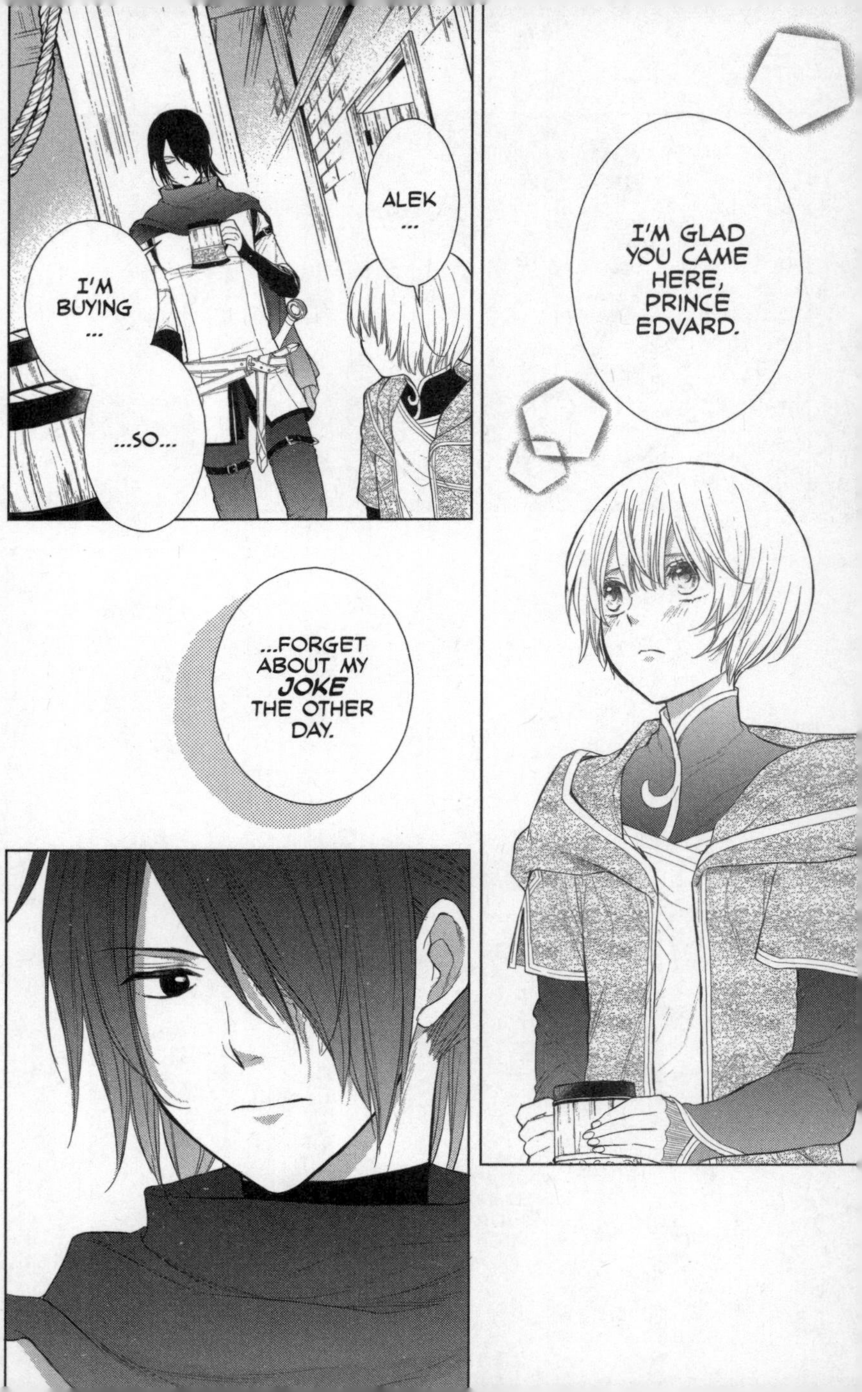
I'M GLAD YOU CAME HERE, PRINCE EDVARD.
ALEK ...
I'M BUYING ...
...SO...
...FORGET ABOUT MY JOKE THE OTHER DAY.

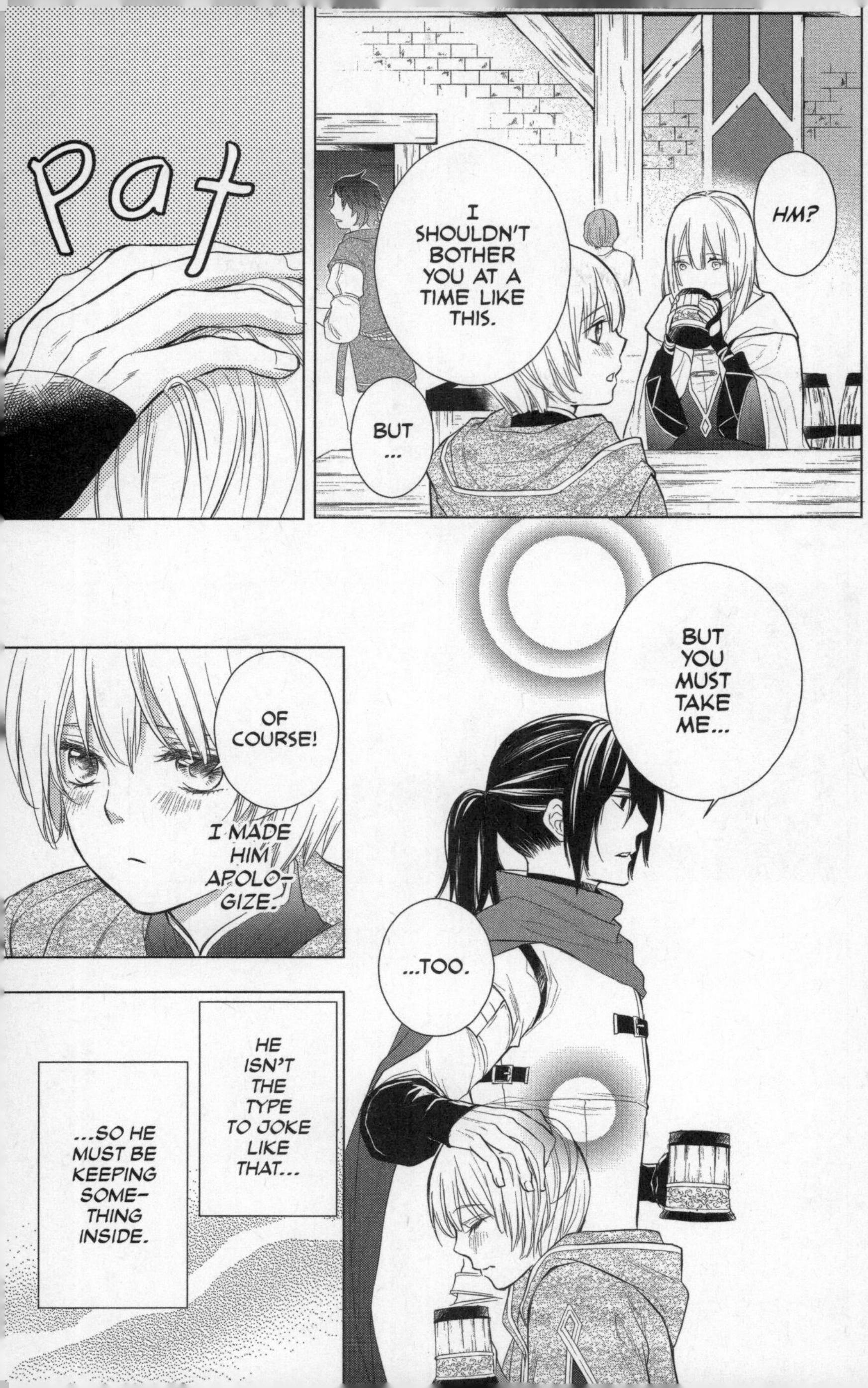
HM?
I SHOULDN'T BOTHER YOU AT A TIME LIKE THIS.
BUT ...
Pat
BUT YOU MUST TAKE ME...
...TOO.
OF COURSE!
I MADE HIM APOLOGIZE.
HE ISN'T THE TYPE TO JOKE LIKE THAT...
...SO HE MUST BE KEEPING SOMETHING INSIDE.

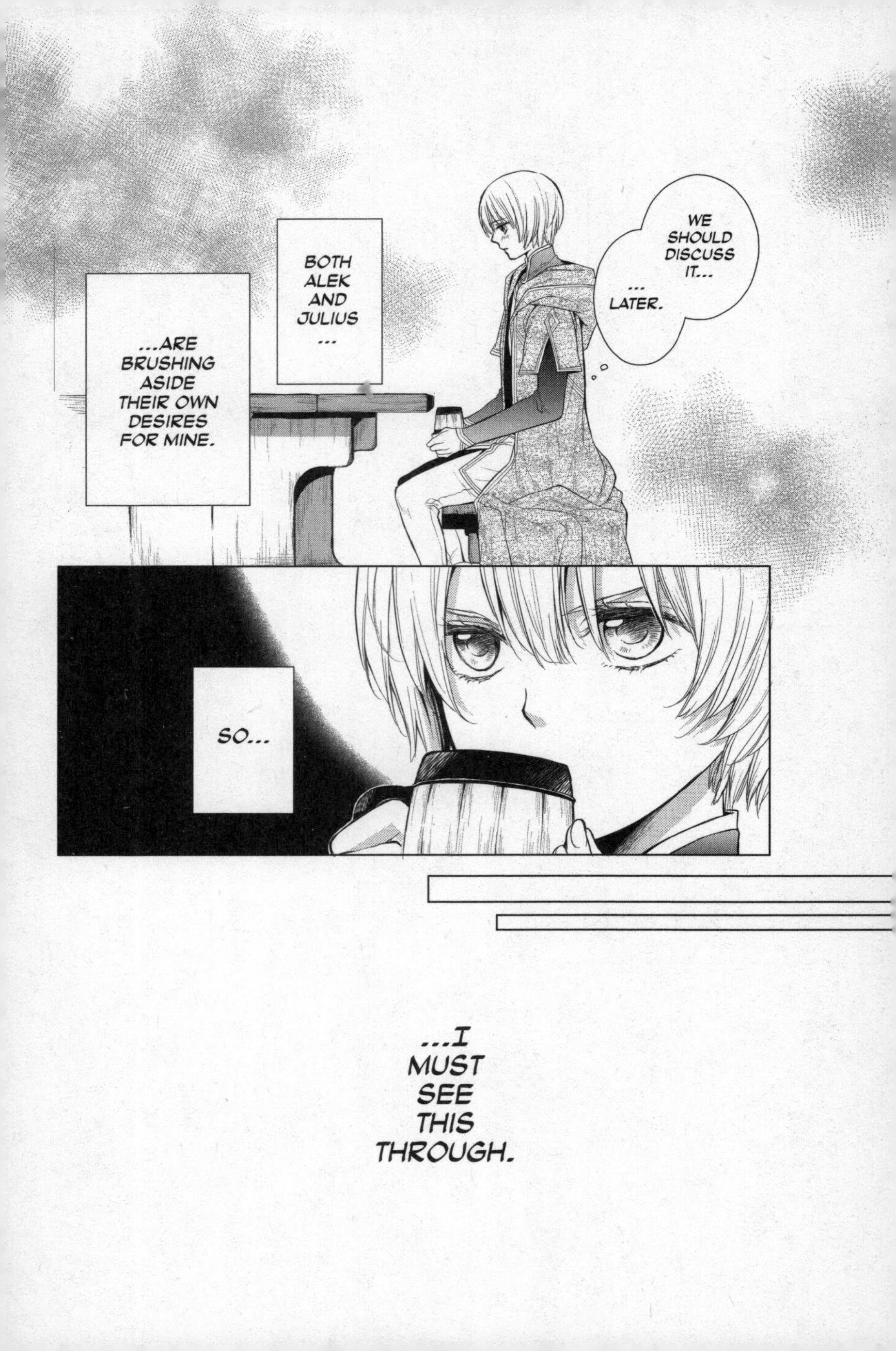
WE SHOULD DISCUSS IT... ... LATER.
BOTH ALEK AND JULIUS ...
...ARE BRUSHING ASIDE THEIR OWN DESIRES FOR MINE.
SO...
...I MUST SEE THIS THROUGH.

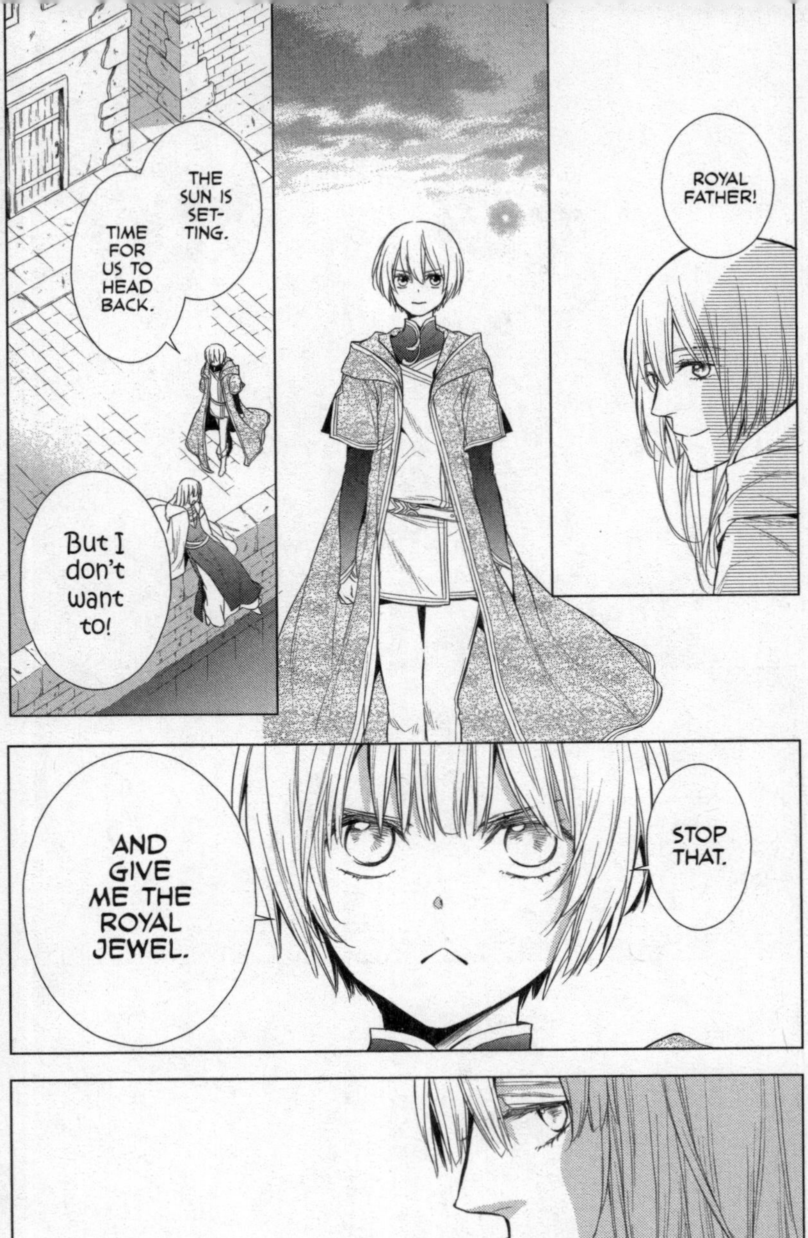
ROYAL FATHER!
THE SUN IS SETTING. TIME FOR US TO HEAD BACK.
But I don't want to!
STOP THAT.
AND GIVE ME THE ROYAL JEWEL.

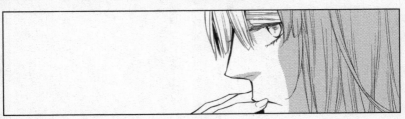

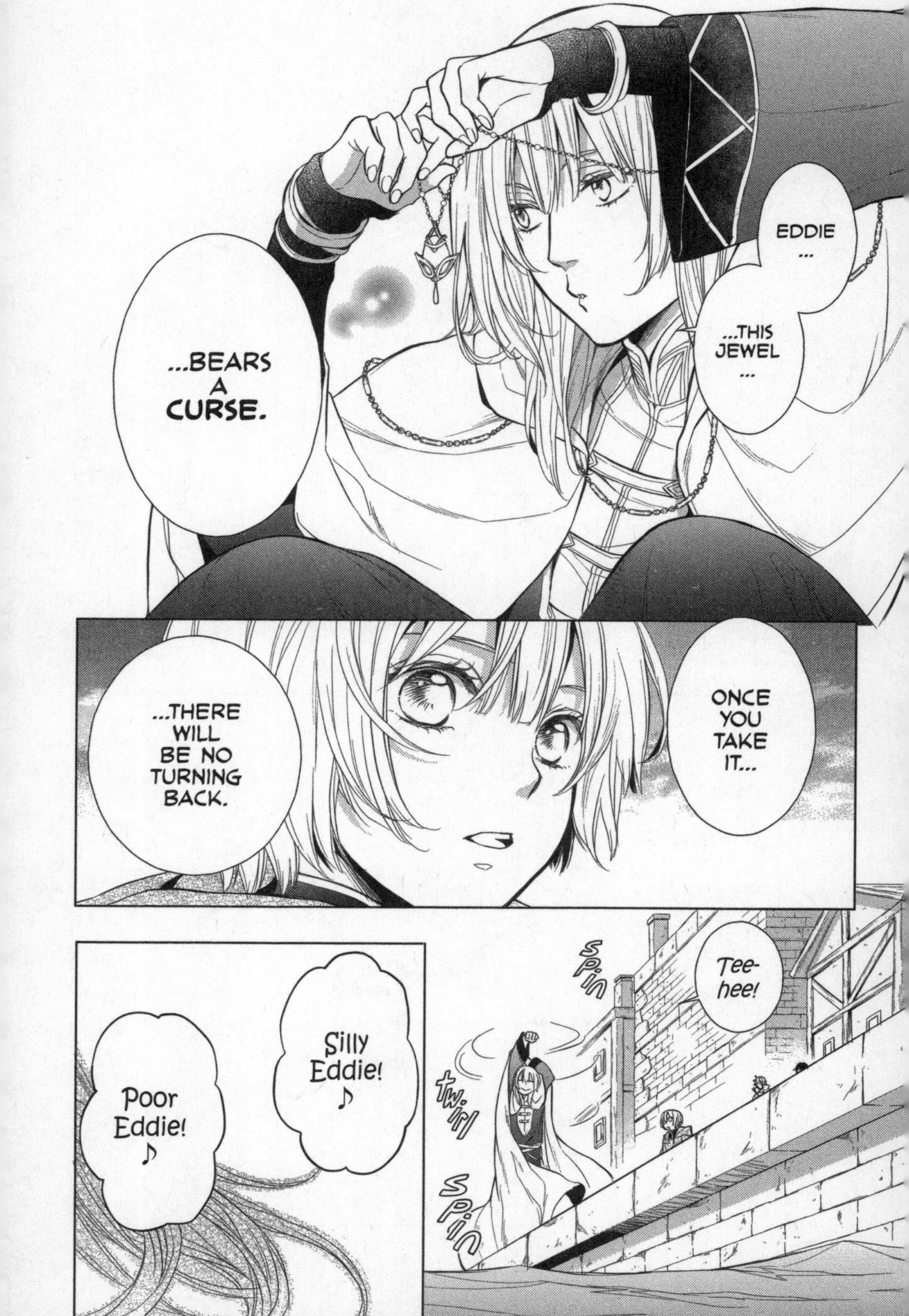
EDDIE ...
...THIS JEWEL ...
...BEARS A CURSE.
ONCE YOU TAKE IT...
...THERE WILL BE NO TURNING BACK.
Tee-hee!
spin
twirl
spin
Silly Eddie! ♪
Poor Eddie! ♪

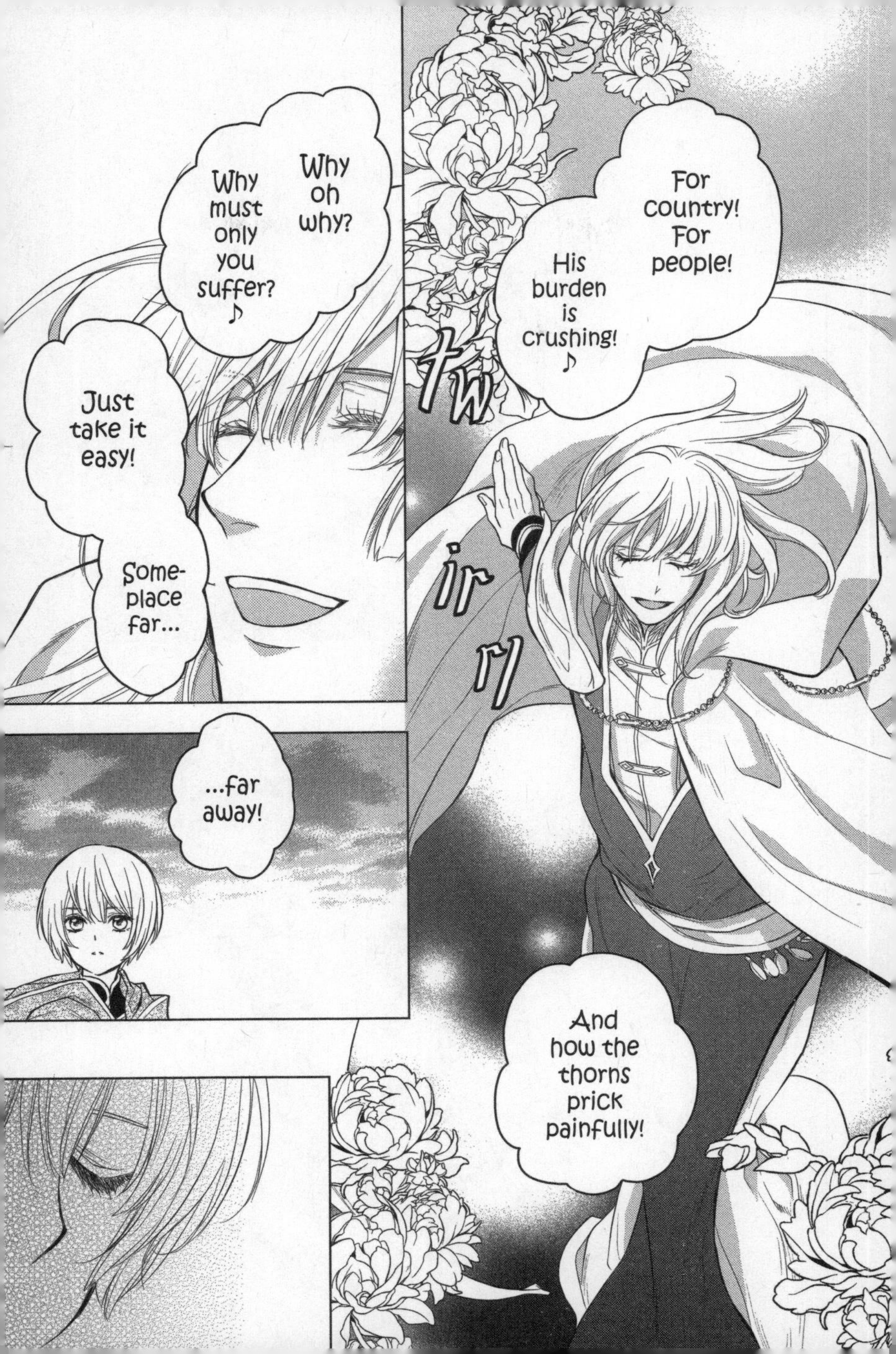
For country! For people!
His burden is crushing! ♪
tw ir rl
And how the thorns prick painfully!
Why oh why?
Why must only you suffer? ♪
Just take it easy!
Some-place far...
...far away!

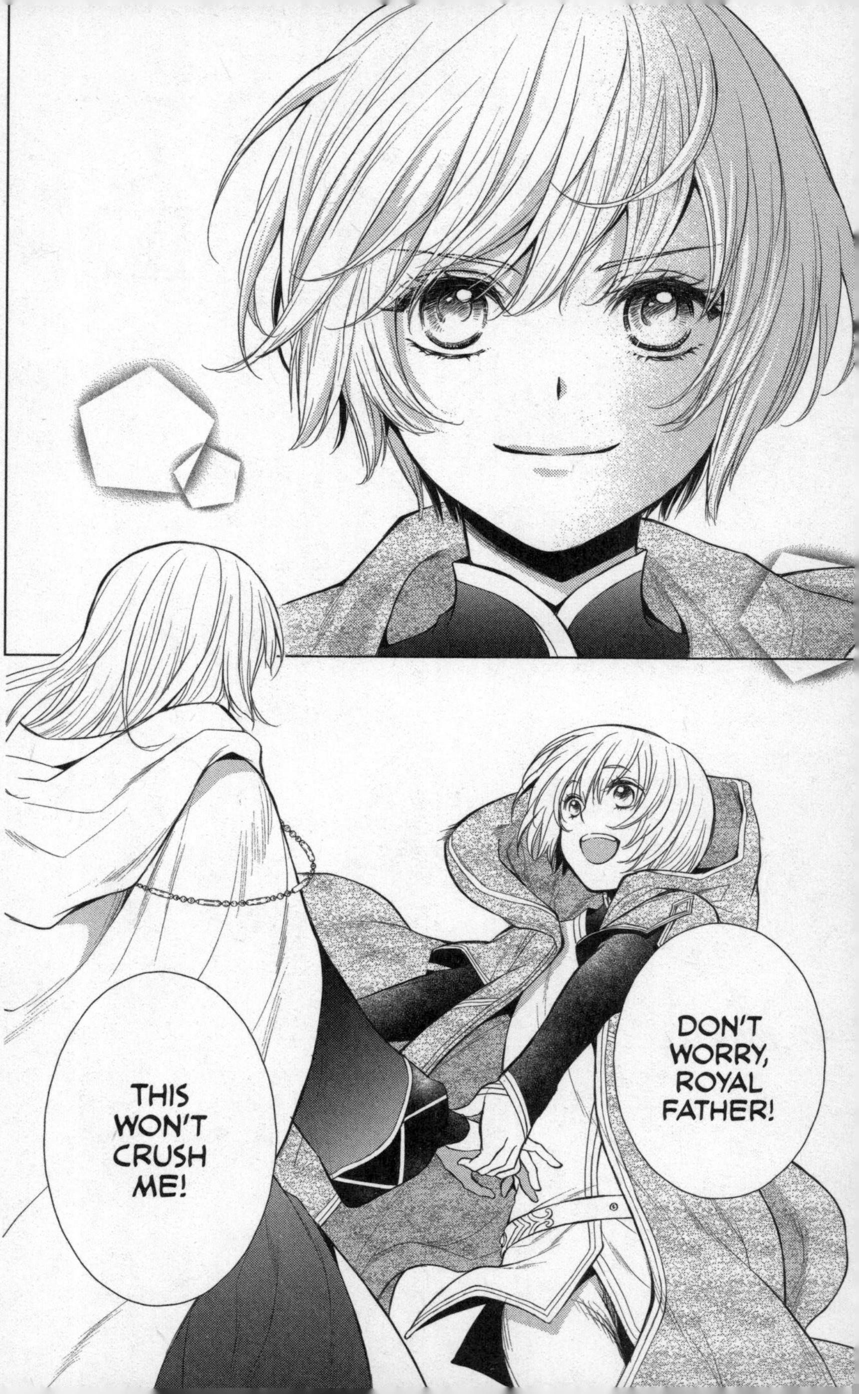
DON'T WORRY, ROYAL FATHER!
THIS WON'T CRUSH ME!

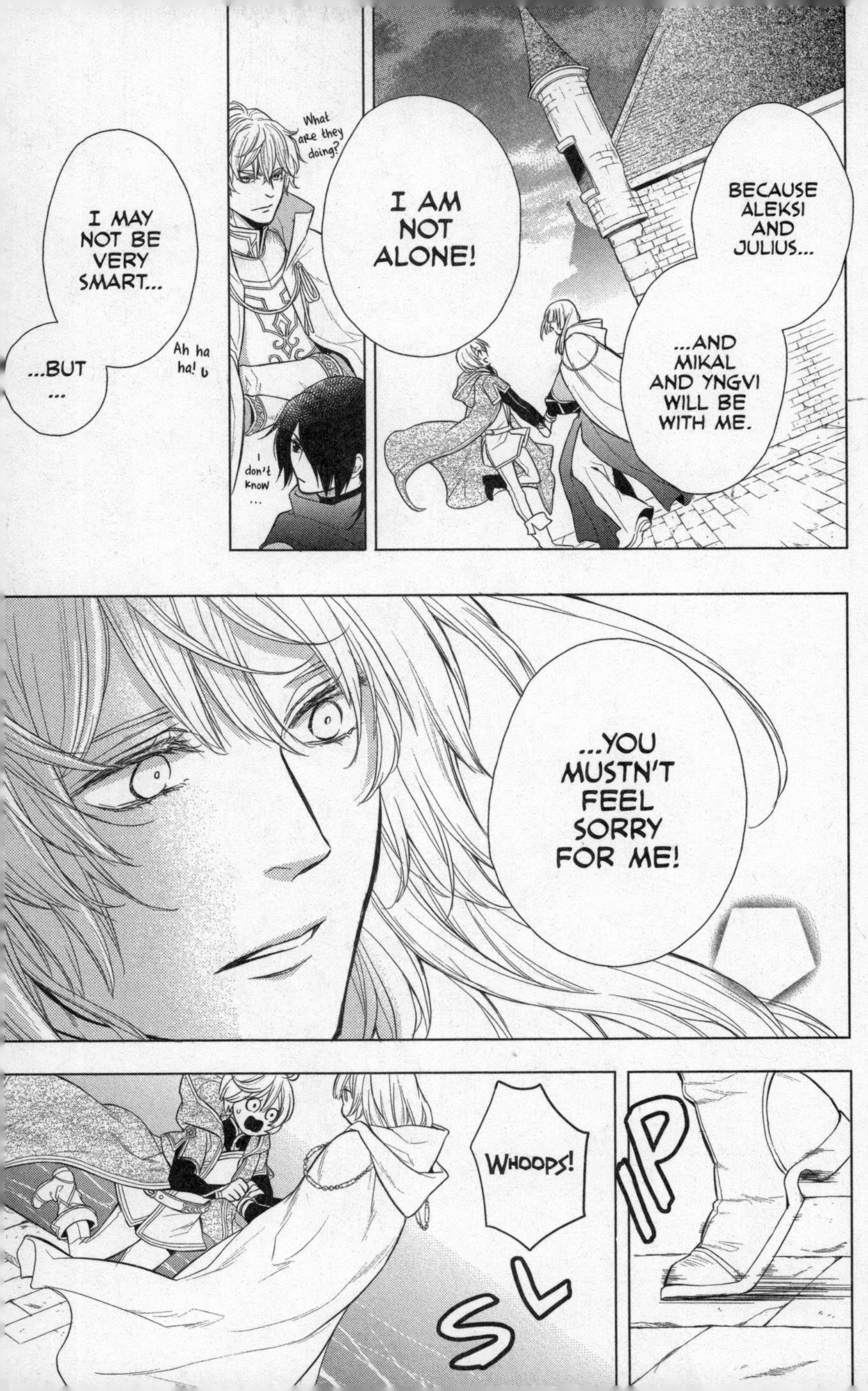
BECAUSE ALEKSI AND JULIUS...
...AND MIKAL AND YNGVI WILL BE WITH ME.
I AM NOT ALONE!
What are they doing?
Ah ha ha!
I don't know ...
I MAY NOT BE VERY SMART...
...BUT ...
...YOU MUSTN'T FEEL SORRY FOR ME!
SLIP
WHOOPS!

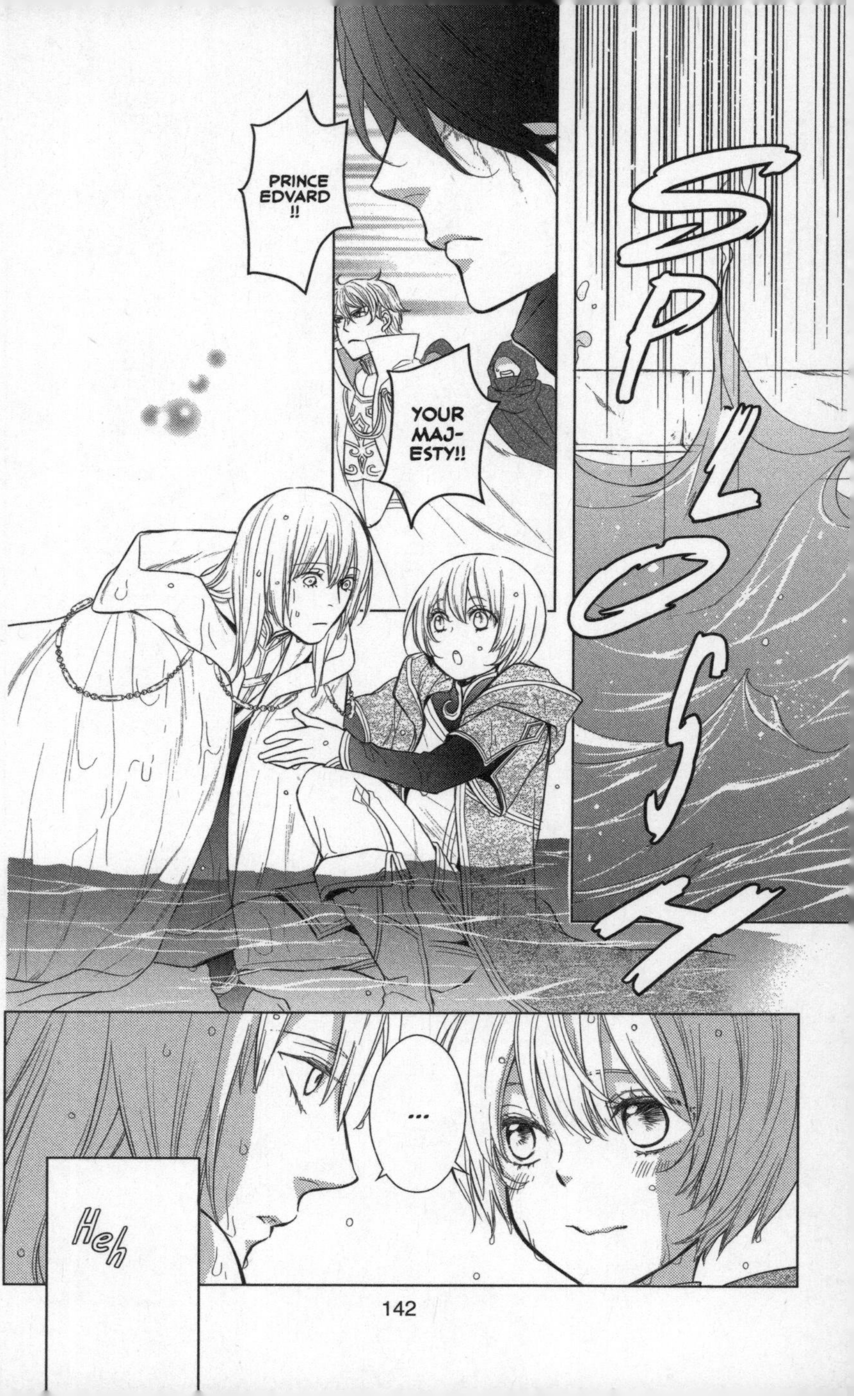
SPLOSH
PRINCE EDVARD !!
YOUR MAJ-ESTY!!
...
Heh

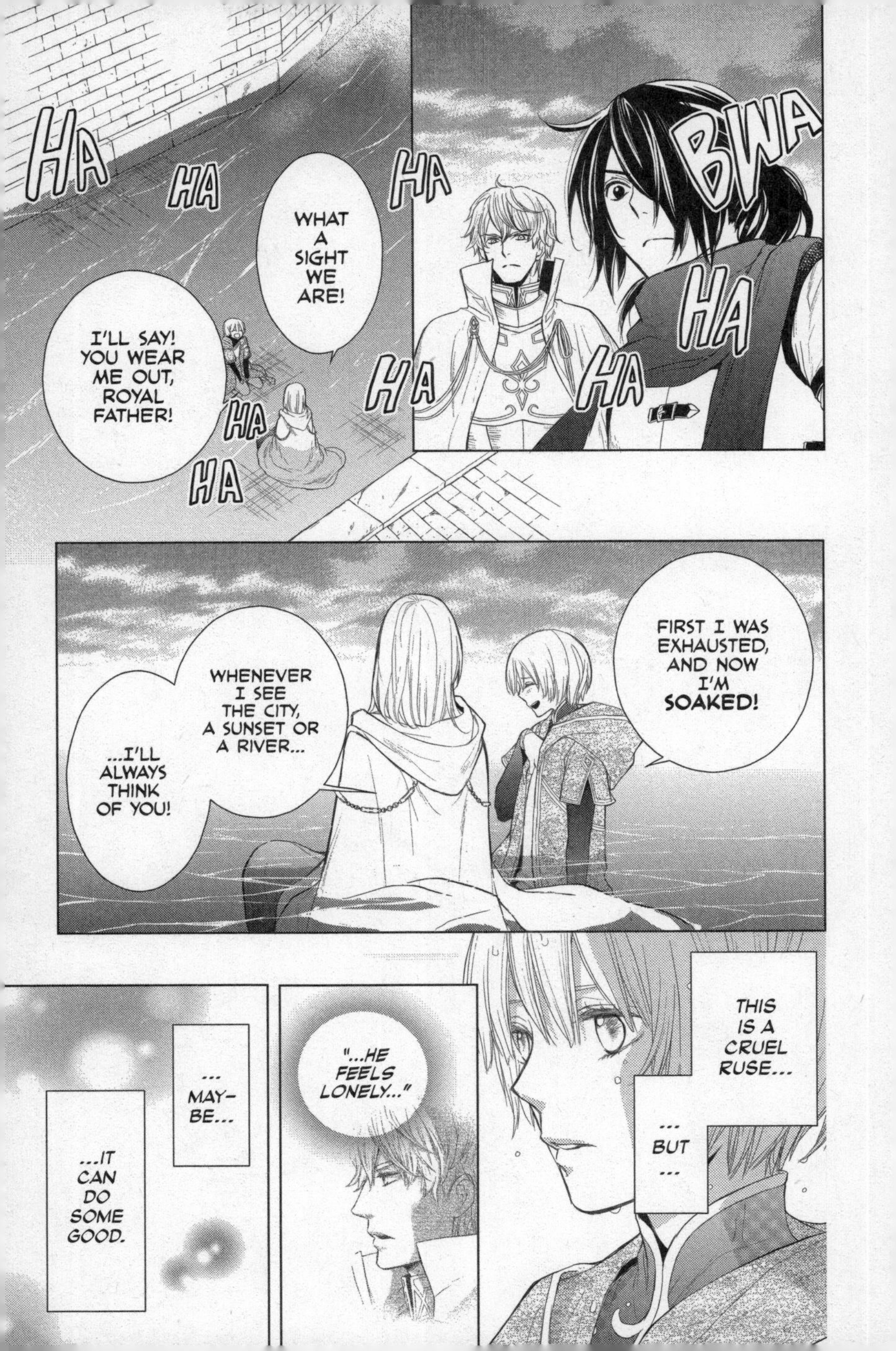
BWA
HA
HA
HA
HA
HA
WHAT A SIGHT WE ARE!
I'LL SAY! YOU WEAR ME OUT, ROYAL FATHER!
HA
HA
HA
FIRST I WAS EXHAUSTED, AND NOW I'M SOAKED!
WHENEVER I SEE THE CITY, A SUNSET OR A RIVER...
...I'LL ALWAYS THINK OF YOU!
THIS IS A CRUEL RUSE...
...BUT...
"...HE FEELS LONELY..."
...MAY-BE...
...IT CAN DO SOME GOOD.

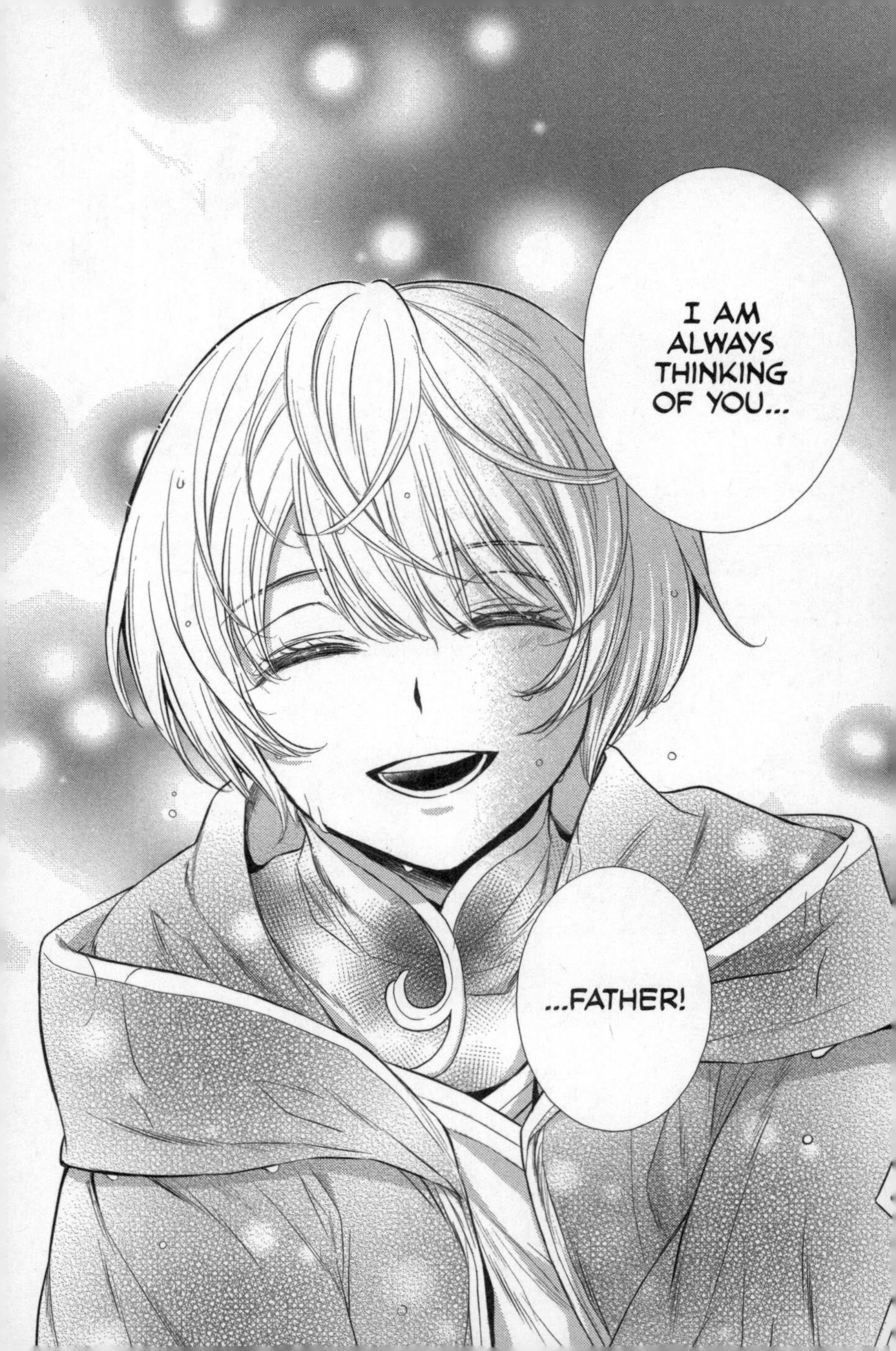
I AM ALWAYS THINKING OF YOU...
...FATHER!

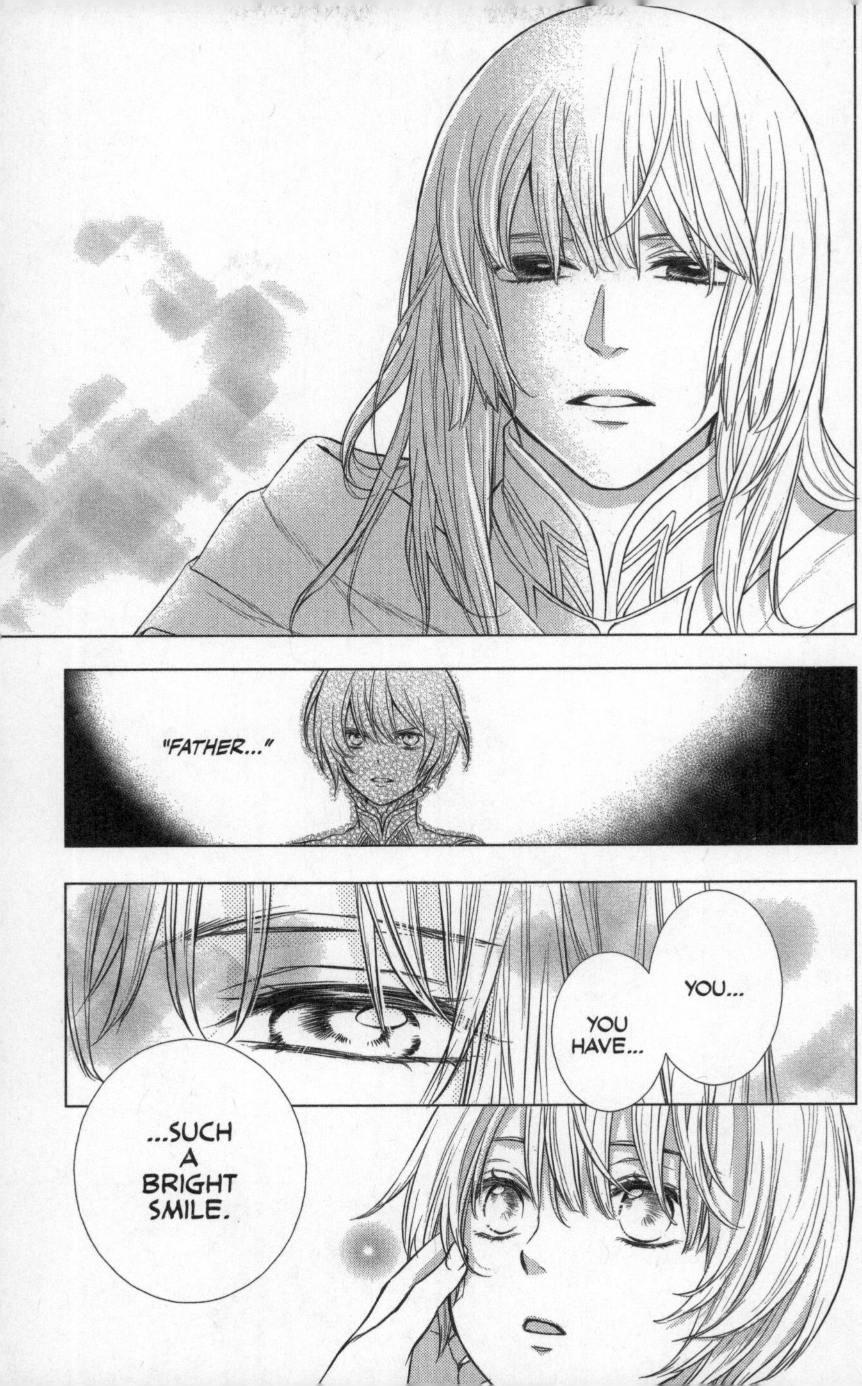
"FATHER..."
YOU... YOU HAVE...
...SUCH A BRIGHT SMILE.

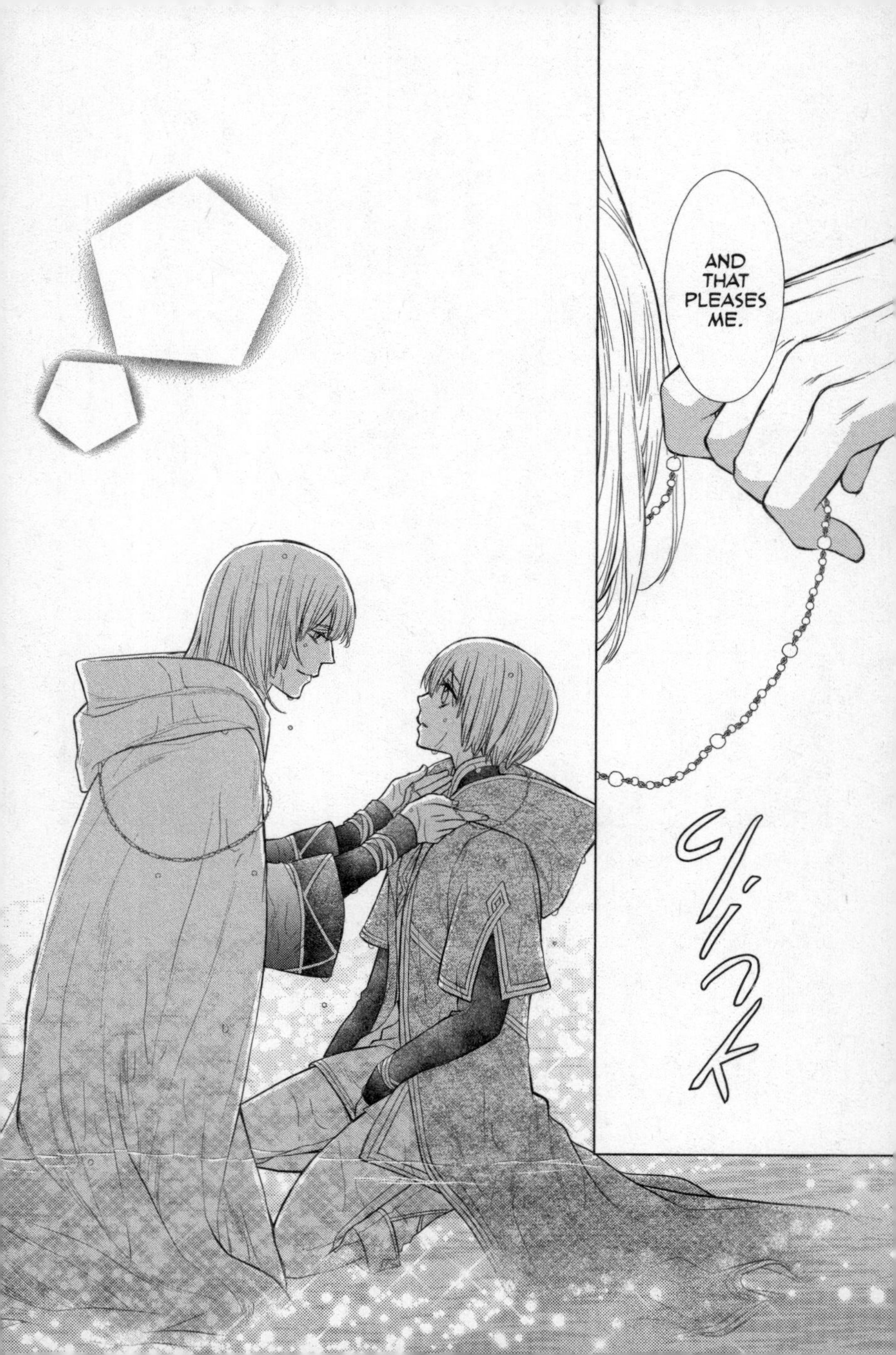
AND THAT PLEASES ME.
CLINK

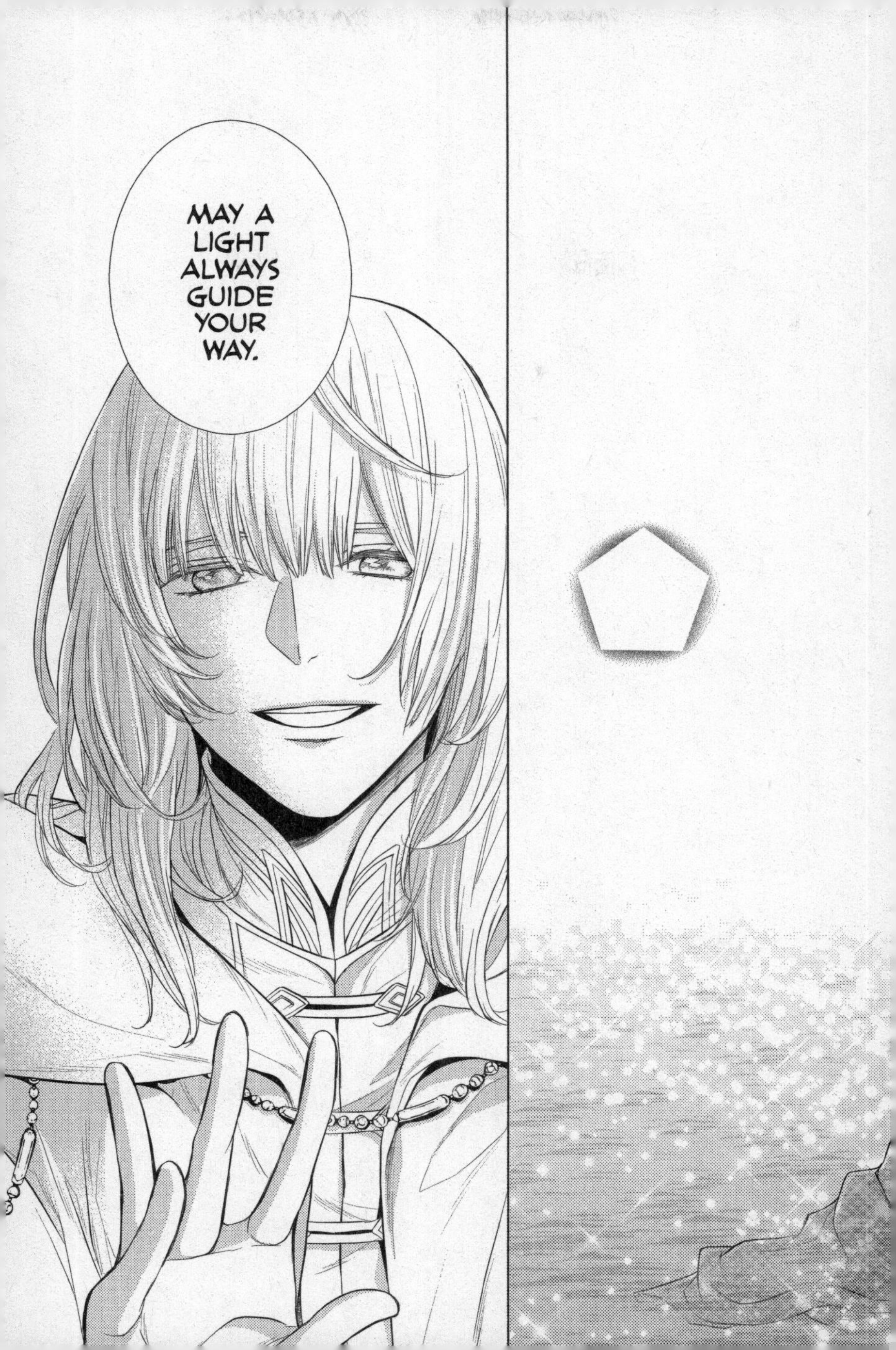
MAY A LIGHT ALWAYS GUIDE YOUR WAY.

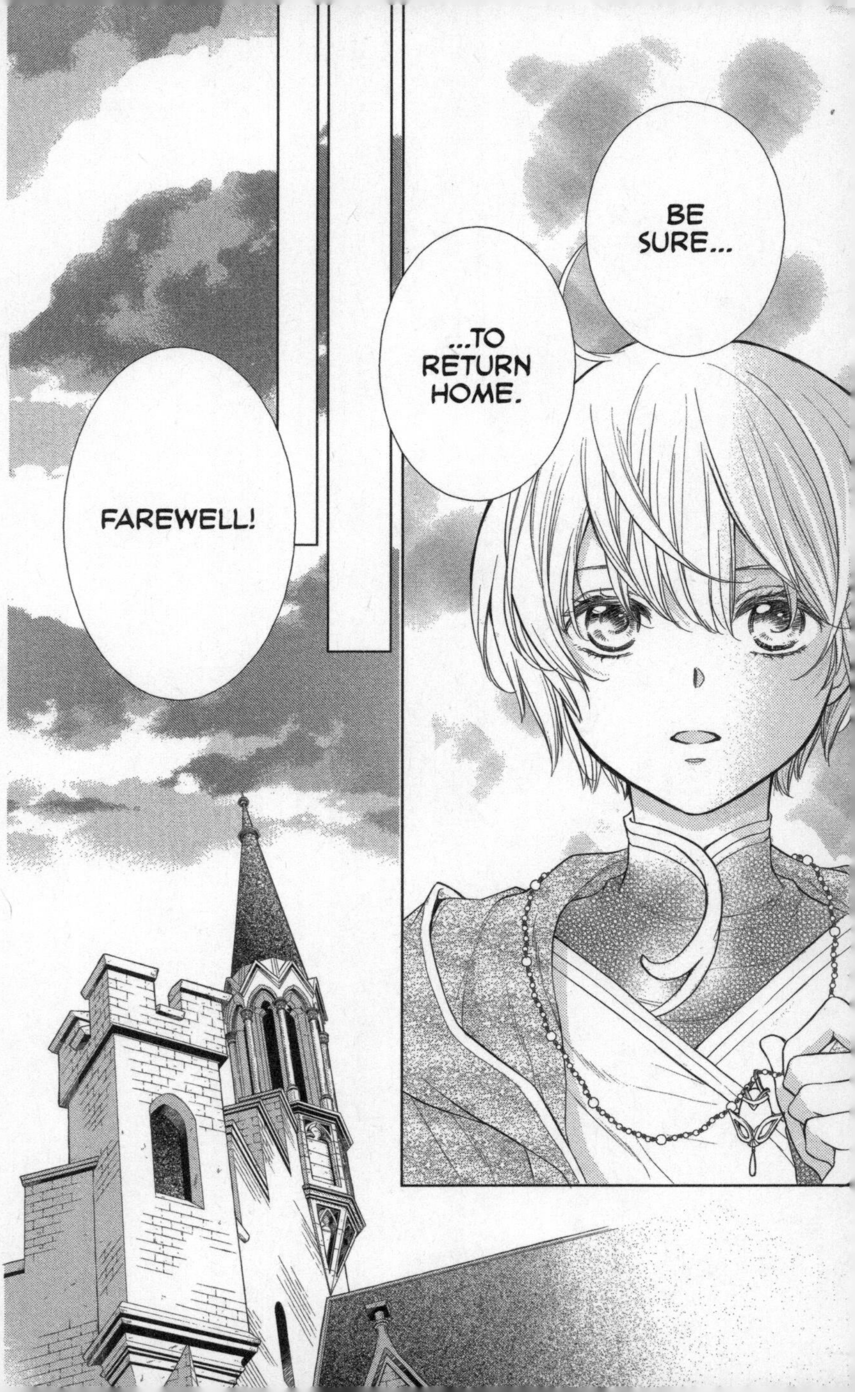
BE SURE...
...TO RETURN HOME.
FAREWELL!

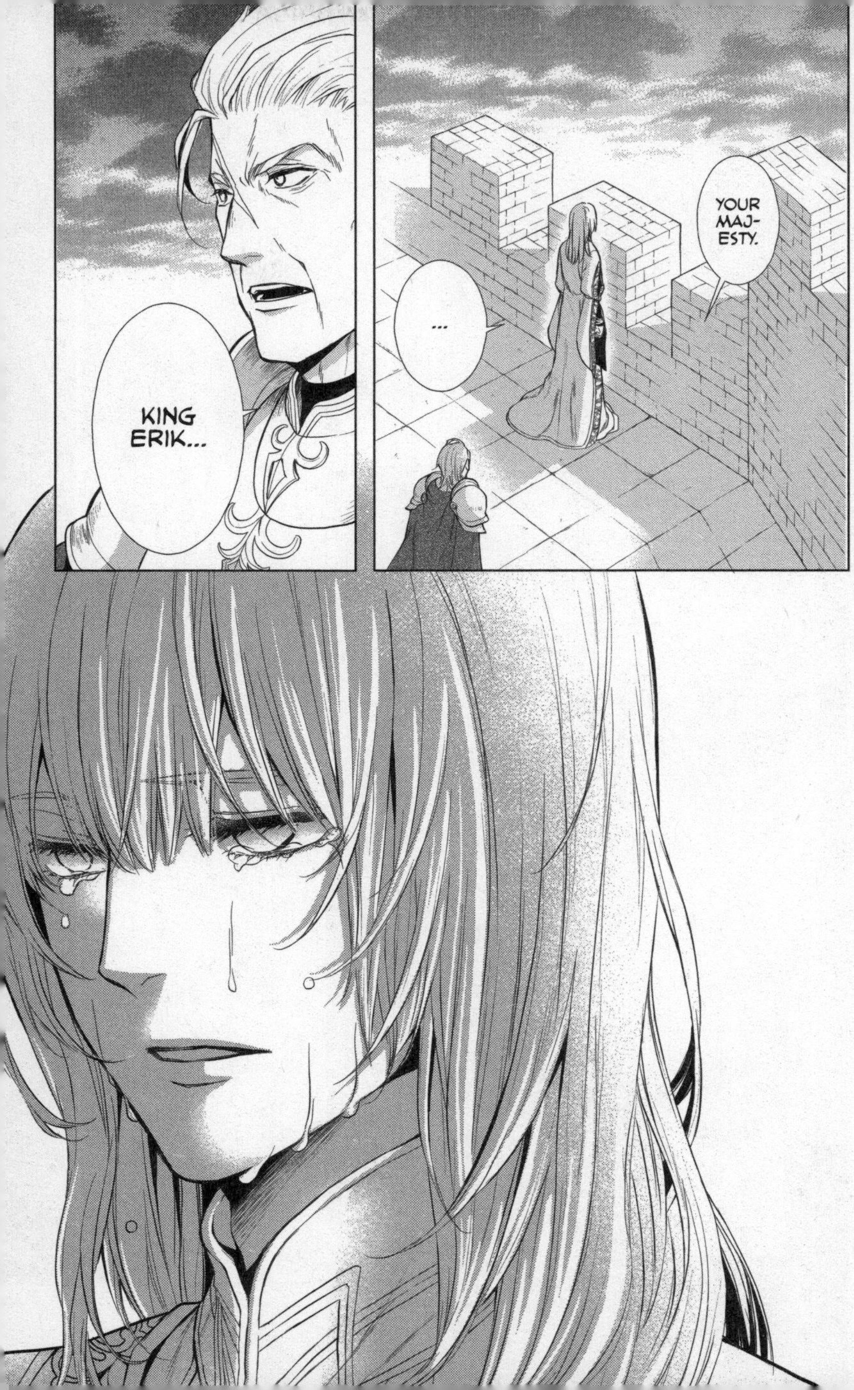
YOUR MAJ-ESTY.
...
KING ERIK...

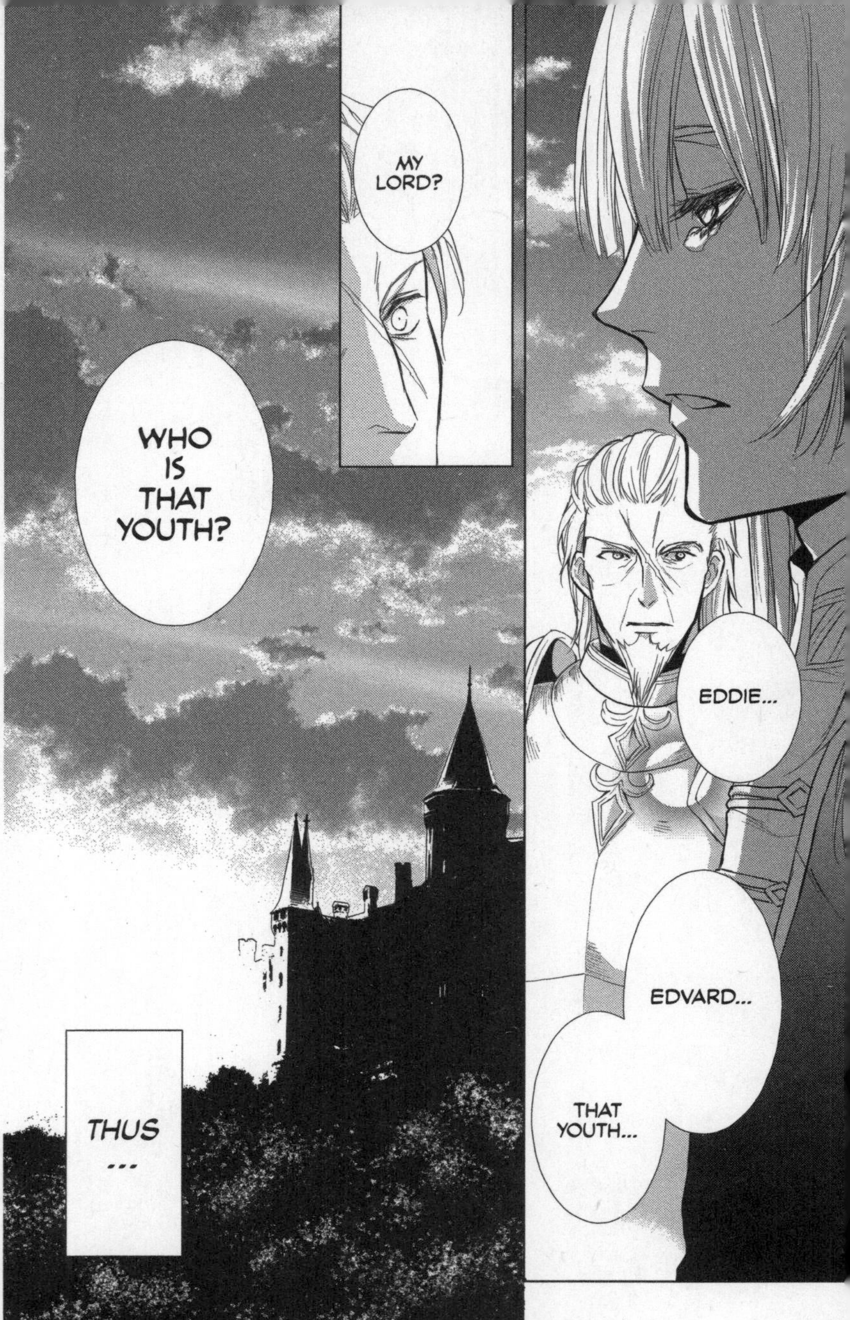
EDDIE...
EDVARD...
THAT YOUTH...
MY LORD?
WHO IS THAT YOUTH?
THUS ...

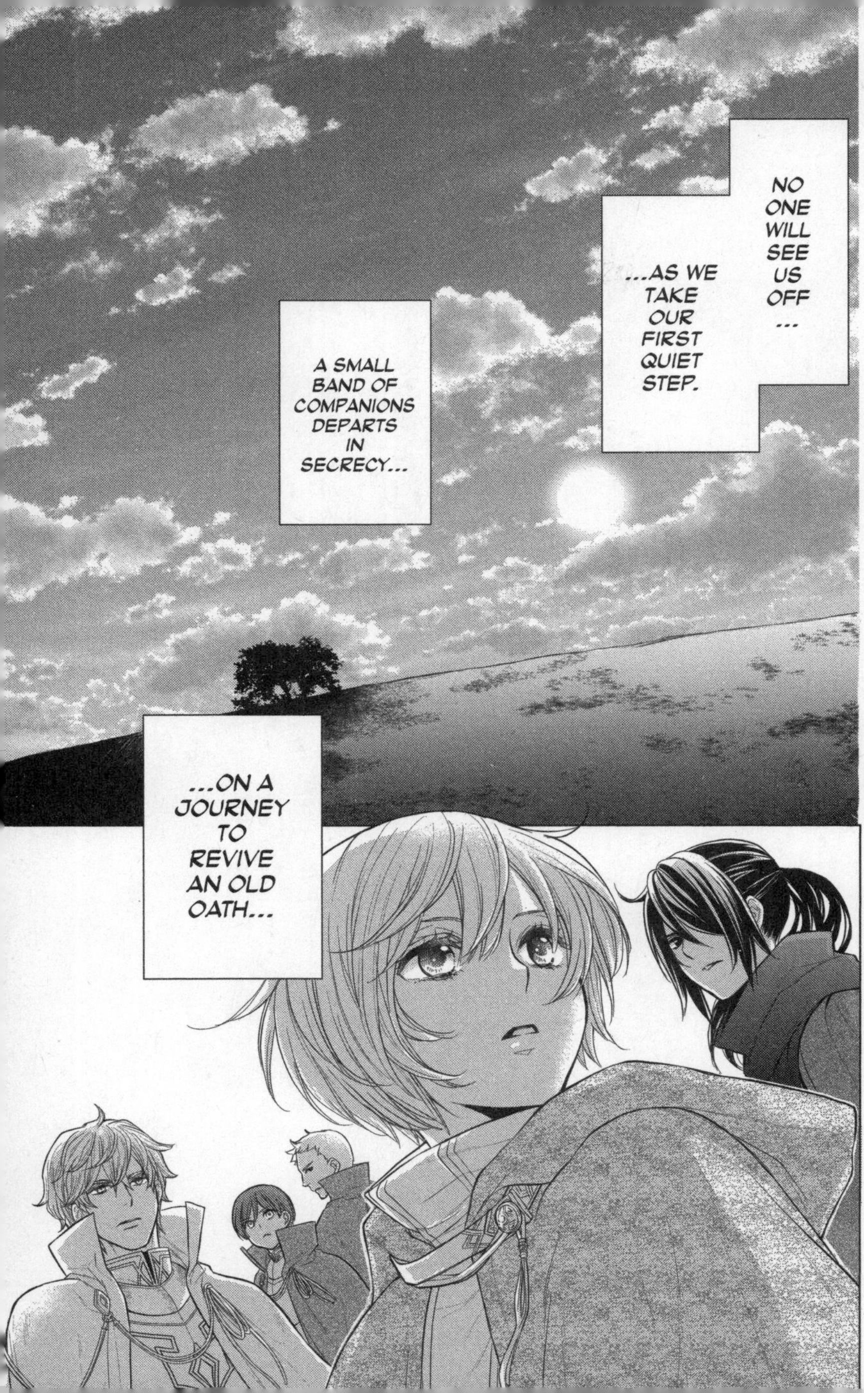
NO ONE WILL SEE US OFF...
...AS WE TAKE OUR FIRST QUIET STEP.
A SMALL BAND OF COMPANIONS DEPARTS IN SECRECY...
...ON A JOURNEY TO REVIVE AN OLD OATH...

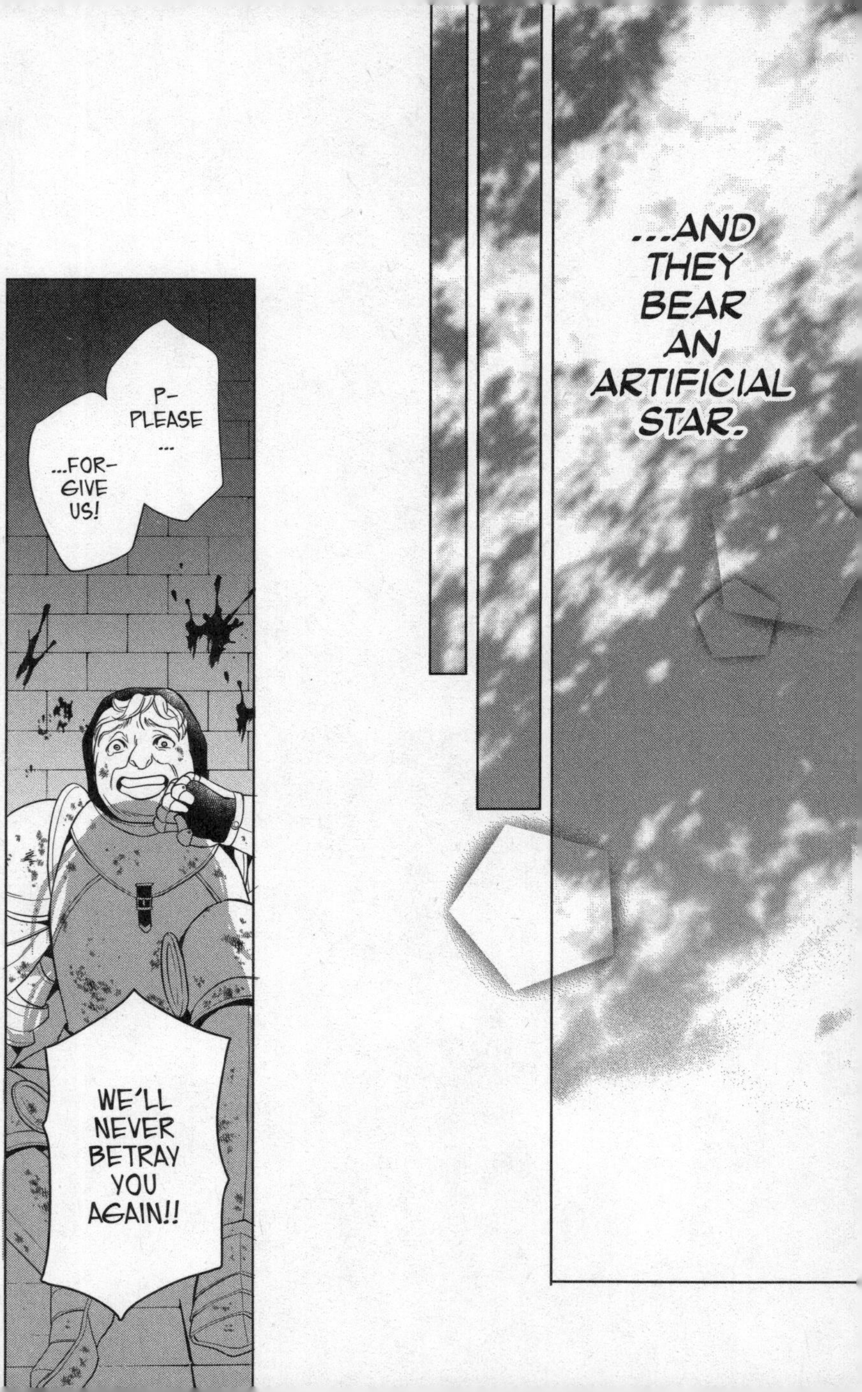
...AND THEY BEAR AN ARTIFICIAL STAR.
P-PLEASE ...
...FOR-GIVE US!
WE'LL NEVER BETRAY YOU AGAIN!!

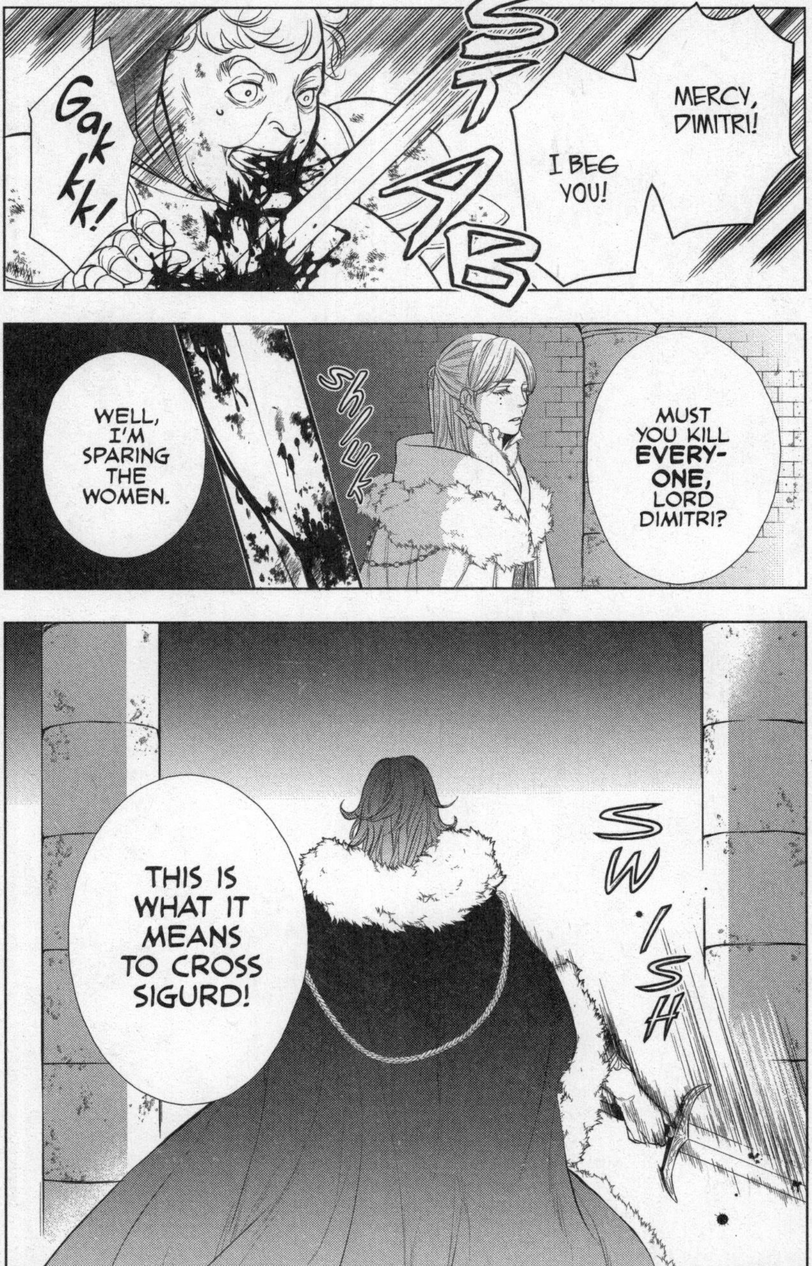
MERCY, DIMITRI!
I BEG YOU!
STAB
Gakkk!
MUST YOU KILL EVERYONE, LORD DIMITRI?
shluk
WELL, I'M SPARING THE WOMEN.
SWISH
THIS IS WHAT IT MEANS TO CROSS SIGURD!

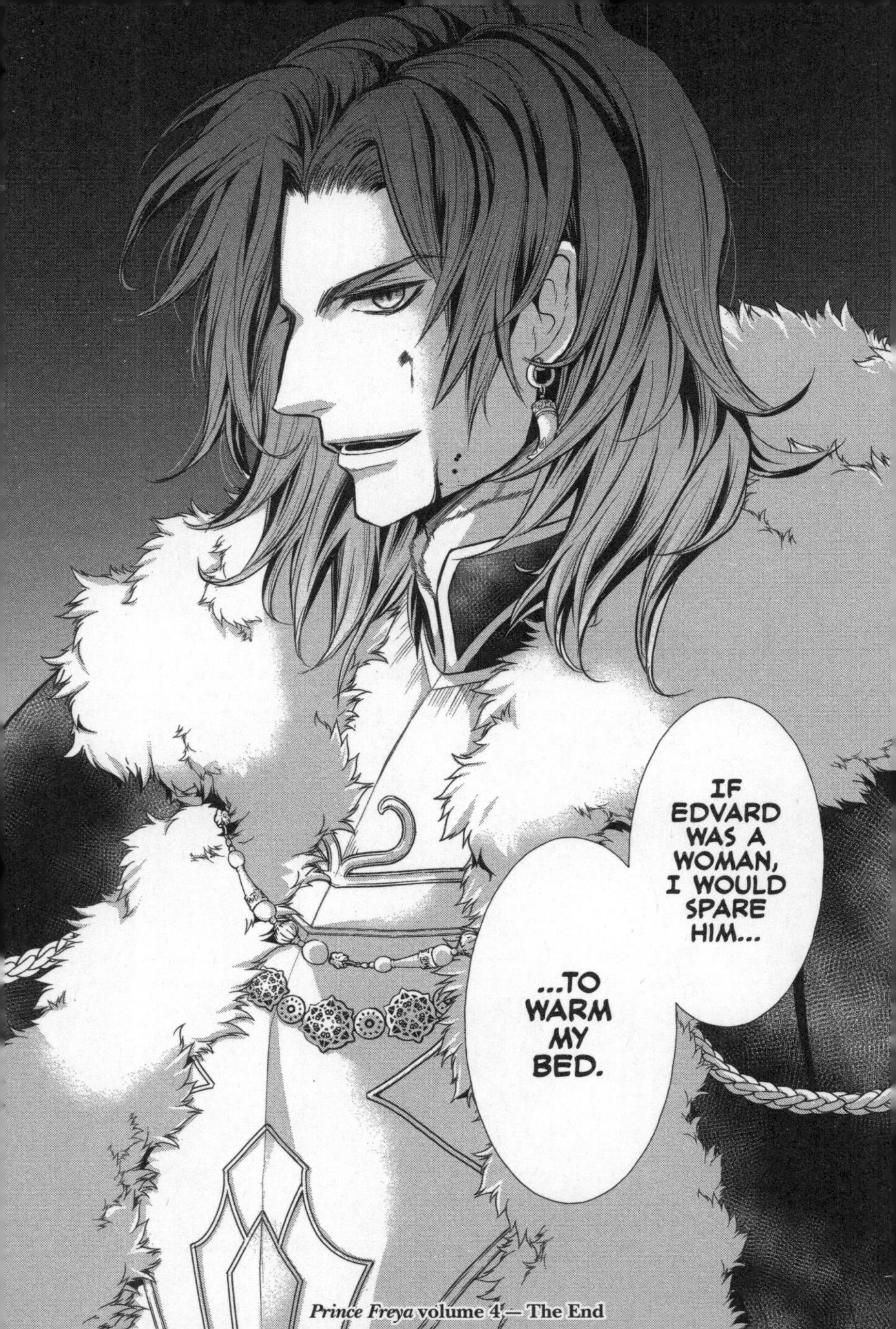
IF EDVARD WAS A WOMAN, I WOULD SPARE HIM...
...TO WARM MY BED.

Prince Freya volume 4 — The End

Afterword

The Making of Freya

石原ケイコ
Keiko Ishihara

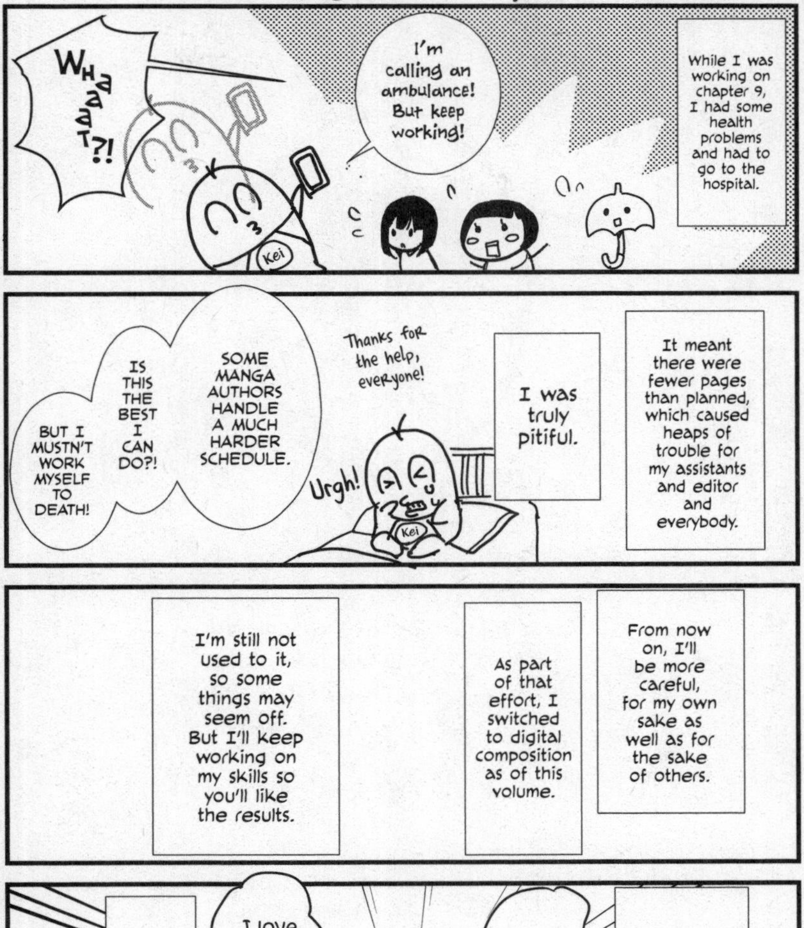

While I was working on chapter 9, I had some health problems and had to go to the hospital.
I'm calling an ambulance! But keep working!
WHAAAT?!
Kei
It meant there were fewer pages than planned, which caused heaps of trouble for my assistants and editor and everybody.
I was truly pitiful.
Thanks for the help, everyone!
Urgh!
Kei
SOME MANGA AUTHORS HANDLE A MUCH HARDER SCHEDULE.
IS THIS THE BEST I CAN DO?!
BUT I MUSTN'T WORK MYSELF TO DEATH!
From now on, I'll be more careful, for my own sake as well as for the sake of others.
As part of that effort, I switched to digital composition as of this volume.
I'm still not used to it, so some things may seem off. But I'll keep working on my skills so you'll like the results.
I didn't go outside for ten days while I was in the hospital.
But it was easy!
I love being holed up alone!
It was mostly like being at home.
Put your health first! ☆
ipad
Manga
Kei

Assistants: Sadayuki Amahara. Miyuki Tsutsui. Misaya Morifuji. U-san. Yoshineko Kitafuku

Thank you so much!

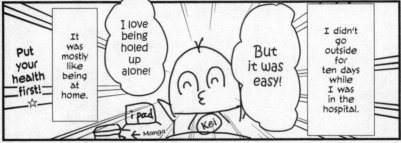

I made a special bonus booklet about *Prince Freya*. Whoo! This was a goal of mine, so I am very happy to announce its release in Japan. It includes illustrations of Freya's friends and some other characters I normally don't draw. Please take a look when you have the chance!

KEIKO ISHIHARA

Born on April 14, Keiko Ishihara began her manga career with *Keisan Desu Kara* (It's All Calculated). Her other works include *Strange Dragon*, which was serialized in the magazine *LaLa*, and *The Heiress and the Chauffeur*, published by VIZ Media. Ishihara is from Hyogo Prefecture, and she loves cats.

PRINCE Freya

VOLUME 4 · SHOJO BEAT EDITION

STORY AND ART BY
KEIKO ISHIHARA

ENGLISH TRANSLATION & ADAPTATION John Werry
TOUCH-UP ART & LETTERING Sabrina Heep
DESIGN Shawn Carrico
EDITOR Pancha Diaz

Itsuwari no Freya
© Keiko Ishihara 2020/HAKUSENSHA, Inc.
All rights reserved.
First published in Japan in 2020 by HAKUSENSHA, Inc., Tokyo.
English language translation rights
arranged with HAKUSENSHA, Inc., Tokyo.

Printed in the U.S.A.

Published by VIZ Media, LLC
P.O. Box 77010
San Francisco, CA 94107

10 9 8 7 6 5 4 3 2 1
First printing, January 2021

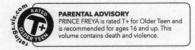

viz.com   shojobeat.com

Snow White
with the Red Hair

Inspired
the anime!

STORY & ART BY
SORATA AKIDUKI

Shirayuki is an herbalist famous for
her naturally bright-red hair, and
the prince of Tanbarun wants her all
to himself! Unwilling to become the
prince's possession, she seeks shelter in
the woods of the neighboring kingdom,
where she gains an unlikely ally—the
prince of that kingdom! He rescues her
from her plight, and thus begins the
love story between a lovestruck prince
and an unusual herbalist.